HISTORIANS AND THE LIVING PAST

HISTORIANS

AND THE

LIVING PAST

The Theory and Practice

of Historical Study

Allan J. Lichtman & Valerie French
The American University

Harlan Davidson, Inc.
Arlington Heights, Illinois 60004

Library of Congress Cataloging-in-Publication Data

Lichtman, Allan J.
    Historians and the living past.

    Bibliography: p.
    Includes index.
    1. History—Study and teaching. I. French, Valerie.
II. Title.
D16.2.L49   1986   907'.2   86-19796
ISBN 0-88295-773-2 (pbk.)

Manufactured in the United States of America
90   EB   7 8 9 10 11

For Our Children
Kara, Signe, and John

In Whom

"Time present and time past
Are both perhaps present in time future.
And time future contained in time past."

T. S. Eliot

CONTENTS

PREFACE

Why do we need to know anything about the past? How do we find out what happened and explain why it happened? How do we convey to others what we have learned? These questions reflect not only our own interest in the method and philosophy of history, but also our recognition that academic history has been less than successful in convincing this generation of students that the study of the past is important, interesting, and useful. We are convinced that history illumines the world as brightly as any field of study, yet current enrollment trends suggest that too few students share our view of history's value and excitement.

Our own enthusiasm and our belief in the relevance of history gave rise in 1974 to a course, "Historians and the Living Past," from which this book draws its name. We created that course to impress upon as many students as possible, not just prospective history majors, the significance of historical study. Our fundamental premise was that everything we think that we know about the past, whether true or false, becomes a frame of reference for our understanding of the present and a guide to the future. We sought to show how politicians, journalists, advertisers, or anyone else advocating a cause invariably ends up appealing to the past by way of explanation and justification. We argued that anyone expecting to analyze and evaluate these claims, or indeed, anyone hoping to understand and deal with today's world, must rely upon an understanding of the past. But such an understanding does not come automatically, even to the most gifted. Thus, we also attempted to teach the skills requisite for thinking critically and communicating ideas effectively. To this end, we explored how historians reconstruct and explain past events; we examined their different approaches to historical study; and we considered their methods for research and writing. We stressed that the same methods historians use to understand and write about the past are applicable whenever anyone tries to draw conclusions from a body of information and convey the results of their thinking in a persuasive way.

Both the course and this book reflect other ideas about teaching, researching, and writing history. History, we believe, includes every aspect of life— politics, economics, social relations, ideas, and art. We believe that for history to have meaning and impact in today's world, it must emphasize these broad concerns as well as the particular events of the past. As historians, we have tried to communicate not only the how and why of historical study and our enthusiasm for our own special fields (the recent United States and classical antiquity), but also the intellectual excitement found in the whole historical enterprise.

ACKNOWLEDGMENTS

All historians have debts to two separate groups of people—to the other scholars whose ideas have influenced the authors' own thought and to the people who have helped prepare an individual article or book. While there is no way to list here our intellectual indebtedness to the many historians and philosophers who have provided insight for us, one scholar deserves special mention—the great French historian, Henri Frankfort. We have relied heavily on his exposition of mythopoeism as a distinctive mode of thought. We have tried to indicate in the text of the book our debts to other scholars whose work we have found particularly illuminating.

Since the people who have been so generous in their help with this book are not mentioned elsewhere, we will take this opportunity to thank them formally. Many of our colleagues at The American University have read much of the manuscript and offered valuable comments and criticisms. For their interest and care, we are most grateful to Professors Ira N. Klein and Richard Breitman. We also appreciate the comments offered to us on specific portions of the book by Professors Laura Irwin Langbein, Jane Lewin, Roberta Rubenstein, and Phillip Scribner; we wish also to thank Kenneth Thibodeau and Sharon Gibbs of the National Archives and Records Service, and Professor Laurence Tribe of the Harvard Law School. Several of our students have read the entire manuscript and identified problems that might

xiii

otherwise have gone undetected. Leslie Winn, Gary Braithwaite, and William Reckmeyer were particularly helpful in this regard. In addition, the hundreds of students who have taken our course, "Historians and the Living Past," have made significant contributions through their questions and comments.

We must also express our appreciation to Professor Arthur S. Link, general history editor of Harlan Davidson, Inc., for his support, encouragement, and helpful critiques, and to the late Harlan Davidson for his patience in awaiting the completion of the book. And, penultimately, for his unstinting assistance in offering trenchant criticism and in turning our too often pedestrian expression into graceful prose, we thank especially our colleague Professor Robert L. Beisner. Finally, we thank our children, to whom this book is dedicated, for understanding that we had to spend time working on the book when we could have been playing with them.

INTRODUCTION

"History is bunk!" "Everyman his own historian." "What experience and history teach is this—people and governments never have learned anything from history." "Nothing is new under the sun."

Henry Ford, an industrialist; Carl Becker, a historian; G. W. F. Hegel, a philosopher; Publius Syrius, a Roman slave—like all of us, they had definite notions about mankind's past, notions that affected not only their comprehension of the past, but also their understanding of their own times and their expectations for the future. Since the ancient Egyptians, humans have sought knowledge of their past. And what we think we know about the past shapes our awareness of the present and guides our decisions about the future. Indeed, history enables us to slip the bonds of our own time and perceive a far broader canvas of human action, thought, and feeling. The study of history has generated some of our finest art and profoundest philosophy.

Historical study is a broadening and humanizing experience. We find it both humbling and inspiring to realize that life in our own times does not begin to exhaust the possibilities of human emotion, thought, imagination, and endeavor. History provides a glimpse of what people have thought and felt in times and places very different from our own. It reveals their successes and their failures, loves and hates. It portrays the splendor of past civilizations and records their decay and decline. History discloses the arrogance and greatness of rulers, the passions and audacity of revolutionaries, and the day-to-day lives of ordinary people. Finally, history helps us to understand our own identity in the present by giving us an understanding of how we came to be what we are.

As with so much that he has done, man has sought to understand his past in a multitude of ways. Everyone asks, "When did this start?" "How did it begin?" "Why did this happen?" These are questions common to all curious people, but their answers range across the full spectrum of human thought. The ancients used mythology; the Hebrews and Christians believed that a divine hand guided their lives; modern men have devised such theories as dialectical materialism or contingent accident to explain their past.

Just as man has developed a wide range of theories to explain the past, so also has he considered many ways of trying to determine what actually happened in the past. The problems of evaluating historical evidence, of deciphering its often hidden messages, and of formulating intelligible statements about the past have both vexed and inspired historians since the invention of their discipline in the fifth century B.C. But questions of historical methodology should not be seen as interesting solely to historians. Methods of inquiry evolved by historians are useful to all those seeking to comprehend the information that bombards them in a complex society. Anyone who has attempted to unravel the bewildering controversies over the Kennedy assassination, the CIA, Watergate, disarmament, and the Middle East has experienced the same frustrations as the historian seeking to understand the fall of Rome or the origins of World War I. Even so mundane an activity as reading a newspaper can benefit from the insight of historical methodology. Every historian must seek ways of understanding conflicting and incomplete information; any thinking person living in the modern world faces the same problems every day.

Before we can begin to discuss the theories and methodologies of history, however, we must state what we believe history to be. It is perhaps surprising that such a well-known word is hard to define. We think we know what we mean when we say "history," yet we commonly use the word to denote at least two different ideas. Men use "history" often as a synonym for the past itself. Just as often, "history" is used to designate the study of the past. Dictionaries give both meanings. But the historian ought to limit himself to one definition. To use the word to signify two different ideas invites confusion. However, defining the word "history" to mean the study of the past is still too imprecise. Antiquarians study the past; so do chroniclers, genealogists, and chronographers. But such people are clearly not historians. We believe that the quality of "reasoned argument" distinguishes historical study from these other types of investigation.

History is reasoned argument about the past by which we seek the fullest possible understanding of actions, thoughts, and feelings. History is argument for two reasons. First, we can never be certain of the absolute truth of any statement that refers to the past. And second, we can know the past only indirectly by analyzing the evidence that survives. Leaving aside our own memories, our only knowledge of the past comes from such things as newspapers, letters, diaries, census reports, tape recordings, films, coins, pottery, and tools—in short, whatever remains that was produced by the people the historian wants to study. To reach a historical conclusion about these people, an argument (i.e., an ordered series of statements leading to a particular conclusion) must be constructed, linking existing evidence to an earlier phenomenon.

For example, suppose a historian wants to investigate early Celtic society. One of its major survivals is the awe–inspiring megalithic monument at Stonehenge, England. The historian can see, measure, and survey these huge monoliths and the circle of some eighty-five stones that surrounds them. But to say something about Celtic society, he must fashion an argument from observations of these mysterious remains. He might construct an ordered series of statements suggesting that Stonehenge was a temple. Or, like the astrophysicist Gerald Hawkins, he might argue that Stonehenge was an astronomical observatory. The stones do not speak; they cannot tell us about the people who quarried and erected them. This is the job of the historian— to reach conclusions about the past by linking surviving evidence to the actions and ideas of the people who produced it.

The process of constructing arguments about the past, however, is fraught with difficulty since historical evidence is frequently biased, incomplete, or contradictory. Moreover, historians frequently deal with complex questions involving human motivation or cause-and-effect relationships; often there are no right or wrong answers to such questions.

Yet to the chagrin of many students, discovering that historical conclusions are uncertain does not mean that all conclusions are equally meritorious. For history is *reasoned,* not random, argument about the past. All historical conclusions should be supported by the widest possible canvass of the relevent evidence and the use of the best available methods for linking this evidence to the statements being made. Whenever anyone makes a statement about the past, he also invites critical commentary. This applies to claims made by students in the classroom or on the pages of examination bluebooks, as well as to the arguments advanced by professional historians in lectures, scholarly articles, and books. If arguments are to be seriously considered by a critical audience, they must be defended through the rigorous analysis of all available evidence. Historical understanding is achieved only under the pressure of continual discussion and debate.

In this book we will explore five major aspects of historical study. First, we will consider questions relating to the procedures and methods used by historians to comprehend past experience (Chapters II and III). Second, we will examine the general approaches that men have employed to explain the past (Chapter IV). Third, we will discuss some of the recent developments in historical study (Chapter V). Fourth, we will investigate how family and local history can bring people closer to their personal heritage (Chapter VI). Finally, we will describe the ways in which all students of history go about doing research and communicating their findings (Chapters VII and VIII).

In the first chapters of this book, we will examine the reconstruction and explanation of what happened in the past. A scientist would readily concede that, in his discipline, a conclusion is only as good as the evidence and logic that support it. This observation applies with equal force to historical study. But the historian who tries to achieve the same degree of certainty as the scientist will soon despair. For the historian must view the past indirectly through a limited amount of surviving evidence. Since the past cannot be altered, the historian does not have the scientist's option to manipulate his data and perform controlled experiments. While a scientist can compare the growth of *E. Coli* bacteria with or without the introduction of penicillin, a historian can only speculate about what might have happened had the South won the battle of Gettysburg or the Persians defeated the Greeks at Marathon. Moreover, the historian must deal with people as whole beings, not with pieces of the whole, like the structure of muscle, the chemistry of blood, or the functions of the liver. He must also consider the societies and institutions that man constructs as well as the kinds of behavior that give purpose and direction to life.

Like the scientist, the historian must connect evidence and conclusion with logical argument, but he must employ a different set of criteria for handling and evaluating complex and unpredictable evidence. Although he is aware that his craft will never have the certainty of science, the historian still must be as *rigorous as possible.* Those historians and philosophers (and there have been altogether too few of them) who have thought seriously about the principles of historical analysis have developed theories and standards for evaluating and using evidence. A responsible historian cannot simply throw up his hands, mumble something about the complexity of human affairs, and ignore such theories and standards for using evidence and fashioning histori-cal explanations. We will describe some of these methodologies, and we will discuss their value and applicability to history as well as to human under-standing in general.

Over the four millenia that have passed since the Sumerians and Egyptians created stories to explain their past, men have taken three general approaches to understanding the past—myth, force, and man. Modern man has difficulty accepting myth, the oldest of these approaches, as a valid and meaningful perspective for comprehending the past. To us, myth connotes legend, ro-mance, fairy tale—in a word, unreality. But for nearly four thousand years, myth was the mode of thought that men used to comprehend their past. Sumerians, Egyptians, Hittites, Assyrians, and Phoenicians lived quite com-fortably, even elegantly, with only a mythic understanding of their heritage.

Though now unfamiliar with myth as a mode of historical explanation, we readily recognize attempts to comprehend the past by looking either at external forces or at the nature of man himself. Some have proposed that forces external to man, such as divine power or the natural environment, direct the general unfolding of human experience. Others reject this view and seek instead to explain historical change by examining the nature of man himself. The latter can be divided roughly into two separate categories: in one, those who believe that man's past conforms to the principles of some general or overarching theory of explanation; in the other, those who insist that each situation must be examined and explained individually, applying whatever theory best fits the particular case.

Moreover, historical study in this century has been further subdivided into specialities based on time, geography, or thematic emphasis. Thus, historians often refer to themselves as ancient, medieval, or modern; European or American; and political, social, or intellectual historians. And in recent years, new specialties have appeared that cut across the traditional fields of study. These new approaches to explanation reflect both advances in human knowl-edge and changes in the cultural and political milieus in which historians work. For example, the revolutionary theories of Sigmund Freud paved the way for psychohistory. Our political concern with the ordinary man and woman fueled interest in "history from the bottom up." The development of sophisticated statistical methods and high-speed computers gave new impetus to quantitative history. Moreover, people's need to find their per-sonal roots in a highly mobile society stimulated the study of family and local history.

In the final chapters of this book, we will examine in detail how historians research the past and communicate their findings to the larger community.

Historical research is analogous, we believe, to the work done by great detectives such as Sherlock Holmes. Historians must find a case to work on, pinpoint the focus of their investigation, locate and evaluate clues that will solve the puzzle, and overcome the problems posed by their evidence. Once their investigation is finished, they must shift from the role of detective to that of writer. They must devise a strategy for presenting the fruits of their research so that readers will both understand and accept their findings and arguments. Like novelists, historians can quickly lose an audience unless they organize their work with care and present it lucidly and gracefully.

Before proceeding to a discussion of these major themes, we must reiterate and demonstrate (in Chapter I) one of the fundamental premises of this book: what we believe about the past powerfully influences our perceptions of the present and decisions about the future. The past is the major repository of information against which we measure and compare observations of our own time. We do not live and act in a historical vacuum. On the contrary, we are intimately connected with our past, whether we are conscious of the bond or not. Both individuals and societies make plans for the future predicated on what they have experienced in the past. Thus, for understanding what we do now and for planning our future, we rely inevitably on the past—a living past. It behooves us, therefore, to seek the best knowledge of the past. We address this book to the task of achieving that "best knowledge."

I

Past and Present:
History and
Contemporary Analysis

Our understanding of the past informs and shapes our view of contemporary life on many levels. The past provides our only source of information for evaluating current affairs and making predictions about the future. Historical knowledge enables us to place our perceptions of the contemporary world into a meaningful context and to discern the cause-and-effect relationships between events that serve as the basis for future expectations. Without such knowledge we would be as bewildered as a quarterback entering the fourth quarter of a football game without knowing the score, the amount of elapsed time, or the successes and failures of plays and players.

More concretely, historical study helps us to understand and criticize decisions made in the realms of journalism, business, and government that critically affect our daily lives. These decisions are usually based, either explicitly or implicitly, upon "lessons of history" drawn from the decision makers' own conceptions of the past. An understanding of history is required either to recognize or to critique the historical analysis that underlies vital policy decisions.

We will illustrate our arguments about the relevance of history by examin-

1

ing a newspaper column on the Nixon pardon by George F. Will, published in the *Washington Post* on September 10, 1974, and a short book by George F. Kennan, *American Diplomacy, 1900–1950,* published in 1952.

Even "instant analysis," like the following article, is permeated with historical argument. Most journalists, especially editorial writers and commentators, constantly use historical arguments to persuade readers of their perspicacity and wisdom. Historical argument is but one of the elements in the skillful journalist's strategic design. He has an arsenal of weapons of persuasion. He can compel the readers' attention with sheer literary brilliance; he can use irony, humor, metaphor, analogy, and other rhetorical figures; he can anticipate his opposition's arguments and deflate them; and, finally, he can draw upon the past as he reconstructs it to buttress his own opinion of current affairs.

WHO HAS ERODED RESPECT FOR LAW

George F. Will

"Man," said Robert Louis Stevenson, "is a creature who lives not by bread alone but principally by catchwords." Americans will have to eat more bread now that President Ford has drained the nutritional value from the catchwords about "equal justice under law."

Those words are chiseled deep in stone over the portico of the Supreme Court building. Rather than try to erase them Mr. Ford should just chisel a big asterisk next to them. Then he should find a surface large enough and chisel on it all the exceptions to that rule.

It is an iron law of politics that when a politician intones support for a principle, he is about to make an exception to that principle for the benefit of a friend. ("I revere the free enterprise system, but the farmers in my district need this subsidy because. . . .") That is why an alert citizen listening to Mr. Ford's statement about pardoning Mr. Nixon knew what was coming when Mr. Ford sailed into the part about believing in "equal justice, for all Americans, whatever their station or former station."

That principle is not the only casualty of Mr. Ford's pardon for Mr. Nixon. The English Muffin Theory of History is now just another theory killed by a fact.

The theory was that a President who toasts his own English muffins for breakfast is somehow different from the general cut of politicians. The lethal fact is that Mr. Ford now has demonstrated that he is just one of the boys: he doesn't mean what he says.

Mr. Ford said he would let the judicial process work regarding Mr. Nixon. Two weeks later, when aborting the judicial process, Mr. Ford said, "I deeply believe in equal justice," etc. Mr. Nixon always said the people could not stand an impeachment process. Mr. Ford says the people could not stand a trial of a former

President: it would shatter "domestic tranquility." Amazing, you think, how solicitous our leaders are about our peace of mind? But it is not really amazing when
a politician decides that people cannot endure whatever he thinks it is not in his
interest to let happen.

In fact, Mr. Ford has done for Mr. Nixon what Mr. Nixon never quite mustered
the gall to do for Lt. William Calley, the officer convicted on charges stemming
from the My Lai massacre. By pardoning Mr. Nixon, Mr. Ford has ingratiated
himself with an intense minority (Nixon bitter-enders) whom Mr. Ford evidently
considers important to his political base.

We judge a politician, at least in part, by his political base, and by what he will
do to curry favor with it. We also judge a politician by his ability to get something
in exchange for something. Mr. Ford either did not seek or could not get Mr.
Nixon to admit, in exchange for the pardon, that he was guilty of any of what Ford
gingerly refers to as the "allegations and accusations" against him. All Mr. Nixon
says is that he regrets not acting "more decisively" about Watergate and he has
never admitted to and will never admit to anything worse than indecision. Of
course, the June 23, 1972, tape shows that he acted decisively to obstruct justice.

Mr. Ford seems to think Mr. Nixon is a sociological not a legal problem.
According to Mr. Ford a Nixon trial, like some social condition, might stir "ugly
passions." Mr. Ford plunges through the looking glass to argue dizzily, that "the
credibility of our free institutions" would be "challenged at home and abroad" if
our free judicial institutions were allowed to work.

Mr. Ford may, as he says, have "the constitutional power to firmly shut and seal"
the Watergate "book." But that does not mean that it was right for him to hastily
slam the book shut before we could read it. That is what he did by rushing to
prevent a judicial examination of Mr. Nixon's conduct, and by giving Mr. Nixon
custody of the best evidence about Mr. Nixon's conduct.

Mr. Ford's motives no doubt included a desire to be compassionate, and a
concern for Mr. Nixon's health. But in government effects and appearances can
be as important as motives. And whether or not it was Mr. Ford's intention, the
effect of his precipitate action appears rather like the effect of what used to be
called, in less polite times, a cover-up.*

Even a cursory inspection of Will's article reveals that his analysis of
President Ford's decision to pardon Richard Nixon rests on a series of historical assumptions and assertions. A closer scrutiny further discloses that many
of the claims that Will puts forth so lightly actually involve interpretations
of the past that are both complex and controversial. Some of these claims are
obviously straw men, set up by Will merely to be knocked down. Others he

---

*Editorial by George F. Will, *Washington Post,* copyright © 1974 by Washington Post
Writers Group. Reprinted by permission.

presents as basic truths about the behavior and beliefs of the American people. Will's own interpretive judgments are sometimes identified, sometimes camouflaged with colorful language. Without clear distinctions, Will refers both to short-term historical trends and to the long run. Will's historical references form an essential component of his persuasive strategy; they enable him to criticize simultaneously the pardon decision, President Ford, the "general cut of politicians," and the American public.

The most notable historical argument included in Will's column is, of course, the "English Muffin Theory of History"—that "a President who toasts his own English muffins for breakfast is somehow different from the general cut of politicians." This homey theory of political life, Will argues, has been disproved by Ford's pardon, becoming "just another theory killed by a fact." Yet Will's message is not nearly as simple as it appears. Will uses the theory and its refutation to classify Ford as just another self-serving politician and to underscore the naiveté of public opinion. The "English Muffin Theory of History" rests on several important assumptions about American political life. First, the theory assumes that politicians generally require the services of others to avoid the mundane tasks that dominate the everyday lives of most of their constituents. Second, it assumes that a politician humble enough to perform such chores for himself is somehow different from most of his brethren. Third, the Muffin theory rests upon the premise that, prior to Ford's pardon of Nixon, most Americans believed in the first two assumptions. Fourth, it assumes that, because of Ford's pardon, the second assumption is no longer held as valid. Fifth, the argument assumes that the pardon exemplifies the general conduct of politicians.

But, as already noted, Will's own assertions about the "English Muffin Theory" also rests upon dubious assumptions about the logic of historical inquiry. First, his own argument implies that a generalization about human behavior and belief can be disproved by a single contrary example—a rather odd reversal of the old adage that "the exception proves the rule." Second, Will suggests a fundamental distinction between a "theory" and a "fact." Facts, it appears, are what debunk theories. Both these suppositions are discussed further in Chapters II and III.

Will also sets up and then knocks down several other generally held beliefs about the nature of man. He begins his piece with Robert Louis Stevenson's wry observation that man "lives not by bread alone but principally by catchwords." Stevenson, of course, was playing on Jesus's saying that man cannot survive solely on physical nourishment but requires love and spirituality as well. Stevenson's parody suggests that the complement of mere existence is neither love nor spirit but empty slogans. By adding this ironic twist to his own argument, Will insinuates that long before Ford's pardon of Nixon, the concept of "equal justice under law"—the spiritual basis of the American legal system—had become more a slogan than a reality. He also suggests that Ford actually performed a public service by puncturing the soap bubble of our illusions.

The paragraph about bread and catchwords is followed by another "Willian" dictum: "It is an iron law of politics that when a politician intones support for a principle, he is about to make an exception to that principle for the benefit of a friend." Supposedly, this is another empirical statement, based on past experience, about the behavior of politicians. The "iron law" explicitly connects knowledge of the past to prediction of the future. Any "alert citizen" with an awareness of political history should easily have been able to predict President Ford's decision. Will's iron law also adds to the cynicism about human motivation that he first suggests by quoting Stevenson and then sustains throughout his article. For example, Will asserts that a politician generally "decides that people cannot endure whatever [the politician] thinks it is not in his interest to let happen." Thus he suggests that politicians have traditionally manipulated John Q. Citizen by misrepresenting attempts to promote their own selfish interests as selfless service for the public good.

Will employs one explicitly historical analogy, the Lieutenant Calley case, to buttress his argument about the pardon and puts it to particularly effective strategic use. By comparing the pardon granted Nixon to the aborted pardon for the convicted mass murderer, Will tars Ford with guilt by association. He also uses the Calley analogy to interpret the motivations not only of Nixon but of Ford as well. By implying that Nixon really wanted to pardon Calley but, in the face of political opposition, never mustered the courage (or gall) to do so, Will underscores the idea that Ford's decision to pardon Nixon rested upon political considerations, rather than on notions of justice or national interest.

Will further suggests that, in contrast to the Calley pardon, the Nixon pardon "drained the nutritional value from the catchwords about 'equal justice under law.'" This contention presupposes, however, that prior to the pardon, these catchwords truly reflected public sentiment about the American legal system. It further assumes that Ford's action (even though characteristic of the "general cut of politicians") so violated the popular view as to reorient fundamentally our thinking about "equal justice" in America.

Will concludes his article by linking Ford's action to an ongoing historical trend—a continuing cover-up of the Watergate scandals, a tendency of government officials to hide their actions from public scrutiny. However,

Will's language here is cagey; perhaps he means to suggest that Ford knowingly aided the cover-up or perhaps that his actions simply created the appearance of complicity. Will's conclusion also heightens the tension that he has deliberately created between two seemingly contradictory ideas: first, that the Nixon pardon was a gross exception to the sacred principle of "equal justice," and second, that this pardon was consistent with the normal behavior of American political leaders.

Although Will's commentary clearly rests in part upon his understanding of the past, he rarely makes the premises of his historical arguments explicit. His conclusions often represent only the final step in a complex chain of implicitly historical reasoning that the reader must dig out on his own. On the other hand, Will does not pose as the impartial scholar interested only in "objective" truth. In his column, history is subservient to political commentary; he uses the past selectively as an instrument for criticizing Ford's decision to pardon Richard Nixon. It comes as no surprise, therefore, that Will the columnist, yet implicitly the historian, devotes little space to evidence that would lend credibility to his historical interpretations (except for a reference to the White House tape of June 23, 1972, the famous "smoking pistol" that decisively influenced the House Judiciary Committee's vote to recommend impeachment).

The reader who seeks to evaluate the use of history in contemporary journalism thus bears a heavy responsibility. He must be able to detect an author's historical propositions and their role in his strategic design. He must also reconstruct the implicit logic of arguments about the past and assess their empirical accuracy. Unless he is content to be snared by the commentator's skills, the reader must be prepared to deploy his own arsenal of analytic weaponry.

George F. Kennan's *American Diplomacy, 1900–1950,* although offered as a study in diplomatic history, is also a far-reaching commentary on the contemporary conduct of foreign affairs. Kennan views American diplomacy during the first half of the twentieth century as a series of well intended initiatives that failed. He attempts to isolate the factors responsible for American inability to cope with world affairs and to use these findings as the basis for proposed changes in both the ideology and institutions of foreign policy in the United States. Indeed, Kennan does not hesitate to discuss the past as it really was, the past as it might have been, and the future as it ought to be. For virtually every episode within the scope of his study, he details the policies followed by American diplomats, suggests the course they should have followed, and draws a moral for the guidance of policymakers in his own time.

Kennan locates the fatal flaw of American diplomacy in a characteristic which had been exalted as a virtue by most previous commentators. He indicts American statesmen, not for lack of intelligence, training, or integrity, but for a proclivity to conduct foreign policy on the basis of moral and legal principles. This proclivity, he claims, did not result from some peculiarity of the foreign policy establishment, but was "deeply rooted in the national consciousness." Unfortunately, the "moralistic-legalistic" approach to international relations contradicted the best interests of the nation and the goal of world harmony. Embedded within the structure of Kennan's historical arguments are several distinct criticisms of a diplomacy that rests on law and morality. The validity of these criticisms, however, depends upon the historical examples that are the focus of Kennan's narrative.

First, Kennan suggests that the application of law and morality to international affairs falsely assumes that nations within the world community behave like individuals within a single nation-state. Whereas individuals generally experience internal pressure to follow the laws and customs of a national culture, leaders feel no such compulsion to follow the rules of international politics. Statesmen do not subordinate the perceived interests of their nation to the requirements of international laws and compacts. Moral principles and codes of agreement are respected only insofar as they promote the already established goals of national policy. Moreover, international agreements, unlike those within a single nation, cannot be enforced with meaningful sanctions. For example, Kennan criticized America's Open Door policy in China, an attempt in 1899 and 1900 to gain international agreement on the principle that all nations should have access to trade and commerce in China, and that the political integrity of China should be respected. Kennan maintains that the Open Door policy had no practical effect on world affairs; foreign diplomats were willing to pay only lip service to a vague, moral principle that included no enforcement mechanisms. He further intimates that this policy was counterproductive, because rival nations suspected that it was merely a cloak for sinister motives on the part of the United States. Similarly, the Open Door policy contributed to the spread of anti-American sentiment since these nations also felt that American diplomats were asking them to sacrifice their vital interests without giving up or risking anything in return.

Second, Kennan believes that considerations of law and morality have genuine meaning only within cultures that share common legal systems and traditions. Moral precepts cannot be applied indiscriminantly to diverse nations and peoples, and policymakers cannot assume that their own ethical systems are equally applicable to alien cultures. Indeed, the attempt to impose nationally conditioned standards of law and morality upon the international community leads to moral perversity, as lives, property, and goodwill are squandered in a futile attempt to alter national traditions and institutions. Kennan argues, for example, that American statesmen after World War I made the great mistake of indulging in "the colossal conceit of thinking that you could suddenly make international life into what you believed to be your own image." They ignored the realities "that a study of the past would suggest" and impudently sought to coerce the defeated Germans into restructuring their traditional institutions. This self-defeating policy served only to plunge Germany into social chaos and to leave her bitter, disillusioned, and thirsting for revenge.

Third, and most important, Kennan maintains that the attempt to conduct foreign affairs according to legal and moral principles leads to the disastrous policies of total war and unconditional surrender. If a nation resorts to force, not to secure a limited, well-defined political objective, but to rectify violations of law or morality, then warfare becomes a crusade, aimed at eradicating evil by any means available. Similarly, when a nation is aroused to undertake a great moral crusade, diplomats cannot easily bargain or compromise with the enemy—the goal of total war is unconditional surrender. Both World War I and World War II were total wars in which the victorious powers demanded the unconditional surrender of their enemies. In both cases, these misguided policies resulted in unnecessary death and destruction and jeopardized the prospects for lasting peace. Kennan emphasizes that Americans need to recognize the folly of using force to alter the nature of foreign regimes or to create a purified world order.

If American statesmen were preoccupied for a half century with legal and moral questions, Kennan suggests that they should have been preoccupied with determining the national interest of the United States. Only a foreign policy designed to preserve and protect America's vital interests would have avoided the contradictions of the moralistic-legalistic approach and responded to the realities of international affairs. Most important to the maintenance of America's security was the preservation of a balance of power among the industrialized nations of the world. By balance of power, Kennan means a situation in which no single nation or tightly aligned group of nations can dominate the rest of the civilized world. War is an almost inevitable result of serious breakdowns in the balance of power. Ironically, the result of both World War I and World War II was to disrupt the balance of power and sow the seeds of a new conflict. Kennan argues that, after World War I, Germany emerged as the strongest, most unified state in the middle of Europe. Germany was flanked on the East by Soviet Russia, whose interests were antithetical to those of the western democracies, and on the West by Britain and France, whose strength had been sapped by the exertions of world conflict. The effect of World War II was to eliminate any effective counterforce to the power of a resurgent Russia, either in Europe or the Far East.

According to Kennan, the failure of American diplomacy between 1900 and 1950 can be rectified only by fundamental changes in the future conduct of American foreign policy. Policymakers must never let moral and legal principles control decisions about war and peace. Warfare can be justified only by a hardheaded analysis of America's security interests. Similarly, American statesmen must recognize that warfare need not be total, and that surrender need not be unconditional. Rather, force can be used in a limited and controlled fashion to help maintain the international balance of power and protect the national interest.

Kennan further suggests that the United States should not blindly oscillate between periods of isolation and total involvement in world affairs. To a great extent, the rhythm of American foreign policy is determined by military strength. A decision to disarm and demobilize after the catharsis of total war would not only restrict America's ability to influence international events, but would also mean that the nation must be summoned to a new crusade before adequate rearmament could take place. Thus America must maintain her military strength even in time of peace and should promote her national interests through active participation in foreign affairs.

Kennan believes that American diplomats should be less responsive to the erratic swings of public opinion and more responsive to the balanced judgment of professionals. He maintains that subservience to popular whims has precluded a rational approach to foreign policy; he fears that ordinary citizens will never be able to transcend their "emotional" and "subjective" reaction to world events. Only an elite corps of professionals would have the knowledge, experience, and detachment to guide the foreign policy of the United States rationally and objectively.

In the final sections of his book, Kennan sketches the broad outlines of a realistic approach to Soviet-American relations, based upon the experience of both nations. The lesson that Kennan draws from Russian history is that the Communist regime will necessarily remain hostile to the United States and other western democracies. The destruction of all effective internal opposition has compelled Russian leaders to justify their dictatorship by stressing the menace of foreign opposition. But, despite their belief in the ultimate self-destruction of capitalism, the Soviets need not engage in dangerous military confrontations. Rather, they can afford to be patient, while relentless. Moreover, since Communist leaders are not bound by the fetters of public opinion, they are able to employ whichever tactical maneuvers appear most suitable at a particular time and to abandon them when circumstances change.

Faced with these grim facts, Kennan believes that the United States can no longer afford the luxury of amateur diplomacy based on fuzzy moral principles. He proposes the policy of containment as a realistic alternative to either war or capitulation. This policy can thwart the expansion of Communism without provoking the enemy into armed conflict. Expert diagnosticians of world affairs can contain "Soviet pressure against the free institutions of the western world . . . by the adroit and vigilant application of counter-force at a series of constantly shifting geographical and political points, corresponding to the shifts and maneuvers of Soviet policy." Under the direction of professionals, the policy of containment cannot "be charmed or talked out of existence," and in the long run, may lead to the internal destruction of the Soviet regime.

Kennan's book is especially important for contemporary minded students of American diplomacy, because the views that he expressed in 1952 were to a large extent adopted by American policymakers. National leaders have seen in the policy of containment as articulated by Kennan an acceptable middle ground between the extremes of appeasement and nuclear war. Indeed, the so-called domino theory—that a Communist takeover in one nation would lead to the toppling of neighboring governments—is but an extension of Kennan's ideas on containment. Similarly, the United States firmly embraced the notion that she could afford neither military demobilization nor isolation from the quarrels of foreign nations. Since 1950, the United States has maintained a vast military establishment and has actively defended its interests in far-flung corners of the globe. No conflict seemed too trivial for American involvement, no area of the world too remote or primitive. The United States has also followed Kennan's dictum regarding the use of force for the achievement of limited political objectives. The covert operations of the CIA, the American sponsored insurrections in Cuba and Guatemala, and the military interventions in the Dominican Republic and Vietnam, all exemplify the policy of limited war. Yet policymakers also seem to have heeded Kennan's warnings about the inability of the public rationally to evaluate foreign policy initiatives; America's military operations, both direct and indirect, are invariably justified to the American people on the basis of the very legal and moral principles scorned by hardheaded statesmen. The American foreign service has also become far more professionalized in the years following World War II. The professional staff of the State Department and other agencies involved in foreign affairs has increased at a fantastic rate; and expert analysts, using the best available information and technology, were intimately involved in the planning of such major enterprises as the Bay of Pigs invasion and the Vietnam War.

All of Kennan's prescriptions for the conduct of diplomacy evolve from his interpretations of past events. Kennan's plans for the future cannot be separated from his vision of the past. Therefore, to the extent that his historical arguments are misguided, his policy recommendations lose their rationale.

Many of Kennan's ideas about American diplomatic history have been disputed by other reputable scholars. While it is beyond the scope of this chapter either to describe competing interpretations in detail or to resolve any of the historical issues involved, we can set forth some of the more important objections to Kennan's views. Historians have challenged the fundamental thesis of *American Diplomacy*—that policymakers have been influenced primarily by moral and legal precepts. For example, a major school of thought, the "revisionists," has emphasized that American diplomats in the twentieth century have consistently sought to advance the economic interests of American business. In this view, the federal government has operated hand in glove with American corporations in an effort to extend the economic and political influence of the United States. "Revisionist" scholars have reinterpreted every one of the episodes discussed by Kennan and have attributed misguided policy to entirely different causes. American leaders do not emerge from the works of revisionist history as naive moralists, disdainful of power politics. Instead, they appear to be shrewd and calculating politicians, rationally pursuing a set of reasonably well-defined economic and political objectives. In contrast to Kennan's recommendations, the revisionist version of American diplomatic history would suggest that the United States should reduce its overseas commitments, slash defense spending, cease intervening in the affairs of foreign nations, seek mutual accommodations with Communist states, downgrade the role of foreign policy experts, and provide the American public the information necessary for an intelligent contribution to the policymaking process.

Kennan's historical analysis is also vulnerable to other substantive objections. Historians have questioned whether public opinion actually has restricted the flexibility of American foreign policy. They have suggested, for example, that leaders have been responsive only to the articulated opinions of a very small group of prominent citizens, and that the general public has been willing to indorse virtually any vigorous presidential initiative in the realm of international affairs. Scholars have also disputed Kennan's sanguine assessment of a diplomacy directed by professionally trained authorities.

Researchers have found that experts have tended to become rigidly committed to particular viewpoints and disinclined to change policies in which they have vested personal interests. Professionals have not been responsive either to new ideas or to changing circumstances. Similarly, experts are often so preoccupied with their own areas of expertise that they ignore the broader context of policy decisions. Historians with a general grasp of world history have also suggested that it is extraordinarily difficult to wage a carefully controlled, limited war, and that armed conflict in pursuit of practical objectives is not necessarily more humane than conflict based on law or morality. They have further pointed out that, over the long-term, the maintenance of a balance of power among nations has not proved to be an effective means of avoiding war.

The logic as well as the substance of Kennan's work raises questions that must be considered by the serious reader. Kennan's analysis of diplomatic history rests on the assumption that it is possible to separate considerations of morality and national interest. Yet judgments of what is and is not in the national interest, no less than judgments of what is moral or immoral, depend upon the system of values being applied. These values determine the individual's view of what "ought to be," an essential component of any judgment about goals or objectives. For example, the different value systems of Barry Goldwater and George McGovern produce very different opinions about what constitutes the national interest. Moreover, Kennan's own work is interlaced with moral judgments about international affairs. He morally condemns the ideologies of both Communism and Fascism as well as the specific regimes established by Adolf Hitler in Germany and Joseph Stalin in Russia. He is morally committed to the Judeo-Christian tradition and, despite some trepidations, to the institutions of American democracy.

Kennan's work also presupposes the existence of an "objective" reality independent of the individual observer. Wise and knowledgable statesmen should be able to discover this reality and guide their policy decision accordingly. Yet most thinkers would agree that our interpretation of the outside world is a function of both external information and the preconceptions we bring to that information. Individuals with different ways of looking at the world might draw different conclusions from the same data; in other words, there are no independent criteria for deciding which conclusions are right and which are wrong. We shall discuss the assumptions that people bring to the study of the past more fully in Chapters III and IV.

The works of Will and Kennan provide striking examples of present minded authors unabashedly using history to understand contemporary issues. Moreover, the disputes engendered by Kennan's analysis particularly point to the desirability of having a firm basis for evaluating historical arguments. Reputable scholars have contended that Kennan's description of how diplomats made decisions on moral and legalistic grounds is not credible; that his view of the influence of American public opinion on foreign policy decisions is not sound; that his assessment of the abilities of specially trained experts is overly optimistic; that a balance of power among nations does not insure against war; and that it is not possible to distinguish neatly between national interest and morality. How is the reader to choose among these conflicting accounts of what happened and contradictory interpretations of the past? The next two chapters address themselves to both of these problems.

Historical Inference: Reconstructing The Past

Sherlock Holmes and the historian have much in common. Each of them tries to reconstruct events he has not actually observed from evidence that he can observe. Neither of them can afford to overlook any possible clue. Both the historian and the detective are prepared to examine evidence ranging from written documents and material objects to oral testimony, photographs, and recordings. Both of them recognize that evidence does not speak for itself but that its story must be drawn out by using logical reasoning and applying other knowledge that the historian brings to the evidence itself. Asked what he can gather from an old felt hat, Watson professes "to see nothing." Holmes instantly concludes that the owner was "highly intellectual . . . fairly well-to-do within the last three years, although now fallen upon evil days," that "his wife has ceased to love him," and that he "leads a sedentary life, is middle-aged, has grizzled hair which he has cut within the last few days and which he annoints with lime-cream." Elementary if you know what you are doing. As Holmes often reminds us, there is no magic in his method, only "pure deductive reasoning" and years of laborious study.

Just as the detective examines evidence to reconstruct a crime, so also the historian investigates evidence to reconstruct the past, to determine what actually happened. Moreover, every one of us reconstructs what happened in our personal lives and in the conduct of current affairs. We rely on our memory and, like the historian and the detective, on what we observe in the present. The methods of reconstruction used by the historian are no different than those we use in daily life.

In many cases, the reconstruction of "what happened" poses no special problems. Consider, for example, a historian who finds several newspaper accounts describing the nomination of a candidate at a political convention. If those accounts were written by reporters known to have differing political views and to work for different newspapers, and if those accounts agreed substantially, the historian could be confident that a reconstruction based on those accounts would reflect what happened. Similarly, if in reading through the personal correspondence of an individual, a historian finds reference again and again to a particular problem, he can be reasonably sure that the individual was concerned about that problem. In these cases, common sense permits the historian to infer what happened from the surviving evidence with comparative ease and certainty. Historians can make these inferences because they use some generally accepted notions about the way people think and act. In the first case, we take it for granted that when several reporters of different political persuasions and from different newspapers have filed the same story describing a major public event, we are reasonably confident that their accounts are correct. In the second case, we believe that if a person writes over and over about the same problem, that problem concerns him. Thus for the most part, the historian's effort to reconstruct the past is devoted to gathering evidence, sifting it, and applying his common sense to determine what happened. He usually feels safe in relying on his common sense. The guidelines he uses are accepted by others; he has no reason to doubt the veracity of his sources; and his evidence all seems to point to the same reconstruction. In short, he believes that any other historian examining the same evidence would reconstruct a similar account of what happened.

From the perspective of common sense, the reconstruction of past events seems simple and straightforward. Yet historians, like detectives, must be wary even of what seems most obvious. As Sherlock Holmes once warned Dr. Watson, "There is nothing more deceptive than an obvious fact." During the presidential campaign in 1912, for instance, the *New York Times* quoted Woodrow Wilson as scorning his opponent Theodore Roosevelt for posing as a "self-appointed divinity." Understandably, historians would be inclined to believe that such a prestigious newspaper would accurately report the words of a presidential candidate. Yet research by Arthur S. Link, editor of the *Woodrow Wilson Papers,* reveals that Wilson actually used the much less offensive phrase, "Providence resident in Washington," and referred to Roosevelt only by implication.

Not only may historians be misled by apparently reliable sources, but cases often arise in which problems of reconstruction are readily apparent. The historian, like the detective, may find precious little evidence to work with, or he may find a single piece of evidence that easily admits of more than one interpretation; or he may find that different pieces of evidence point to different reconstructions. When confronted with such problems, the historian can no longer rely on common sense alone, for it cannot solve the puzzles presented by his evidence.

Consider the historian facing the following dilemma. He is investigating the Spanish Inquisition and has been lucky enough to discover several accounts of the same inquisitorial proceedings in one district. One of the accounts was written by a clerk of the inquisitorial board; another came from a Jew whose brother was eventually condemned to burn at the stake; and another came from a priest who ministered to those accused of heresy. Having found these three accounts written by people who were eyewitnesses to the events they describe and who saw the inquisitorial proceedings from three perspectives, the historian initially may feel fortunate indeed. But, when he tries to reconstruct what happened in that Spanish district, he may be stymied. He may find that all three accounts purport to tell the same story, but contradict one another in their very descriptions of what happened. How does the historian decide what actually happened? If he has no reason to suspect the honesty of any of the three writers, he has no grounds simply to dismiss one or more of them. If he has no other documentation for the event, he must use the evidence at hand. Merely applying common sense to this problem will be inappropriate if the historian has no generally accepted notions that tell him what different types of Spaniards involved in the Inquisition were apt to do or to think. Only by drawing on his knowledge of how people are likely to behave and how the world works, can the historian make arguments that enable him to reconstruct the past, to determine what happened. Indeed, what we call the application of common sense is simply an implicit rather than explicit operation of the process of reconstruction.

Historians should approach their evidence skeptically, prepared to go beyond intuition or common sense to advance arguments that justify the conclusions drawn from inspection of source material. This chapter will explore the process by which historians move from their evidence to a reconstruction of the past. We will consider the nature of historical evidence, the kinds of questions historians ask of their evidence, and the methods used by historians to elicit a story from this evidence. This chapter will discuss only historical inference—the process of reconstructing past events, of determining what actually happened, from historical evidence. We are using the word *reconstruction* here in a narrow sense. In historical writing, "reconstruction" often connotes not only a description of what happened but also an explanation of past events. Because the process of determining what happened must precede and remain distinct from the process of explaining what happened, we discuss these problems separately and confine the meaning of "reconstructing the past" to "determining what happened." Our next chapter will explore the problem of *explaining* what we know about the past.

Historical Evidence

Much as he would like to have them, the historian has neither a videotape nor a time machine that enables him to observe the past directly. Since the historian is unable to observe the events he describes, he cannot, like the sportscaster, simply tell it "like it is." The historian must depend upon objects that survive from the past—historical evidence—to make even the most rudimentary reconstruction of the past. If he wants to know something about ancient Egyptian family life, the French Revolution, or the Great Depression, he seeks items that might allow him to infer something about those events.

Too often, historians have confined their studies to documentary evidence. Written materials are easy to use and can be conveniently gathered, reproduced, and deposited in libraries. But if we stop and think for a moment, we will realize that much more survives from our past than written material. The earth itself—its topography, its soil, its climate—affected the lives of men and women in the past as much as it affects our own. If the historian is studying a battle, for example, he probably ought to visit the site of the battle to see for himself the terrain and to infer from its present state the physical conditions under which the battle was fought.

In addition, what past societies have built often survives at least relatively intact. Although much of ancient Rome has been destroyed, many of its most important buildings still remain—the Forum, the Coliseum, monumental arches, and aquaducts. The historian can and should use these physical artifacts just as archaeologists do. Even such mundane things as floor plans of houses can reveal much to the historian who is interested in the way people lived. Moreover, historians need not confine themselves to buildings and cities. Anyone who has gone through a museum knows that a startling variety of small, everyday objects from the past have survived. Some of exquisite beauty—coins, jewelry, vases, and silverware—are out on display. But in the storerooms of many museums are countless other, less beautiful objects, that can be just as useful to the historian. Pots and pans, household furniture, lamps, remnants of clothing, and tools—all can be used to reconstruct the past.

Historians conventionally classify their sources as either primary or secondary. They usually refer to evidence produced at the time of the event as "primary," and accounts written later as "secondary." We prefer a more precise differentiation, classifying the source materials historians use to reconstruct the past in three categories: primary, secondary, and tertiary. Primary sources consist only of evidence that was actually part of or produced by the event the historian is studying; secondary sources consist of other evidence pertaining to and produced soon after the event; and tertiary sources are "historical" accounts written afterward to reconstruct the event. For example, a historian investigating how the American military responded to the attack on Pearl Harbor would use as primary source material such things as the entries in the ship logs that survived the attack, radio messages sent during the bombing, and films and pictures taken during the raid. His secondary sources might include such materials as newspaper accounts, diaries describing the attack, and memoirs of military and political leaders. Finally he would examine his tertiary sources—books and articles that scholars have already written. Obviously, the historian will normally attempt to work with as much contemporary—primary—evidence as possible. The farther removed his evidence from the event in question, the more likely it will be distorted or biased.

Only recently have historians begun to make use of another potentially rich source of historical evidence—oral and visual material. Every generation carries around in its head vast quantities of information about its own experience. Yet rarely do individuals take the time to write this information down; consequently, when the generation dies, so too does the information. Moreover, when an individual sits down to write, he invariably begins to analyze his thoughts and selectively chooses what he wants to record and what he wants to omit. Writing rarely lends itself to free association. Access to this normally irretrievable information and to the free associations that can be so helpful in understanding an individual's attitudes and feelings about his own experience has been the goal of "oral" historians. They seek to interview and record on tape the recollections of a wide variety of individuals, both important leaders and anonymous followers.

In addition to taped interviews, historians are also beginning to use such visual materials as photographs, movies, and drawings, even doodles and graffiti. Taken together, these oral and visual sources can significantly enrich the body of evidence available for the reconstruction of the past.

The following chart indicates the enormous range of materials available to the historian in his quest to reconstruct the past.*

Archaeology:

Inscriptions
Entire or part remains
(buildings, walls, etc.)
Pots and other artefacts

Coins

Public written sources,
    whether on stone, papyrus,
    parchment or paper:
Royal Charters
Laws
Surveys
Official government papers

Other official or semi-official
    sources:

Cabinet records
Diplomatic dispatches
Ambassadors' reports
Poll books
Local government records
Manorial records
Legal cases and reports
Parish registers
Parish poor relief records
Police reports
Trade Union minutes and
reports

Private written sources:

Letters
Diaries
Contracts

Estate records
Wage returns
Monastic records and chronicles

Printed sources:

Pamphlets
Treatises and polemical writings
Parliamentary debates
Newspapers
Published autobiographies
and reminiscences

Industrial archaeology:

Entire or part remains of factories
Old machinery
Workpeoples' houses
Remains of transportation systems

Place names

Maps

Aerial photography

Other photographs

Film

Oral traditions: folk songs, etc.

Architecture

Novels

Poems

Painting

Sculpture

----

*Chart from Arthur Marwick, *Primary Sources* from *Humanities: A Foundation Course,* copyright © 1970 by The Open University. Reprinted by permission.

In brief, historical evidence can be anything that provides a clue to the occurrence of past events. As the great French historian Marc Bloch put it, "Whether it is the bones immured in the Syrian fortification, a word whose form or use reveals a custom, a narrative written by the witnesses of some scene, ancient or modern, what do we really mean by *document,* if it is not a "track," as it were—the mark, perceptible to the senses, which some phenomenon, in itself inaccessible, has left behind?"

Historical Reports

To learn about the inaccessible past from the accessible evidence, historians must ask questions of that evidence. The simplest ones that historians ask in their attempts to reconstruct the past require answers similar to those contained in the opening paragraph of a standard news story. These questions turn on the four basics—What? Where? When? Who? Henceforth the term *historical report* will refer to any statement about the past that answers one or more of these basic questions. *Historical reports,* as we use the term in this book, are limited to those statements about the past that establish and describe the events that actually happened. Those events may include not only external occurrences—wars, elections, coronations, earthquakes, and the like—but also internal events, the thoughts and feelings of individuals who experienced those external occurrences.

Because historical reports answer only the questions What? Where? When? and Who?, they are often equated with the facts of history, those solid little nuggets of information that can be used to build interpretations of the past. Reports simply tell us what happened, provide us the "facts" of history that form the core of most history textbooks. But, given the problems of confidently deciding what actually happened in the past, we prefer the term historical *report* to historical fact. Indeed, upon close examination, historical facts are often far less substantial than we generally assume. For example, we may never be able to determine the time and circumstances of the burning of the palace complex at Persepolis by the army of Alexander the Great. The burning of this Persian palace, one of the most dramatic incidents of ancient history, took place some time in the spring of 330 B.C., but its exact date remains a mystery. Also, we do not know whether Alexander himself or a drunken courtesan, a Greek campfollower Thais, set off the fire. The skimpy evidence available does not allow the historian to give a sure answer to either the question "Who?" or "When?"

Verifying historical reports is a problem not only when dealing with remote periods of history or with events for which we have unusually sparse evidence. Experience has shown that it can also be difficult to provide reliable accounts of well documented events close to our own time. Few historical events, for example, have stirred the passions of Americans as much as the assassination of President John F. Kennedy. Beyond a reasonable doubt, we know that the President was killed; we know where he was killed; and we know when he was killed. Many students of the assassination would argue, however, that we do not yet know who killed the President.

A presidential commission, headed by Chief Justice Earl Warren and including some of the nation's most distinguished public figures, investigated the Kennedy assassination. The commission issued a summary report of 888 pages and twenty-six volumes of exhibits and testimony. In addition to its own staff of fourteen lawyers, the commission used the investigative agencies of the federal government. It had access to 30,000 interviews, autopsy reports, physical evidence, and even a color movie of the President's movements as he was shot. It called upon expert witnesses in such fields as medicine, ballistics, photography, and acoustics. The findings of the Warren Commission have been combed by a varied assortment of private individuals —some seeking publicity and profit, others clearly seeking the truth. Their work has produced a continuing cascade of books and articles.

Despite the incredible amount of time, energy, manpower, and resources devoted to the investigation of the Kennedy assassination, the basic reportorial question of who killed the President remains a matter of intense controversy. Imagine, then, the difficulties that the historian faces in seeking accurate reports of events in a remote period. He is confronted by linguistic and cultural barriers; often works in isolation; is unable to interview witnesses or examine films; and lacks eyewitness accounts.

Thus, although simple and straightforward in appearance, questions about the basic events of history are often impossible to answer reliably. The application of common sense alone cannot solve the problems. When confronted with situations in which his common sense cannot provide a sure guide for reconstructing the past, the historian must reframe his inquiry in a way most likely to elicit answers that establish the most credible reports possible. Instead of asking simply, "Who did this?" he can set up an hypothesis and then test it against the evidence he has gathered. As Holmes reminds us, "One should always look for a possible alternative and provide against it. It is the first rule of criminal investigation." A historian of the Kennedy assassination might recast the question, "Who killed President Kennedy?" into the hypothesis, "Lee Harvey Oswald, acting alone, assassinated President

Kennedy." He would then examine his evidence to try to ascertain whether it sustains this hypothesis more credibly than some alternative hypothesis—perhaps that "Lee Harvey Oswald, together with another, unknown assailant, assassinated President Kennedy." If the original hypothesis is not rejected, in turn, it can be compared to yet another alternative. Hypotheses survive or die in competition with each other.

In fact, the process of reasoning used to move from observation of evidence to a reconstruction of the past is identical whether the historian employs his common sense or consciously tests alternative hypotheses. Once he has arrived at a tentative answer to one of the interrogatives, he decides whether to accept that answer by judging whether it is more credible than any other answer; he turns his tentative answer into an hypothesis and tests it against other hypotheses. This reasoning process occurs so quickly that we are usually unaware of it. Only when confronted by situations in which this reasoning process does not work easily and reliably—when we can neither formulate nor have confidence in a tentative answer—do we usually become conscious of the reasoning that we employ to reconstruct the past.

There are two situations, then, in which the historian must consciously adopt the posture of hypothesis tester rather than inquiring reporter, although as we have argued, the process of inference is the same for both. The first of these arises when the historian cannot easily and reliably answer one or more of the basic interrogative questions. The second occurs when a historian seeks to prove that his reconstruction of the past is the most credible one possible, and that the inferences he has drawn from the evidence are the ones most likely to establish the historical reports that most accurately describe what actually happened. Since historians are already familiar with the use of common sense as a guide for reconstructing the past, we will devote the rest of this chapter to a discussion of the issues involved in testing hypotheses about historical reports. Indeed, we would recommend that historians consciously check the reliability of their common sense answers by subjecting them to formal testing as hypotheses.

The Twin Foundations of Historical Reports:
Knowledge and Logic

To learn about the past from observations of historical evidence, historians not only must use logical methods, but also must possess a considerable range of knowledge. In fact, this very knowledge permits the historian to construct historical reports upon a foundation of evidence, and provides the generaliza-

tions needed to build a logical argument. Generalizations describe the properties and processes that characterize groups of individuals and objects. Any
statement that applies to all members of a group is a generalization. For
example, we might generalize about all children, all Greeks, all monks, all
ships, and all trees.

Through their knowledge of generalizations, historians and detectives alike
can connect descriptions of the properties of evidence to the occurrence of
past events. Watson knows about the methods Holmes uses to solve crimes,
but he cannot make them work because he lacks Holmes' storehouse of
generalizations. To Dr. Watson, and even Inspectors Lestrade and Gregson,
a bit of cigar ash at the scene of a murder is just filth. To Holmes it may
reveal the identity of the culprit. For the generalizations at his command
include knowledge of the properties of the ashes left by every variety of cigar
and the kinds of people who smoke each one of them. Even Holmes would
be as incompetent as Watson or Lestrade if asked to make deductions from
evidence in realms beyond his knowledge, say astronomy or literary history.
He would face the same dilemma as the historian of the Spanish Inquisition
who lacked enough knowledge of how fifteenth century Spaniards thought
to decide which of the accounts he had discovered made it possible to
reconstruct what actually happened.

For all his knowledge of crime, Holmes relies on the rules of logic to solve
his cases.* If Holmes occasionally commends others for their perceptive
intuitions, his own methods are supremely logical. Holmes can always explain
how he reaches any of his conclusions. The flawless logic of these
explanations makes his conclusions seem obviously correct. As Watson has
remarked, "When I hear you give your reasons, the thing always appears to
me to be so ridiculously simple that I could easily do it myself, though at each
successive instance of your reasoning, I am baffled until you explain your
process."

The methods of logic also help us choose among contradictory reports. If
conclusions about the past were indeed reached by a purely intuitive or
unconscious process, then no one could justify his conclusion to another or
benefit from another's criticism of the process by which the conclusion was
reached. Holmes reaches conclusions so quickly that many are misled in
believing that even he operates by intuition. But conclusions spring instantly
to his lips only because "from long habit the train of thoughts ran so swiftly

---

*We do not draw the traditional distinction between deductive and inductive forms of
reasoning. The model of inquiry we propose is equally applicable to reasoning from evidence
to report (inductive) and from report to evidence (deductive).

through my mind that I arrived at the conclusion without being conscious of intermediate steps." But there always are such steps and, if pressed, Holmes can always reproduce them.

The historian and detective can infer the unknown from the known by use of logical methods. These methods enabled Holmes to infer a man's age, his intellectual capacity, and his marital problems from observations of his hat. They enable historians to infer reports of past events from their observations of historical evidence. Formal logic is simply a set of rules for drawing conclusions from statements (called "premises") that express what we already know. Taken together, statements of premises and conclusions form an argument. An argument is logically valid if the truth of its conclusion necessarily follows from the truth of its premises. However, if one or more premises of a logically valid argument are not true, the truth of the conclusion is in doubt. Aristotle (384–322 B.C.), the father of formal logic, offers the following example of a logically valid argument:

Premise I:	Socrates is human.
Premise II:	All humans are mortal.
Conclusion:	Socrates is mortal.

The argument about the mortality of Socrates exemplifies a general form of argument called a syllogism. The conclusion of a syllogism follows from two premises. Statements of premises fall into three categories: (1) singular statements about particular things or individuals, for example, "Socrates is human"; (2) less than universal statements about members of a category, for example, "some humans have red hair"; and (3) universal statements about members of a category, for example, "all humans are mortal." The two premises of a syllogism must have a term in common. This middle term (the term "human" in Aristotle's example) establishes a connection between the other or outside terms in each of the premises (the terms "Socrates" and "mortal" in Aristotle's example). These outside terms are related to each other by virtue of their common relationship to the middle term. The two premises "Socrates is human" and "all foxes love to catch chickens" cannot entail any conclusion because there is no common term by which to relate the two statements.

At least one of the premises of a syllogism must be a universal statement about all members of a category. If neither premise was universal, the connection between the outside terms would be problematic. If, for example, we knew that Socrates is human and that some humans are mortal, we could conclude only that Socrates may or may not be mortal.

The arguments that Holmes uses to reach his conclusions can be displayed as syllogisms. These arguments include as premises statements expressing Holmes' observations of a particular individual or object and generalizations linking these observations to the conclusion. When Mr. Jabez Wilson enters the Baker Street apartment at the beginning of the story of "The Red-Headed League," Holmes calmly notes that "Beyond the obvious facts that he has at some time done manual labour, that he takes snuff, that he is a Freemason, that he has been in China, and that he has done a considerable amount of writing lately, I can deduce nothing else." When pressed by his astonished visitor to explain "how he knew all that," Holmes quickly recounted his arguments. The following syllogism, for example, reveals how he knew that Mr. Wilson had been to China:

Premise I:	Mr. Wilson has a tattoo of a fish on which the scales are stained a particular shade of pink.
Premise II:	All tattoos of fish with scales stained this shade of pink are made only in China.*
Conclusion:	Mr. Wilson had been to China.

Holmes professes reluctance to disclose his arguments because they undermine his reputation as a wonder worker who leaps magically to unexpected conclusions. Indeed, after listening to Holmes' explanations, Jabez Wilson laughed and confessed that "I thought at first that you had done something clever, but I see that there was nothing in it, after all."

The arguments used to infer historical reports from historical evidence also can be displayed as syllogisms. Historical arguments conclude with reports about the past and begin with premises about the properties of historical evidence. For example, a detailed description of a clay tablet found by an archeologist might be one premise of an argument which concludes with the report that the ancient Babylonians produced this tablet. But a historical argument is incomplete unless its premises include a universal generalization (one which applies to all members of a category) linking statements about evidence to reports about the past. These generalizations must apply to all members of a category to establish more than a problematic connection between the evidence and the report. Unless the historian knew that all tablets with certain properties were produced only by the ancient Babylonians, he could not have inferred his report from a description of the evidence.

---

*Holmes has "made a small study of tattoo marks and even contributed to the literature of the subject."

Arguments of this form also enable historians to infer a historical report from another historical report. One of the reports would be a premise of the argument, whereas the other report would be the conclusion. To complete the argument, its premises would also include a universal generalization linking the two reports. If, for example, we knew that Piers Plowman was a medieval peasant and we also knew that all medieval peasants were illiterate, we could conclude that Piers Plowman was illiterate.

The generalizations used to infer historical reports may simply reflect our knowledge of the correlations (the degrees to which the occurrence of one event is associated with the occurrence of another event) among events of the world. For instance, the hypothetical example used above assumes a perfect association between being a medieval peasant and being illiterate. Generalizations of this type are often termed "empirical generalizations." Other generalizations may be derived from "causal laws," theories that express our fundamental beliefs about the causal relationships among events. For example, economists have developed theories that assert causal connections between changes in supply and demand and changes in prices. Psychologists have advanced theories that describe human and animal behavior as responses to stimuli in the environment. Generalizations of this second type are sometimes called "covering laws." For purposes of establishing historical reports, it makes no difference whether the generalizations included in historical arguments are based only upon observed correlations or are founded on causal laws. Any true generalization, universal in form, can get us from here to there—from what we know about historical evidence to what we seek to know about past events. Covering laws, as we shall demonstrate in the next chapter, are necessary only for historical explanations.

We have seen then why evidence does not speak for itself and why the historian must formulate arguments that include as premises generalizations as well as descriptions of evidence. We also have seen why Holmes is usually right and Watson, Lestrade, and Gregson are usually wrong. The doctor and the inspectors leap to conclusions without following the step-by-step procedures of formal logic. These gentlemen also lack Holmes' vast knowledge of the generalizations that must be included in any logical argument. Their ignorance causes them to miss crucial details of evidence and to draw erroneous conclusions from the details that they do perceive. As Holmes once remarked of a promising French detective, "He possesses two of the three qualities necessary for the ideal detective. He has the power of observation and that of deduction. He is only wanting in knowledge."

Students of history may require even broader knowledge than the aspiring detective. Because history encompasses all of human experience, its study is especially exciting and demanding. The practitioners of a particular science or social science deal with limited ranges of natural or human behavior. The problems of inference relevant to their discipline can often be placed into standard categories and attacked by a relatively limited number of generalizations. Chemists, for example, have standard methods for determining the composition of a compound, economists for measuring supply and demand. But historians deal with the subject matter of virtually every other discipline. The relevant problems of historical study cannot be categorized easily, or approached through a limited number of generalizations.

Although historians possess no convenient set of generalizations that can be inserted mechanically into historical arguments, they have identified many of the issues raised by the effort to infer reports from historical evidence. Knowledge of these issues aids the historian by suggesting what he should think about when reconstructing the past from various kinds of evidence. A critic might use these same issues as a guide for evaluating the relative credibility of competing reports about historical events. Since historians so often rely on written accounts of past events, we will briefly consider some of the issues involved in drawing inferences from this type of secondary evidence. These issues are analogous to those addressed in the rules of evidence used in courts of law. Broad considerations of this kind, of course, are not necessarily identical to the generalizations that the historian actually includes in an argument designed to infer reports from specific pieces of evidence. But they do indicate how the historian combines the scrutiny of evidence with other knowledge to learn about what happened in the past.

Historians should approach their secondary sources with skepticism, always suspicious of appearances and sensitive to conflicting interpretations. Scholars have learned from painful experience that even the most generally reliable witnesses make mistakes and sometimes even lie. And they have found that even untrustworthy witnesses sometimes tell the truth. The careful historian, like the experienced detective, takes no one at his word.

On occasion historians must authenticate written evidence, demonstrating that a document is what it appears to be rather than a clever forgery. For example, if a newly discovered letter about events of the Civil War bears a person's signature, the writing should be checked against other samples written by that individual. The paper, ink, penmanship, and word usage should be verified as contemporary with the date of the letter. Historians and detectives consider these and many other issues of authenticity before accepting and using documentary evidence.

Once a document is authenticated, the historian must ponder the credibility of the witness. How does the source know what he claims to know? What does he want the reader to believe about himself and the events he describes? To answer these large questions, the historian draws upon knowledge about the witness and upon internal criticism of the story related in the document. If the historian does not already know much about the witness, he should consult the works of those who do, often other historians. But the historian must realize that even the most matter-of-fact reports about witnesses are themselves inferences drawn from evidence and must be regarded skeptically. Historians must carefully balance those inferences about the witness's credibility that are based on reports about the witness himself with the inferences that are based on a reading of the story itself. In some cases, of course, historians will know virtually nothing about the witness and must rely upon internal analysis of what the witness has said.

A number of subsidiary considerations guides the historian's effort to learn how a witness came to know what he claims to know and what might have influenced him to present his story as he did. Historians usually try to determine whether the source actually observed what he reports or relied upon the accounts of others. If the source was an eyewitness, was he paying close attention to what he saw or heard? Was he in a good position to make accurate observations? Was he a bystander or a participant in the events described? Was he too distracted, frightened, or excited to be a reliable reporter? Historians also attempt to assess the competence of a witness. Was he observing events that he could not be expected to understand? Was he commenting on matters beyond his range of knowledge? Moreover, historians consider whether what a witness expected to see and hear influenced what he said he saw and heard. For instance, Holmes had been suspicious of reports from those influenced by the legend that a "Hound from Hell" pursued descendents of the Baskerville line. Only after he heard for himself the baying of a hound in the moors near Baskerville Hall was the detective sure that there really was a "Hound of the Baskervilles."

If the source used by the historian was not an eyewitness, the historian must try to ascertain how the source obtained his information. Although courts of law have fairly strict sets of rules about hearsay evidence, the historian works with hearsay evidence all the time. A researcher must be aware, however, that a source almost never reproduces an eyewitness account in full; he selects and edits the oral or written material from which he draws his own account. Newspaper reporters, for example, may consciously or unconsciously distort what a person actually said. Even written accounts found in collections of personal correspondence may have been selectively edited prior to release. When the daughter of John Fiske, the noted historian of eighteenth–century America and popularizer of Darwin, published his correspondence, she obliterated all references to his weight (he struggled all his life with obesity), his financial problems (he was frequently in debt), and the phrases of endearment addressed to his wife (he called her "Puss"). Unfortunately for the solicitous daughter, but fortunately for Fiske scholars, the ink eradicator that she used to wipe away offensive passages was not permanent. On the manuscript letters themselves, the original writing has reappeared.

Historians also recognize that the reason why someone has bothered to write something down can affect the reliability of an account. Historians try to find out whether a witness had a personal interest in gaining acceptance for a certain version of an event, whether the witness was biased, whether the witness might be trying to protect someone (himself, family members, friends, or a group to which he belonged), or whether the witness might be trying to enhance his own image and stature. In some cases, witnesses may have something to gain from telling the truth; in other cases, from deliberately lying. The historian using written descriptions of events also becomes a literary critic, endeavoring to determine whether the style of the written account colors or slants the story. He also considers to whom the witness addressed the account and tries to assess how the witness may have tailored his account to meet the demands and expectations of his audience. As a detective, Holmes knows well that people have confessed to crimes they did not commit simply to satisfy their inquisitors or to afford themselves a sense of importance.

Whenever possible, historians try to corroborate the account of any witness by searching for other evidence that helps him to choose among competing reports of the events being described. Not every additional piece of evidence weighs equally in the attempt to infer a historical report reliably. Obviously two separate descriptions of an event are less convincing when written by two people with similar expectations, interests, and biases than by two people with differing outlooks, backgrounds, and objectives. Moreover, when two secondary sources are not eyewitnesses to an event, the historian must make sure that both accounts are not based on the same original source.

To infer reliable reports from accounts of events, whether based on hearsay or direct observation, the historian must simultaneously consider all issues relevant to determining a witness's credibility. He cannot simply examine one or two of those issues and reach a sound judgment about what can be drawn out of the account. Moreover, the balancing of various issues—proximity to the event, competence of the witness, prior interests, and biases and expectations—may not yield a conclusive verdict. A witness in an excellent position to observe an event may be of questionable competence, whereas a perfectly competent witness may not have been able to observe clearly what was happening. The historian must be able to cope with uncertainty in the credibility of witnesses and therefore in the historical reports inferred from their testimony.

Historical Reports and the Problem of Uncertainty

One more concept—the concept of probability—needs to be introduced before completing this discussion of how the historian infers reports about the past. Think for a moment about the generalization used to infer the illiteracy of Piers Plowman. Is it credible? Were all medieval peasants really illiterate? Surely some of them must have learned to read. To rescue this generalization and virtually all other generalizations historians use, one must apply the theory of probability.

A knowledge of the meaning and application of probability theory is essential to the comprehension of modern science, philosophy, and social science. We believe that probability theory is equally relevant to the study of the past. Anyone who has bet on a horserace, speculated about the arrival of a late train or airplane, or wondered if he or she loves me or loves me not, has implicitly applied the concept of probability. Yet most people dimly understand this concept, in part because our language leads us to think in terms of such polarities as yes and no, right and wrong, true and false, and good and bad.

Sherlock Holmes relies on probabilistic knowledge. He is well aware of the difference between "mere guesswork" and probabilistic inference, founded upon knowledge and logic. By examining a watch belonging to Dr. Watson's brother, Holmes is able to infer intimate details of the brother's life. When informed by the disconcerted Watson that every detail is exactly correct, Holmes remarks on his "good luck," explaining that "I could only say what was the balance of probability. I did not at all expect to be so accurate." "But," Watson interrupts, "it was not mere guesswork." "No, no," Holmes replies, "I never guess. . . . What seems strange to you is only because you do not follow my train of thought or observe the small facts upon which large inferences may depend."

Of course even Holmes could have been mistaken, not only in his inferences, but also in his description of the watch. Similarly, uncertainty may pervade not only the generalizations used in historical arguments, but also the descriptions of the evidence being considered. These descriptions may be incorrect. For example, a historian using the Zapruder film to infer reports about the Kennedy assassination may be mistaken in his description of the physical characteristics of the film. Thus the probable truth of the conclusion of a historical argument depends not only upon the likelihood of the connection asserted by the generalization, but also upon the likely truth of the descriptive statements that set forth the properties of the historical evidence.

Probabilities are relevant to historical study because we cannot be certain about the truth of statements referring to the real world. For purposes of this discussion, probability is a measure of our uncertainty regarding any empirical statement. In quantitative terms, the value of a probability judgment varies from 0 to 1. A probability of 0 corresponds to the belief that a statement is certainly false; a probability of 1 corresponds to the belief that a statement is certainly true. Intermediate probabilities correspond to intermediate degrees of belief in the truth of a given statement. The stronger our belief that a statement is true, the closer its probability will approach 1. A probability of .01, for instance, means that we believe a statement has a 1 in 100, or 1 per cent chance of being true; a probability of .90 means that we believe a statement has a 90 in 100, or 90 per cent chance of being true.

Probabilities can be applied to the generalizations used to infer reports about past events. For example, rather than saying that all medieval peasants were illiterate, we could say that a medieval peasant was very likely to have been illiterate. Probabilities can be expressed in this approximate verbal form or set forth more precisely as numerical values. If we had sufficient information, we could say that the probability is 90 per cent that a medieval peasant was illiterate. In most cases it is possible to establish only a probabilistic connection between the terms included in generalizations used by historians. If such a connection were stated in absolute rather than probabilistic form, the relationship could almost certainly be proven false by example.

The use of probabilistic generalizations does not alter the logical form of historical arguments. Logically valid inferences can be drawn from probabilistic generalizations as well as from those stated in absolute form. The only difference is that for arguments including a probabilistic generalization, the historical report must also be stated in probabilistic form. Such arguments only establish the likely truth of a particular report; they do not enable the historian to conclude that a report is definitely true or false. If the probabilistic generalization is stated in numerical form, the probable truth of the historical report can also be stated in numerical form. If, however, the probabilistic generalization is stated verbally, then the probable truth of the historical conclusion must also be stated verbally. Both of the syllogisms below yield logically valid conclusions, even though they include generalizations that are probabilistic in form:

Syllogism I

Premise I: Piers Plowman was a medieval peasant.
Premise II: The probability is 90 per cent that a medieval
                    peasant was illiterate.
Conclusion: The probability is 90 per cent that Piers Plow-
                    man was illiterate.

Syllogism II

Premise I: Piers Plowman was a medieval peasant.
Premise II: A medieval peasant was very likely to have
                    been illiterate.
Conclusion: Piers Plowman was very likely to have been
                    illiterate.

The more information included in the first premise, of course, the more likely we are to assess probabilities accurately. We might know, for example, that peasants from certain areas of Europe were 99 per cent likely to have been illiterate, but that peasants from other areas were only 80 per cent likely to have been illiterate. Thus, if we knew where Piers Plowman lived, we could better evaluate the probability that he was illiterate.

Those accustomed to thinking in polar categories of right or wrong and true or false may feel uncomfortable with probabilistic knowledge. When dealing with human behavior, however, probabilistic knowledge generally is the best we can achieve. The American legal system recognizes this limitation. Despite the resources at its command, the prosecution in a criminal case need not prove beyond any doubt that a defendant is guilty as charged. Rather, the prosecution need only demonstrate guilt "beyond a reasonable doubt," something short of certainty. In civil cases, a litigant generally needs to show only that his claims are more likely to be true than those of his opponent. And the standard for the relevancy of evidence set forth in the *Federal Rules of Evidence* is openly probabilistic: "Relevant evidence means evidence having any tendency to make the existence of any fact that is of consequence to the determination of the action more probable or less probable than it would be without the evidence."

Probabilistic knowledge is a perfectly legitimate kind of knowledge that significantly advances our understanding of the world and enables us to act intelligently. Let us consider a contrived but graphic example of the value of probabilistic knowledge. Assume that a philosopher king, sensitive to the population problem, presents all potential immigrants to his kingdom with two sealed envelopes, one red and one green. In one of the envelopes is a permit for the prospective settler to enter the kingdom; in the other is an order for the individual's head to be cut off. Over the long run, we would expect that the number of people choosing the envelope with the permit would be about equal to the number of people choosing the envelope with the execution order. Assume, however, that the king had a soft-hearted minister who surreptitiously informed each individual that 99 per cent of the time the king placed the execution order in the green rather than the red envelope. Assuming the petitioners trusted the minister, this probabilistic information would save the heads of many prospective immigrants. All of the petitioners would choose the red envelope and all but a very few of them would proceed with their anatomy intact. Similarly, the historian who knows that a historical report is 99 per cent likely to be true knows far more than the individual who has no idea whether or not the report is true.

Like all forms of knowledge, probabilistic knowledge should be as accurate as possible. To illustrate the dangers of using probabilistic information that is inaccurate, return again to the realm of our philosopher king. But this time assume that he has an evil minister who convinces the petitioners that 99 per cent of the time the execution order is in the red envelope when the order is actually in the green envelope 99 per cent of the time. In this case, the prospective immigrants will choose the green envelope, and only a small remnant is likely to survive. Similarly, the historian who has studied medieval history and knows that a peasant was far more likely to be illiterate than literate knows far more than the individual who has no basis for assessing the probable literacy of medieval peasants. In recognition of the value of accurate probabilistic knowledge the United States Supreme Court now insists upon legal counsel for any individual accused of violating the criminal law. The clash between counsel for the prosecution and counsel for the defense increases the likelihood that both sides of the case will be presented and that the jury will not be misled by incomplete or biased evidence and dubious generalizations.

Confronted with uncertainty in the premises of their arguments, historians must abandon the quest for certainty in their reports about the past. At best, historians can attempt to evaluate the "odds" that a given report is true rather than false. The concept of odds should be familiar to anyone who has ever played the stock market, bet on a horse race, or followed the machinations of "Jimmy the Greek." The odds in favor of a report about the past can be interpreted in the same way that we interpret the odds that a particular horse will win a particular race. For example, the odds of one to three that a horse will win the Kentucky Derby means that the probability of that horse's victory is three times the probability that any one of the other horses would win. Similarly, odds of one to three in favor of a historical report means that the probable truth of the report is three times greater than the probability that any other report is true. The greater the probable truth of a particular report, and the smaller the probable truth of alternative reports, the shorter the odds in favor of that report.

Verifying Historical Reports

The probable truth of historical reports depends upon the probable truth both of statements about evidence and of the generalizations linking the evidence and the report. For purposes of illustration, let us consider, in detail, the problem of learning about the Kennedy assassination. A historian of the assassination might use the Zapruder film to infer reports about the circumstances of the President's murder. As with written documents, the historian using visual material must first determine whether or not the material actually portrays what it seems to portray. The standard way to answer this question regarding the authenticity of evidence is to infer reports about the circumstances of its creation through the formulation of a historical argument. The process of inferring reports pertaining to the authentication of evidence is identical in form to the process of inferring any other report. The only difference is the function the report serves. Reports authenticating historical evidence simply enable historians to infer other reports from the evidence in question. From the characteristics of the Zapruder film, one could argue either that somebody on the scene of the assassination shot the film, or that clever technicians forged the film after the assassination had taken place. Any historian could propose logically valid arguments linking a description of the Zapruder film to either historical report. The credibility of these arguments, however, depends upon the probable truth of the generalizations connecting description and report.

The historian is not interested in these arguments for their own sake, but rather because they enable him to evaluate the credibility of reports about the past. If the first report about the formation of the Zapruder film is correct, further inferences about the Kennedy assassination can be made from the film. If the second report is correct, further inferences are likely to be misleading.

To determine which of the two reports is more likely to be true, it is necessary to describe in detail the Zapruder film. Possibly only one of the two reports can be inferred with high probability from an accurate and thorough description of the film. The historian's knowledge of generalizations relevant to the authentication of visual material tells him roughly what details to expect if the film were genuine and what to expect if it were a forgery. Just as Holmes' immense knowledge of crime tells him what to look for at the scene of a murder, a historian's ability to authenticate evidence will enable him to know what to look for in describing the Zapruder film. It might be important, for instance, to find out whether there is agreement between events portrayed in the film and other accounts of these events; where the film came from, how it was obtained, and what its physical condition was; whether anyone would benefit from a forgery; whether the time sequences within the film are internally consistent; and whether the events in the film agree with the known laws of science.

For the knowledgeable historian, the more detailed his knowledge of evidence, the more reliable his inferences about past events. A historian, for example, who knows both the history of a film and its physical characteristics is in a better position to assess its authenticity than a historian who knows only its physical characteristics. A plausible generalization might state that a film is very likely to be genuine if the events it portrays do not contradict well–established laws of science and are generally consistent with other accounts; if no one would benefit from a forgery; if the film's history is well-known and reputable; if its time sequences are consistent; and if physical inspection discloses no trace of doctoring.

Like the well–trained historian, Sherlock Holmes thrives on details. For Lestrade and Gregson, the fine details of a crime only "complicate matters," creating doubt and confusion. But for Holmes, these details increase his confidence in the conclusions he reaches:

> things which have perplexed you and made the case more obscure have served to enlighten me and to strengthen my conclusions. . . . The most commonplace crime is often the most mysterious, because it presents no new or special features from which deductions may be drawn. This murder would have been infinitely more difficult to unravel had the body of the victim been simply found lying in the roadway without any of those outré and sensational accompaniments which have rendered it remarkable. These strange details, far from making the case more difficult, have really had the effect of making it less so.

This discussion of the Zapruder film indicates the difficulty of performing even the first step of historical inquiry. The historian must be familiar with the logic of historical arguments and with the generalizations that can link descriptions of the evidence to reports about the past. To complete a detailed description of the evidence, he must have historical knowledge (for example, knowledge of the film's history and of the accounts rendered by witnesses to the assassination); scientific knowledge (for example, knowledge of the methods used to doctor film); and technical expertise (for example, mastery of the techniques used to inspect film). If the historian does not possess the requisite information and skills, he must seek expert consultation or risk grave errors of analysis.

After authenticating his evidence, the historian can begin to use the evidence to make further inferences about the past. The historian must use a generalization to connect characteristics of the evidence to reports about the past. A sequence from the Zapruder film, for instance, shows the President's body moving sharply backward after being struck by the first shot. Some students of the assassination argue that a bullet striking the President from the front rather than the rear of the automobile produced this movement. Others argue that a bullet fired from the rear produced this movement. They justify their seemingly counter intuitive argument by claiming, first, that the President's body moved slight forward before flying backward and, second, that a bullet entering the rear of a neck and emerging from the front would produce a reaction similar to that of "whiplash"—our neck whips backwards when we are hit by another automobile from the rear.

On the basis of evidence from the Zapruder film alone, the choice between the two conflicting reports of the direction from which the first shots were fired is very difficult. Each report can be inferred from the film through highly plausible generalizations; the odds are not heavily in favor of one or the other report.

To decide which report is more credible, the historian must examine additional evidence. The most useful evidence consists of photographs and X-rays of the President's body. Only the report that the first shot came from behind Kennedy's automobile can be inferred from this evidence through a plausible generalization. Experts who have examined this evidence testify that information portrayed on the photos and X-rays is consistent only with the report that the first shot was fired from the rear. No sign of an entrance wound in the front of the body was discovered; and a small hole in the rear of the President's skull is identified clearly as an entrance wound. According to expert testimony, a bullet coming from the front of the car could not possibly produce this wound. When the evidence from autopsy materials is added to the evidence from the Zapruder film, the odds shift dramatically in favor of the report that the first shot that hit President Kennedy was fired from behind his automobile.

If historical inference had demonstrated that shots had come from both behind and in front of the presidential limousine, historians would have been forced to conclude that more than one assassin had fired at the President. Any other conclusion would violate the laws of physics. But the finding that all shots were fired from the rear leaves open the question of whether or not there was more than one assassin. Equally plausible generalizations could link reports describing the direction of the bullets to the presence of either one or more than one assassin. To resolve this controversy, historians would have to make inferences from evidence other than the Zapruder film and the photos and X-rays of the late President.

The question of the number of assassins is related to the broader question of whether there was a conspiracy to assassinate the President. Information about the personality of Lee Harvey Oswald—assuming, of course, that he actually was guilty—obviously is relevant to this broader issue. A historian could use generalizations based on his knowledge of human psychology to infer reports about Oswald's personality from authenticated evidence about his thoughts, feelings, and behavior. Using other generalizations taken from his knowledge of conspiracies, a historian could attempt then to determine the probability that someone with Oswald's personality traits would have been the central figure in a plot to assassinate the President. Scholars opposing the conspiracy hypothesis have maintained that Oswald was an unstable and unreliable individual whom a band of conspirators would not have trusted.

The linkages between descriptions of historical evidence and reports about the past are illustrated by Figure I. Each historical report in Figure I is obtained as the conclusion of a historical argument. Historical reports 1 and a are the conclusions of arguments whose premises include a description of historical evidence and a generalization linking the evidence and report. In turn, reports 1 and a serve as premises of other historical arguments that conclude with other historical reports. Again, the premises of these arguments also include a generalization connecting the two reports. The process of inferring new reports may continue indefinitely since every report may be a premise for an argument leading to a further report.

For purposes of illustration, we may assume that historical evidence 1 is the Zapruder film and that historical evidence a is the photos and X-rays from the President's autopsy. Report 1 could be the report that the film was taken on the scene of the assassination; report 2, that the President's body moved

FIGURE I

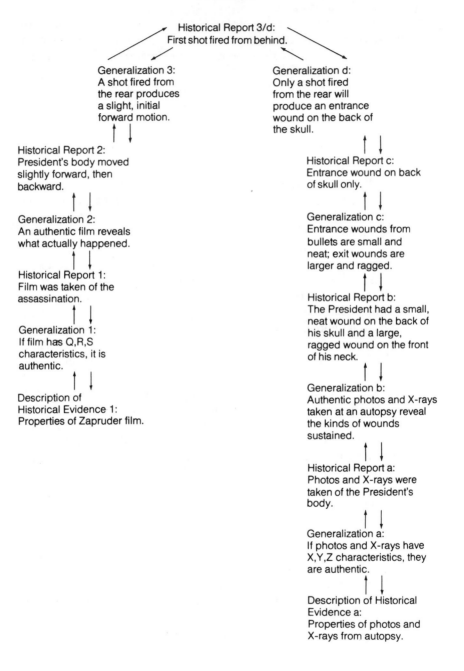

Historical Report 3/d:
First shot fired from behind.

Generalization 3:
A shot fired from
the rear produces
a slight, initial
forward motion.

Generalization d:
Only a shot fired
from the rear will
produce an entrance
wound on the back of
the skull.

Historical Report 2:
President's body moved
slightly forward, then
backward.

Historical Report c:
Entrance wound on back
of skull only.

Generalization 2:
An authentic film reveals
what actually happened.

Generalization c:
Entrance wounds from
bullets are small and
neat; exit wounds are
larger and ragged.

Historical Report 1:
Film was taken of the
assassination.

Historical Report b:
The President had a small,
neat wound on the back of
his skull and a large,
ragged wound on the front
of his neck.

Generalization 1:
If film has Q,R,S
characteristics, it is
authentic.

Generalization b:
Authentic photos and X-rays
taken at an autopsy reveal
the kinds of wounds
sustained.

Description of
Historical Evidence 1:
Properties of Zapruder film.

Historical Report a:
Photos and X-rays were
taken of the President's
body.

Generalization a:
If photos and X-rays have
X,Y,Z characteristics, they
are authentic.

Description of Historical
Evidence a:
Properties of photos and
X-rays from autopsy.

forward slightly, then backward, after being hit by the first shot; and report
3/d, that the first shot was fired from behind the presidential car. Generalization 1 would represent the set of generalizations used to infer that the film
was authentic. Generalization 2 would represent the set of generalizations
used to infer the report about the backward movement of the President's
body from a description of the Zapruder film. Generalization 3 represents
the generalizations used to infer the report about the direction of the first
shot from the report about the movement of the President's body. Report
a could be the report that the photos and X-rays were actually taken during
the autopsy; report b could be that the President had a small hole in the back
of his skull and a larger hole in the front of the neck; and report c, that there
was an entrance wound but no exit wound on the rear of the President's skull.
Generalization a represents the generalizations used to authenticate the
autopsy materials. Generalization b represents the generalizations used to
infer descriptions of wounds from photos and X-rays. Generalization c represents the generalizations used to infer the report that there was an entrance
wound but no exit wound on the rear of the President's skull from statements
about the autopsy materials. Generalization d represents the generalizations
used to infer the report about the direction of the first shot from the report
about the wounds on the President's skull.

The bidirectional arrows in Figure I indicate that the derivation of historical reports is a reversible process. A historian may begin with hypothetical
reports about the past and use generalizations to infer descriptions of historical evidence that would corroborate or deny this hypothesis. The great
classicist Heinrich Schliemann, for example, began his research with the
belief that Homer's epic poem, the *Iliad,* was based on a real event, the
Trojan War, rather than on an entirely fictional story, a view then held by
most classicists. He reasoned, therefore, that the city of Troy must have
existed, and then launched an archeological expedition to test his hypothesis.
Schliemann's familiarity with Homer and the topography of Asia Minor
enabled him to select the site most likely to have been the renowned ancient
city, and he found the evidence needed to confirm his hypothesis on his first
try. Few historians have that kind of luck!

A historian may also begin with historical evidence and use his knowledge
of generalizations to formulate hypotheses about the past whose credibility
depends in part upon statements about this very evidence. Whenever a
historian is unexpectedly presented with new evidence, he performs this
process of reasoning. He would use this evidence to reevaluate earlier statements about the past and to formulate new hypotheses that can be tested by
examination of the evidence.

Since the two processes of reasoning are logically equivalent, the process a historian actually follows is usually impossible to determine. We know only the form in which the historian chooses to present his final argument. For example, whether the historian began with historical report 3/d in Figure I and discovered historical evidence 1, or began with historical evidence 1 and inferred historical report 3/d, the probable truth of historical report 3/d would remain a function of the probable truth of the historian's description of historical evidence 1 and the likelihood of the connection set forth in generalizations 1, 2, and 3. Regardless of which process he actually followed, the historian could present his argument in exactly the same way.

This general model of historical inquiry also demonstrates that generalizations are necessary for the historian even to begin an investigation of the past. The historian learns nothing about the past merely by inspecting evidence. Without a knowledge of generalizations, the historian examining evidence would be as helpless as the illiterate trying to read Shakespeare. Each would be able to describe in some fashion the objects they observe. But the historian would be unable to use his description to infer statements about the past, and the illiterate would be unable to use his description to decipher the meaning of the symbols.

The historian's knowledge of generalizations also enables him to weave statements about the past into meaningful and coherent patterns. The simple pattern portrayed in Figure I can be indefinitely extended in any direction. Additional statements could be inferred from any of the historical statements already included in the model; new statements could be inferred from new evidence and connected to any of the included statements.

Even those who deal with natural phenomena that can be observed directly cannot acquire knowledge merely by passive observation. As the physicist D. F. Presly has pointed out, the observations of the natural world also depend upon a commitment to generalizations: "The physicist or chemist must know not only how to take readings and how to interpret them but also what readings to take and when to take them, and this depends on his knowledge of accepted techniques, systems of measurement and theories, and of their relevance to the work he is doing. . . . To quote Mr. Mackie: 'Observation includes thinking and relies on background knowledge.' "

The model portrayed by Figure I can also be used to illustrate the grounds for factual dispute in history—that is, dispute over the probable truth of historical reports. The following check list indicates the issues that might be raised in assessing the truth of historical reports.

1. Is the historical evidence described accurately?
2. Is the evidence described completely?
3. Does a sound generalization link evidence and report?
4. Is additional evidence relevant to evaluations of the report?

If Holmes and Watson had lived through the 1960's, we might imagine a discussion of the Kennedy assassination that touches all these bases. Allowing poetic license for details, the conversation might have proceeded as follows:

It's astounding, Holmes, these reproductions of the Zapruder film they published in the *Sunday Times*. Why, the film shows the fellow's body propelled backward after being shot. Surely this means that he was hit from the front of the auto. Must have been those blokes on the grassy knoll.

My dear Watson, I believe you've done it again.

Nothing to it, old boy. Just pure deductive reasoning. I trust that I have overlooked nothing.

Yes, Watson, it's amazing how entirely erroneous deductions can suggest the true solution to a problem. Surely, dear fellow, you are a remarkable conduit of wisdom. Look at the film a bit more closely, Watson. Here, borrow my glass. Can't you see that the President's body moved forward just a trifle before flying backwards.

Egad, Holmes, I think you're right! But surely, if the shot came from the rear, the body still wouldn't move backwards like that.

Sorry, old fellow, but I've studied the whiplash effects of high-powered projectiles on the human body, even contributing a small monograph on the subject. If a man were struck in the back of his neck by a high-powered bullet, we would precisely expect his body to move slightly forward before being thrust backward by the force of the exiting bullet.

Amazing, Holmes.

And look here, Watson, these are the photographs which you seem to think show two gunmen lurking behind a bush on the grassy knoll. Observe what happens when we blow up the photographs on the screen over there. Those gunmen become harmless shadows from the trees nearby.

Holmes, you astound me.

Interesting, though elementary. Watson, hand me my violin.

Watson begins with evidence from the Zapruder film (both Watson and Holmes assume the film to be genuine and do not discuss that issue) and infers a report about the direction of the bullets fired at President Kennedy. Taking this report as a hypothesis to be evaluated, Holmes suggests an addition to Watson's description of the evidence. He notes that the good doctor's account fails to mention a detail of the Zapruder film relevant to determining the truth of the hypothesis in question. Holmes then challenges the credibility of Watson's generalization linking the now more complete description to Watson's report about the direction of the bullets. The detective introduces another generalization linking this description to an alternative report. He then considers other evidence relevant to assessing the probable truth of the historical reports. Holmes corrects an erroneous description of this evidence, showing that the corrected description cannot be connected credibly to Watson's report of the assassination.

This discussion of historical inference also demonstrates that there are no historical facts in the sense either of certain knowledge or knowledge that depends only on reports of observations. In history we have no facts, only inferences from evidence. Even the simplest reports of past events are derived from historical evidence through the process of historical argument. In disputing the probable truth of historical reports, historians may question the accuracy and completeness of statements about evidence, introduce new evidence, and question the credibility of generalizations used to link the evidence and the historical report.

The truth of a historical report is well established only when this report and no other report can be linked to available evidence by a generalization that sets forth connections that are highly probable. In this instance, the odds would heavily favor the truth of this report as opposed to the truth of any other contradictory report. On the other hand, inadequate evidence can produce one of two results. First, the evidence may establish that one report is more likely to be true than any other contradictory report; but no report has a very high probability of being true. Second, the evidence may not establish any particular report as most likely to be true. Instead it may establish only that several reports are equally likely to be true.

Particular evidence, of course, may be considered good evidence for one historical question and poor evidence for another. For instance, the Kennedy autopsy materials would enable the historian to determine the direction of the first shot to strike the President. But these materials alone would not enable a historian to determine whether or not the gunman was involved in a conspiracy to assassinate the President.

Historians may come to regard certain well-established historical reports as historical fact, not because these reports are true beyond any doubt, but because there is sufficient agreement about their truth to dry up controversy. We claim that a report is a fact because enough available evidence supports it for us to believe that further research would neither increase nor decrease our confidence in the report. For example, most historians do not believe it worthwhile to question the report that George Washington was the first President of the United States, or the report that Duke William of Normandy conquered England in 1066. But historians are a heterogeneous lot; what some historians regard as fact, others may regard as fiction. Some students of the Kennedy assassination still deny the report that Lee Harvey Oswald fired even a single shot at President Kennedy. Moreover, at any time, what was previously regarded as fact could be called into question. New evidence could be discovered, errors could be found in the description of existing evidence, or the relevant generalizations could be reevaluated. Even the simplest reports about the past are always subject to revision.

Thus historians cannot rigidly maintain the traditional distinction between fact-finding and interpretation. Given the same evidence, reasonable men could reach different conclusions about the likely truth of historical reports. Given such disagreement, it is perfectly legitimate to state that historians have offered different interpretations of the past based on the same evidence.

In addition, historians may bias their work in favor of a particular point of view. A historian may consciously or unconsciously present only the evidence that sustains particular historical reports or slant the description of evidence in order to make particular reports seem more plausible. To combat bias in his own work, the historian should go over in his mind every possible objection to the conclusions he has reached. In effect, he should recapitulate mentally the give-and-take of the debate between Holmes and Watson.

Bias in historical work must be exposed through open debate and discussion, as well as self-scrutiny. Historians must be able to criticize and evaluate each others' work. To many readers, the meticulous way in which historians cite and describe their evidence in detailed footnotes may appear to be mere pedantry, an ostentatious parading of overly rigorous canons of scholarship. But those footnotes, as lengthy and cumbersome as they may seem, are essential to the historian's work. How can a reader evaluate the credibility of the historian's reconstruction of the past, let alone his explanations or interpretations, without knowing how the historian arrived at that particular reconstruction as opposed to some other reconstruction? Who would believe Holmes' reconstruction of a crime if he did not carefully explain to Watson, Lestrade, or Gregson the logic and knowledge he employed? Just as the detective must show that his reconstruction of the crime is the most probable one before making an arrest, so too the historian must demonstrate that his reconstruction of what happened is preferable to any other.

Since historians put their reputations on the line whenever they claim knowledge of the past, they need to be familiar with the methods of historical inference. An understanding of these methods is likewise important for all of us concerned about gaining insight into our own thinking. The procedures used by historians to reconstruct the past should help us to acquire more reliable knowledge and to defend what we think we know against challenges from those with different points of view. The process of challenge and response leads to greater refinement and sophistication of our efforts to comprehend the world, both past and present.

III

Historical Explanation

Puzzles have always fascinated people. Even small children delight in "putting the pieces together." Perhaps one of the reasons why history is so fascinating is that historians have to solve puzzles in putting together a picture of the past. But in history, making a picture of the pieces is only half the job. A historian who shrinks from offering explanations of what happened risks being dismissed as a mere chronicler or antiquarian. We want to know *why* the pieces fit together the way they do. And the "why?" of history is often the hardest puzzle of all to solve.

A explanation may be defined simply as a solution to a puzzle raised by the question "why?" Two types of explanations are especially important for historical work—causal explanations and explanations of the moral consequences of past events. A causal explanation proposes a solution to the puzzle of why something happened; a moral judgment proposes a solution to the puzzle of how to evaluate what happened. To understand these two forms of explanation is to gain insight into how we think about all events, both past and present. Most of us implicitly organize the ordinary events of daily life into patterns of cause and effect. When confronted with something that we did not expect, like a cold shoulder from a friend, we consciously try to figure out its cause. Most of us also make value judgments about the events that we observe. Without considering the moral implications of what we do, we would neither be able to guide our own conduct nor evaluate the conduct of others.

Both causality and morality are tricky concepts that need to be thoroughly understood before they can be applied by historians. No matter how energetic or resourceful, a historian cannot plunge into the problem of explaining or judging past events without first knowing precisely what is being sought. As with reports of historical events, explanations are justified by the formulation of arguments. These arguments link causes to effects and historical events to moral evaluations. Like the arguments used in historical inference, the premises of causal and moral arguments include a universal premise— that is, a generalization pertaining to all members of a class or category. But we shall see that the generalizations used to justify historical explanations must satisfy some very special requirements.

We will turn first to causal explanations and later to explanations of moral consequences. For the puzzles of causality, we will define the meaning of a cause and a causal explanation; discuss the type of generalizations that sustain causal arguments; and show how the empirical credibility of a logically valid causal argument can be assessed. We hope to demonstrate (1) that an explanation of even a particular event commits a historian to some general theory about human behavior, (2) that to explain why something happened is to explain why something else did not happen, and (3) that the probable truth of an explanation depends upon the probable truth and applicability of a general theory as well as the probable truth of the historical reports that constitute the cause and effect in question.

Causes and Causal Explanations: Basic Definitions

The problem of cause and effect has befuddled historians ever since man began to think systematically about his past. Some despairing historians have sought to banish causality from the temple of history, only to slip it through the back door disguised by clauses beginning with "because" or "since" or by words such as "factors," "impulses," "mainsprings," "forces," "foundations," "reasons," etc. The philosopher of history, Michael Scriven, found that a single page of an encyclopedia article on English history included almost thirty claims of causal connections, only two of which were identified by the word "cause." Our everyday language is so possessed by the spirit of causality that it cannot be exorcised.

The concept of causality intimidates historians in part because they have not analyzed closely the requirements of causal explanations of events. Typically, historians are interested in explaining why a particular event has occurred at a particular time or why patterns or sequences of events have occurred over periods of time. Historians have struggled to explain the fall of the Roman Empire, the rise of European nationalism, and the national revolutions of our own century. A few ambitious historians, like Arnold Toynbee (1889–1976), have even tried to explain repeated cycles in the rise and fall of civilizations.

However complex, both single events and sequences of events are explained by citing other events. We call the event to be explained, the effect; the events included in the explanation, causes. Generally, causes occur prior to effects. Some philosophers have argued that this need not always be true, that cause and effect can occur simultaneously. For example, in opening a door, the movement of one's arm occurs simultaneously with the movement of the door. A historical explanation asserts that the effect occurred because of the occurrence of the causes. According to an explanation, if the causes had not occurred, then the effect would not have occurred either. A historian might claim that the South's secession from the Union was a cause of the Civil War. Or he might claim that the North's victory was a cause of the restoration of the Union. For any effect, there are an indefinite number of causes—events whose occurrence we believe was required for the occurrence of the effect. Depending upon the puzzle that the historian is trying to solve, a given explanation may cite one or more events as causes.

A historian, of course, is free to hypothesize any explanation he pleases. But he also must be prepared to solve the puzzle within the puzzle—to explain why the proposed causes of his explanation actually are required for the occurrence of the event in question. If challenged, he can retire from the field, appeal to unspoken intuition, or set forth an argument that links the causes and effect. Of course, the premises of this causal argument may be challenged, and the historian then will have to mount additional arguments. Such challenges can continue indefinitely until the historian reaches the roots of all arguments—axioms that are presumed to be true and cannot be tested empirically.

Some might wonder why we should spend so much time and energy analyzing causal explanations. After all, many historians are content to rely on their personal experience or knowledge of life to draw connections between causes and effects. While they might be very concerned with systematically verifying the historical reports of causes and effects (getting the "facts" of history right), they would not be particularly interested in verifying explanations. Indeed, the neglect of the theories that establish causal relationships between historical reports finds sanction in the work of philosophers anxious to lay down an approach to historical inquiry that faithfully reflects what historians actually do. Michael Scriven, for example, has maintained that even if historians "cannot do without some kind of general knowledge about human nature . . . this simply does not need to be of the kind 'cited in theoretical treatises.' The most abysmal truisms suffice."

According to Scriven and like-minded thinkers, historians are granted liberties denied all other students of behavior. Imagine the reaction to an economist who tried to explain American inflation by reference to "the most abysmal truisms" about money, or a psychiatrist who tried to explain a case of schizophrenia by reference to equally abysmal truisms about insanity. They would be dismissed as the worst kind of charlatans. Social scientists devote scholarly lifetimes to formulating and testing explanatory models. Why should the historian be licensed to ignore their methods and findings? If the tables were turned, would historians grant a similar dispensation to social scientists using historical data? Imagine the reaction to a philosopher who assured us that "although social scientists cannot do without some general knowledge about past events, this simply does not need to be of the kind 'cited in historical works.' The most abysmal truisms about the past will suffice."

Frequently historians will assume that reports of past events can be squeezed into some general notion—a truism—of what causes various kinds of events. These notions usually reflect a historian's training and experience rather than carefully tested theories of human behavior. A historian might believe that men may murder out of passion or anger; to achieve a moral objective; or to attain power, wealth, or prestige. This historian would probably feel justified in explaining any given act of murder by reference to any one of these theories of human behavior.

There are serious problems with this personal or commonsense approach to explanation. Our experiences necessarily are limited. We may not be able to figure out how to explain certain types of events merely by extrapolation from personal experience. Most people, for example, would have little intuitive sense of how to explain the growth of the iron industry in the United States or the development of the germ theory of disease. The growth of industries and the formulation of scientific theories are simply not part of our ordinary experience. Even for events that fall within our range of experience, our common sense may leave out important approaches to explanation. Actually, many psychological insights might run counter to our intuitive understanding of what motivates people to do certain things. In addition, our commonsense view of the world is acquired within a particular culture and time period and cannot necessarily be extended to all periods of the past. Finally, what is common sense to one person may be common nonsense to another. Unless the implicit theories of common sense are made explicit and systematically tested, historians will be unable to resolve disputes that flow from different commonsense views of human behavior.

Generalizations in Causal Arguments

Both reports about past events and causal explanations of these events are founded on historical arguments. But there are distinctions between the premises included in each type of argument. The arguments that sustain historical inference conclude with a report of the occurrence of an event. The premises of these arguments must include either a description of historical evidence or a report of another historical event. The premises must also include a generalization linking either the evidence or the report to the occurrence of the event cited in the conclusion. The probable truth of the concluding report depends upon the probable truth of all the premises that make up a particular, logically valid argument.

In contrast, a causal argument concludes with the claim that one or more events are required for the occurrence of yet another event. Its premises must include reports of the occurrences of all these events. Obviously we could not claim that one event caused another event without first claiming that both events actually occurred. The premises of causal arguments must also include a generalization linking the occurrence of the causes to the occurrence of the effect. Without such a generalization, the conclusion that the causes are required for the effect would not logically follow from the claim that these events occurred. Merely reporting the occurrence of two events does not establish that one of these events was a cause of the other. One might believe, for example, that the Civil War occurred in 1861 and that the volcano Krakatoa exploded in 1883 without believing that either of these events had anything to do with the occurrence of the other. The probability that the conclusion of a causal argument identifies an actual cause of an actual event depends on two things: (1) the probable truth of the reports about the causes and the effect and (2) the probable truth of the generalization linking cause and effect.

Because the generalizations that sustain causal arguments assert a cause-and-effect relationship between events, they much satisfy more stringent requirements than the generalizations that sustain arguments concluding with historical reports. An historical report states only that an event occurred.

If a historian is interested simply in determining the probability that an event took place, he need not ponder the causal implications of generalizations included in his arguments. Assume that a historian inferred that a particular medieval peasant is likely to be illiterate by using the generalization that almost all medieval peasants were illiterate. The credibility of this inference does not depend upon the causal relationship between being a peasant and being illiterate. Being a peasant may be a cause of being illiterate; being illiterate may be a cause of being a peasant (perhaps those who did not learn to read and write were relegated to peasantry), or being a peasant and being illiterate may be common effects of some third factor (for example, a lack of intelligence). To establish the likelihood that a particular peasant was illiterate, the historian need only know the literacy rate of peasants; he does not need to know *why* most peasants were illiterate.

For a generalization to be able to sustain a causal argument, it must meet two additional requirements: (1) the generalization must be derived from a general theory about the ways in which people and things behave; and (2) the generalization must set forth connections between cause and effect that are necessary rather than probabilistic. These requirements reflect two distinct and necessary notions embedded in the concept of causality. First, the logical relationship between a cause and an effect is such that, in the same circumstances, the occurrence of the cause must be accompanied by the occurrence of the effect. Second, the substantive relationship between cause and effect is such that their mutual dependence is set forth in a theory expressing our ideas about how the world functions. Thus causal relationships imply more than a correspondence or correlation between events.

Causal arguments can be sustained only by generalizations derived from theories about behavior. People sometimes use the word theory to signify hypotheses that have not yet been accepted or rejected. We use the word here with a more positive connotation—to indicate a set of statements that define terms and set forth relationships between these terms. Theories are the building blocks of knowledge because they are not derived from any prior propositions. Many of us have a passing acquaintance with some of the more notable theories of physical science, for example, the theory of gravity and the theory of relativity. Historians, of course, rely primarily on theories of human behavior which are less formal and rigorous than the theories of physicists. Like scientific theories, however, the theories that interest historians serve two purposes. First, these theories state the terms used to describe various types of events. For example, certain economic theories use such terms as supply, demand, and price. Second, theories express the relationships that prevail among the types of events so stated and defined. Thus, economic theory might state the influence of changes in supply and demand on changes in prices. These relationships are set forth in axioms—propositions that are assumed to be true.

Since theories include only terms, definitions of terms, and axioms,* the appropriate question to ask is not whether the theory is true or false, but under what conditions it accurately portrays the real world. In science, for example, observations contradicting the classical laws relating the temperature, pressure, and volume of a gas did not demonstrate that these laws were false. Rather, it was found that the laws were inapplicable under some conditions and only approximated real physical relations under other conditions.

To test the applicability of a theory, an investigator must invoke "transformation rules" that relate the terms of the theory to actual events, by describing the observations that correspond to each term. For example, what real world observations correspond to such economic terms as price, supply, and demand? If these terms had no real world equivalent, theories using the terms could not be tested. Such theories would remain pure abstractions, unconnected with what actually goes on in the world. Transformation rules also define the real world observations that correspond to statements of the conditions under which theories are alleged to hold. Again, without these rules we would never know when a theory is supposed to fit an actual situation and when it is not.

Theories operate at several different levels in the process of causal explanation. The very notion that events follow patterns of cause and effect is itself a theory about the world in which we live. Similarly, theories define for us the ways in which we go about explaining the events of experience. Specific theories, of course, must be invoked to explain the events that concern historians. What, for instance, causes people to commit murder? to join political movements? to emigrate from their homeland? The generalizations included in all historical arguments are grounded on such theories. Only by referring to a theory about human or natural behavior can a historian assert that the occurrence of an event is required for the occurrence of another event. Without reference to a theory, he can establish only that events regularly occur together, but not that this regularity reflects a cause-and-effect relationship between the events.

Philosophers often refer to theories that are applied to particular explanations as "causal laws" or "covering laws." They use the phrase "covering law"

---

*From these terms, definitions, and axioms further propositions called theorems can be logically derived. These theorems then become part of the theory.

because the general causal principle embodied in the law "covers" the particular explanation being offered. An economic historian might explain a rise in the price of a particular commodity at a particular time by reference to the covering laws of supply and demand. A biographer might explain the behavior of a particular individual at a particular time by reference to covering laws derived from the theories of Sigmund Freud. Or a political historian might explain the repeated occurrence of revolutions in the twentieth century by reference to covering laws pertaining to group behavior.

Covering laws generally are implicit rather than explicit in historical explanations. Historians usually are content to say that something happened because of something else without indicating the covering law that sustains the explanation. Nonetheless, covering laws derived from general theories are an essential component of every logically valid historical explanation.

Covering laws do not, however, link events in their full complexity to one another. Every event is unique in that no other event duplicates all its features. But every event also has characteristics which are shared by other events. Covering laws link the characteristics of a causal event to the characteristics of the event to be explained. Consider a covering law connecting the secession of the southern states to the outbreak of the Civil War. Such a law could not refer specifically to secession or to the Civil War. But it could refer to an act of defiance against an established government and to the initiation of armed conflict.

Covering laws, because of their general nature can never refer to unique events. Indeed, if two events were truly unique in the sense that they were in no way similar to any other events of our experience, we would never know whether or not these events were causally connected. We would have no grounds for asserting that one event affected the other because we cannot determine the relationship between events that resemble nothing else that we know about. Imagine that a starship transported us to a planet in another galaxy inhabited by beings that do not resemble any earthly form of life. Assume that we observed the beings performing a series of acts followed by another series of acts. Unless we presumed some similarity between the behavior of the space beings and some familiar form of life, we would have no way of knowing which, if any, of the earlier acts were causes of the later acts. Many fine science fiction tales have hinged on the misunderstandings that arise when beings from different planets try to explain each other's behavior.

No matter how they choose to express their explanations, historians cannot escape a commitment to a generalization that links events of the kind mentioned in the cause to events of the kind mentioned in the effect. Those who try to escape can be as maddening as "Old Chicken Colonel Turner," once a pitching coach of the New York Yankees. As Jim Bouton recalls in *Ball Four,* Turner could explain every situation without worrying about the consistency of his explanations:

> If [pitching coaches] shout enough advice they can't be wrong. . . . Old Chicken Colonel Turner was a master at this. He'd sit in the dugout and shout to Stan Bahnsen, "Now, keep the ball down, Bahnsen," and Stan would throw a letter-high fastball that would get popped up into the infield and The Colonel would look down the bench and say, "The boy's fastball is moving. The boy's fastball is rising." Two innings later, same situation, the very same pitch, home run into the left-field seats. The Colonel looks up and down the bench and says very wisely, "Got the ball up. You see what happens when you get the ball up?"
>
> Then you'd get a weak lefthanded hitter up in Yankee Stadium and somebody would throw him a change-up and he'd hit it for a home run into the short porch [right field] and the Colonel would say, "You can't throw a change-up to a lefthanded hitter, boys. Not in this ball park." A week later a guy would throw the same pitch to the same kind of hitter and the guy would be way out in front and The Colonel would say, "Changeup. One of the best pitches in baseball. You can really fool the hitter with it."
>
> Whatever the result, the colonel always knew the cause.*

Similarly, a historian who claims that an explanation is unique in that it does not involve a general principle (for example, never throw a change-up to a lefthanded hitter in a ball park with an exceptionally short right field fence) can explain things without worrying about being proven wrong—or right. All causal explanations are founded on the assumption that the same effects follow from the same causes. Neither historians nor pitching coaches can finesse the implications of this assumption.

The covering laws linking causes and effects must be based not only on theories of what causes types of events to occur, but also must set forth connections between cause and effect that are necessary rather than probabilistic.† A necessary connection occurs all of the time; the covering law lays down a probability of 100 per cent. A probabilistic connection does not

---

*Excerpt from Jim Bouton, *Ball Four,* copyright © 1970 by Jim Bouton. Reprinted by permission.

†Some have argued that the findings of quantum physics, which suggest that, in principle, we can only determine the probable outcomes of certain types of events, dissolve the notion of causality. But even for quantum level phenomena, the same *probability function* must follow the same set of prior events. Thus, the principle of same causes, same effects, is preserved.

occur all of the time; at best, the theory lays down the probability that the connection will occur. A causal explanation expresses the belief that given the causes, the effects certainly will follow. The notion that the same effects must follow the same causes under the same conditions is fundamental to the concept of causality itself.

The following diagram, sketched in Figure II, shows how historical evidence, generalizations used to infer historical reports from that evidence, and causal generalizations (or covering laws) are linked together into a causal explanation. The direction of the arrows between historical reports reflects the flow of causality. Thus historical report 1 is a cause of historical report 2. The model, of course, could be extended indefinitely in either direction. Historical report 1 or 2 could be effects of other causes or causes of other effects. The credibility of the explanation depends upon the credibility of the inferences from historical evidence to historical reports as well as the credibility of the causal connection between the reports. To understand precisely how the historian demonstrates such a causal connection, additional ideas need to be considered. The diagram below represents only the skeleton of causal explanation.

FIGURE II

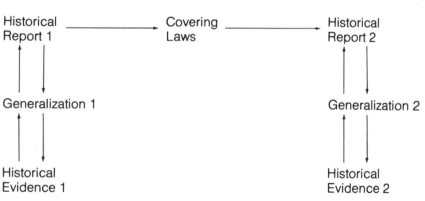

Historical   Covering   Historical
Report 1   Laws   Report 2

Generalization 1   Generalization 2

Historical   Historical
Evidence 1   Evidence 2

Events and Contrasting Events

Historians well may argue over whether or not an event was a cause of another event. But more often they debate the importance of various causes. Some historians, for example, have cited Abraham Lincoln's desire to appease antislavery opinion in European nations as a cause of his decision to issue the Emancipation Proclamation. Historians have asserted that this desire motivated Lincoln to issue the proclamation. However, the election of Lincoln as President of the United States also was a cause of his decision to issue the Emancipation Proclamation, for only as President could Lincoln have issued a proclamation of this nature. But no historian would consider this cause worthy of attention because it does not provide a solution to what has puzzled scholars about Lincoln's decision to issue the Emancipation Proclamation.

Thus we need to sharpen our understanding of what is meant by explaining the occurrence of an event. Obviously, the occurrence of a particular event means that all possible alternatives to this event have not occurred. To understand what we are trying to explain about an event, we must specify with care both the event to be explained and a contrasting event. Only by citing a contrasting event can we understand what is being asked for in a causal explanation. The contrasting event reveals what is puzzling about the occurrence of the actual event. Historians may want to explain why Lincoln decided to issue the Emancipation Proclamation in 1862 instead of making no new statements on the slavery question. This statement of the event and its contrasting event takes for granted Lincoln's ability to issue the Emancipation Proclamation as well as his ability to issue other statements on the slavery question. The puzzle it raises could be resolved by pointing to Lincoln's desire to appease European opinion, but not by pointing to his election as President.

A famous explanation of Queen Elizabeth's use of the term "etc." in stating her full title illustrates the importance of specifying a contrasting event as well as the event to be explained. The late F. W. Maitland has contended that the use of this vague expression gave Elizabeth maneuvering room on religious questions that were troubling England during her reign. The use of a phrase meaning "and so on" enabled the Queen to expand or contract the scope of her authority in response to different circumstances. Maitland's argument helps to explain why Elizabeth used a general term rather than completely spelling out her title. It does not, however, explain why she used the particular term "etc." rather than some other general term, such as "et alia." Maitland's explanation has satisfied most historians, because the puzzle of greatest interest is why she used a general term rather than spelling out her full title.

Historians who barrel ahead to explain the occurrence of events without first specifying a contrasting event may commit grave errors of analysis. These historians do not make clear either to their readers or to themselves exactly what they are trying to explain.

Like effects, causes must also be cited in conjunction with other events. To say that the occurrence of a cause is necessary for the occurrence of an effect is to say that if the cause had not occurred, then the effect also would not have occurred. To signify what we mean by the nonccurrence of the effect, we have noted that it is necessary to set forth a contrasting event (for example, Lincoln saying nothing about slavery rather than issuing the Emancipation Proclamation). But what do we mean by the nonoccurrence of a causal event? If a causal event had not occurred, then some alternative event would have occurred. Thus a particular alternative to each cause must be included in a causal explanation of any event. The claim that the occurrence of a cause is necessary for the occurrence of a later event rather than some contrasting event is founded on the belief that if an alternative to the cause had occurred, then a contrasting event rather than the actual event would also have occurred. The alternative to the cause must specifically be mentioned because the event to be explained might follow the occurrence of some of the possible alternatives to the causal event. The two-by-two table in Figure III illustrates what we mean when we say that one event is a cause of another.

FIGURE III

	Later Event Occurs (e.g., Elizabeth I adds the general term "etc." to her title.)	Contrasting Event Occurs (e.g., Elizabeth I does not add any general term to her title.)
Earlier Causal Event Occurs (e.g., Elizabeth I desires a title that does not limit her authority in religious matters.)	Yes	No
Alternative Event Occurs (e.g., Elizabeth I is not concerned about her authority in religious matters.)	No	Yes

The problem of causal explanation challenges historians to identify what it is about causal events that makes their occurrence necessary for the occurrence of an effect. The table portrayed in Figure III indicates that the causal events cited in a causal explanation must possess some property that, under the circumstances prevailing at the time, leads to the occurrence of the effect. The alternative events lack this property, but instead possess properties that under the same circumstances lead to the occurrence of the contrasting event.

It might be argued that the secession of the southern states caused the dispute between North and South to escalate into full-scale war. The historian offering this explanation might claim that if the South had accepted the compromise proposal framed by Senator John J. Crittenden of Kentucky, the Civil War would not have occurred. This same historian also might recognize that if the South had not seceded, but instead had proclaimed its right to nullify any legislation against its interests passed by the national government, the Civil War still would have occurred. The historian could justify this position by arguing that both the secession of the South and a proclamation of nullification were flagrant acts of defiance against the Union, whereas acceptance of the Crittenden compromise was an act of conciliation. Given the circumstances, the historian would maintain that any act of defiance against the Union would have led to war.

If historians of the Civil War would specify clearly both events and contrasting events, some of the confusion frequently noted by historical critics could be dispelled. The Civil War is an extremely complex event that can be analyzed in many different ways. The first step in explaining the coming of the war would be to break down this amorphous concept into particular events and contrasting events. Without performing this analysis, a historian would not know what is being asked for in an explanation. A historian might want to explain why the South seceded from the Union in 1860–1861 rather than ten years before or ten years later; why conflict between the North and South took the form of armed hostility rather than legal and political confrontation; why the men and women of the North and South followed their leaders into war rather than refusing to fight; and why Lincoln decided to reinforce rather than abandon Fort Sumter. Different explanations would clearly be required for these events and contrasting events. By clearly and precisely setting forth both events and contrasting events, the historian can begin to limit the number of preceeding events that might have been causes. If the historian wants to know why the South seceded in 1860–1861 rather than 1851 or 1871, he need not concentrate on the causes of secession per se, but can address himself to the timing of secession.

Evaluating Causal Explanations

How does the historian evaluate a particular causal explanation? Sometimes historians will speak of verifying historical explanations. At other times they will speak of evaluating, justifying, warranting, testing, corroborating, or confirming explanations. All these terms refer to the same thing—judging the probable truth of the solution offered by the historian to the puzzle of why something happened. We will try to indicate the ways in which historians determine this probability.

Causal explanations are based on the necessary connections between events. When the historian claims that one event was a cause of another, he must show that both events actually occurred and that the occurrence of the earlier event was required for the occurrence of the later event. Thus the credibility of his explanation depends upon the probable truth of all the premises of his causal argument—the probability that the reports of both cause and effect are true and the probability that the connection asserted in the covering law linking these reports is likewise true.

Consider a historian seeking to explain the behavior of voters in the American presidential election of 1928. The election pitted the Republican nominee Herbert Hoover against the Democratic nominee Alfred E. Smith. Hoover was Protestant, rural in origin, and a supporter of prohibition. Smith was Catholic, urban in origin, and an opponent of prohibition. A historian might plausibly claim that an individual voted against the Democratic candidate because that individual was Protestant rather than Catholic, a rural dweller rather than an urbanite, and a supporter rather than an opponent of prohibition. The greater the odds that the individual actually voted for Hoover rather than Smith and the odds that he actually was Protestant, rural, and dry, rather than Catholic, urban, and wet, the greater the odds in favor of the explanation. Similarly, the greater the probability that this information about the voter actually explains his behavior, the greater the odds in favor of the explanation.

It is fairly obvious that the probable truth of a causal explanation depends upon the probable truth of reports about causal events. Events that never happened cannot explain the occurrence of an event that did happen. But we often fail to recognize that the probable truth of a causal explanation also depends upon the probable truth of reports about the effect. If the effect is misrepresented, the explanation will be obviously incorrect. Some early critics of the Warren Report, for example, have argued that the presence of a gunman on the grassy knoll overlooking the President's automobile explains why the first shot to hit the President struck Kennedy in the front of his neck.

Unfortunately for critics of this persuasion, the evidence suggests that all the bullets that struck the President were fired from behind his limousine. The event these critics seek to explain never seems to have occurred.

Historians determine the probable truth of reports about causes and effects in the same way that they would evaluate the probable truth of any report about the past. These reports are the product of a chain of inferences that begins with historical evidence and uses generalizations to forge links between the evidence and the reports. To demonstrate the causal connection between these reports, however, the historian must apply and evaluate a covering law. Since covering laws link types of events to one another, the historian must be sure that the particular causes and effects in his explanation are indeed events of the type mentioned in the covering law. Recall that every theory must include transformation rules that describe the reports about the world that correspond to the terms of the theory.

To evaluate a covering law invoked in an explanation, the historian must determine whether or not the covering law really applies to the situation being studied. As we indicated, covering laws are never true or false, only applicable or inapplicable under various conditions. To begin an analysis, the historian must first of all identify the covering law or laws employed. If the explanation sets them forth explicitly, so much the better. But as we have remarked previously, covering laws are almost always implicit, hidden beneath the surface. Thus, before we can even begin to evaluate a causal explanation, we must first determine the covering laws used to sustain the causal argument.

In testing the applicability of covering laws to particular situations, historians reach probabilistic judgments. Although the covering laws invoked in support of causal explanations assert invariable connections between events, the historian never can be certain that a law actually applies to the considered situation. To evaluate a covering law included in an explanation of a historical event is to evaluate the probability that the law has been correctly applied. Even though the covering law itself cannot be expressed in probabilistic form, the strength of one's belief that the law is applicable can, of course, be expressed as a probability judgment. In other words, a historian can never be certain that a particular explanation really covers a particular case, for the conditions of that case might not conform to the conditions under which the law actually applies.

To determine the probability that a covering law invoked by a historian actually covers the situation in question, the historian must express the law as an "explanatory model" of the event being explained. An explanatory model is simply a way of expressing a covering law so that its applicability to a situation can be tested by reference to reports about the world. The model would specify the event to be explained and the contrasting event as well as the proposed cause and its alternative. The model would also include a statement of the conditions that led the historian to believe that the covering law linking cause and effect can be applied to the case being considered.

A statement of conditions is the key to the application of covering laws to the explanation of historical events. This statement connects theory to the real world. Without such a statement we would not have a model at all, but only a covering law that could not be tested by example since we would not know the conditions under which the law is supposed to apply. Just as the historian must use transformation rules to demonstrate that reports about the cause and effect correspond to events of a covering law, he must also use transformation rules to show that reports about the conditions of the particular case correspond to conditions under which the law is supposed to hold. Figure III on page 53 shows us what we would expect if a model were correct for all situations that fulfill the conditions set forth in the model. The effect should follow the cause, but not the alternative to the cause; similarly, the contrasting event should follow the alternative to the cause, but not the cause.

Historians often have unfairly criticized each others' explanations without being sufficiently sensitive to the statement of conditions that is at least implicit in every explanatory model. For example, historians have criticized the contention that Holland became a great power through "conquering the challenge of the sea." Critics ridiculed this explanation by pointing to other nations that became great powers without meeting this challenge. Yet a historian advancing this explanation could respond by arguing that the conditions of his explanatory model pertain to Holland in the era of her ascendancy but not the other nations cited by his critic. Of course, the historian would have to specify these conditions so that his model could be tested by reference to empirical data.

In their analysis of causal explanations, both historians and philosophers of history have raised clouds of confusion by failing to distinguish between how the historian might state a causal explanation and how it must be justified through the construction of a model. As a hypothetical example, consider an explanation of Brutus' murder of Caesar. Allan Donagan, a distinguished philosopher of history, suggests that a historian can explain Brutus' act of murder by saying that Brutus would perform any act that was necessary to preserve the Roman Republic, and that Brutus perceived that only by murdering Caesar could the Republic be saved.

Donagan's explanation is stated as though he were explaining a unique event (Brutus' decision) by reference to other unique events (Brutus' devotion to the Republic; his conviction that joining the conspiracy to murder Caesar was necessary to preserve the Republic). But the assertion that Brutus would perform any act to save the Republic is not a report about a particular event. Rather, this conditional or "if/then" statement, although apparently tied to a particular person, is similar to an explanatory model in that it states that if the cause occurs (i.e., Brutus' perception), under certain conditions (i.e., Brutus' character and circumstances), the effect will also occur. The conditional statement seems reasonable to us only because we believe that a man like Brutus might well behave in this fashion. A conditional statement, identical in form, asserting that Cassius would perform any act to save the Republic would seem less reasonable because from what we know about Cassius' character, he was not dedicated to the Republic per se but to maintaining his position of political power and influence. Thus we believe that if Cassius thought he could preserve his personal position under Caesar's rule, he would not have joined the conspiracy to assassinate Caesar. The probable truth of such conditional statements about Brutus depends upon the likelihood that an effect of the type specified will follow a cause of the type specified whenever the conditions of the particular case are duplicated.

Continuing to follow explanations of why Brutus murdered Caesar, we will consider how the historian might set forth a model that portrays a particular explanation. Figure IV below portrays the structure of an explanation asserting that Brutus murdered Caesar (effect) rather than taking less drastic action against him (contrasting event), because he was certain (causal event) rather than uncertain (alternative event) that Caesar would make it impossible to preserve the Republic.* The diagram reveals that this explanation is justified by the following covering law: A man (in this case Brutus) will murder another man (in this case Caesar) if he is certain that the other man will block an objective (in this case preserving the Republic); but the man will take action short of murder if he is uncertain that the other man blocks this objective. The transformation rules relating this covering law to reports about Brutus and Caesar would simply define them as men and "preserving the Republic" as an objective.

At this point in the development of the model, a critic sharing Donagan's view of historical explanation might object that the entire exercise is absurd. We surely know that most of the time people do not murder those who block

---

*See the Appendix for a complete elaboration of this causal explanation.

FIGURE IV

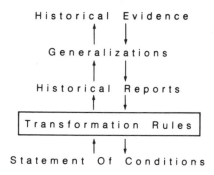

Historical   Evidence

Generalizations

Historical   Reports

Transformation   Rules

Statement   Of   Conditions

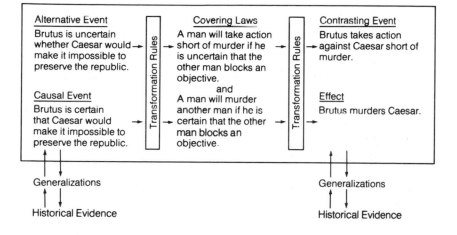

Alternative Event	Transformation Rules	Covering Laws	Transformation Rules	Contrasting Event
Brutus is uncertain whether Caesar would make it impossible to preserve the republic.		A man will take action short of murder if he is uncertain that the other man blocks an objective.		Brutus takes action against Caesar short of murder.
		and		
Causal Event		A man will murder another man if he is		Effect
Brutus is certain that Caesar would make it impossible to preserve the republic.		certain that the other man blocks an objective.		Brutus murders Caesar.

Generalizations   Generalizations

Historical Evidence   Historical Evidence their objectives. Such a ridiculous "law," the critic would declare, could not possibly explain why Brutus murdered Caesar. Recall, however, that a covering law is simply a theoretical statement that connects general terms to each other. As the diagram indicates, the covering law invoked by the historian is supposed to hold only under a specified set of conditions. For the law used here, these conditions might include the means and opportunity to commit murder, the degree of dedication to the objective, and the willingness to disregard the personal consequences of murder. Surely it no longer sounds absurd to claim that, given the means, the opportunity, an incredible dedication to an objective, and a disdain for personal consequences, a man would murder another man who he was certain would prevent the realization of the objective.

Thus, the full explanatory model must include the covering law and the conditions under which the law is supposed to apply. The model is tied to the historian's particular case by transformation rules connecting the covering law and conditions to historical reports inferred from available evidence. Such rules would define the kind of man who was highly dedicated to an objective and who would dismiss the personal consequences of murder. The two–headed arrows linking historical reports and conditions indicate that the historian could begin with reports about Brutus and then transform these reports into a statement of conditions. Or he may begin with a notion of what the conditions should be and then use transformation rules to see how well Brutus actually fits the conditions. No matter how the historian arrives at his statement of conditions, the model as a whole is credible only if the connections set forth in the covering law actually hold under the stated conditions. To see whether the law does indeed hold, the historian must examine situations other than the one to which the model is applied.

Historians usually concentrate on inferring reports relevant to establishing causes, effects, and conditions. Rarely do historians actually try to evaluate a casual model by showing that a covering law connecting cause and effect correctly portrays what happens whenever the stated conditions are met. Usually the covering laws implicitly used by historians come from common sense, the historian's knowledge of life, or are borrowed from the social sciences. Traditionally, historians have not conceived their mission to be the testing of laws about human behavior. Yet the probable truth of an explanation does depend upon the likelihood that the connections set forth in the covering law hold under the proposed conditions. Moreover, historians should reconsider the importance of using historical research as a means of testing notions about human behavior that are part of our common sense or the explicit theories of psychology, economics, and other social sciences.

Given the broad scope of their work, historians have a unique opportunity to examine causal theory under a wide variety of disparate conditions.

Whether a historian decides to test the applicability of a model or not, he should understand how models can be tested with empirical information. In principle, there is no reason why we could not use the methods of experimental science to test the soundness of models that causally connect reports of past events. Since these models cannot be tied to particular events, they must assert that under certain conditions events with certain properties are related to each other as cause and effect. We could test this assertion by duplicating the relevant conditions in two experimental situations. We would recreate the cause in the first situation (e.g., A believes B blocks an objective of A), and the alternative to the cause (e.g., A is not certain whether B blocks an objective of A) in the second situation (often called the experimental control). As Figure IV indicates, the model would be verified only if the effect (e.g., A murders B) occurs in the first situation, and the contrasting event (e.g., A takes less drastic action) occurs in the control situation.

Yet the models that interest historians generally cannot be tested by the methods of experimental science. For several reasons these models usually can be evaluated only by reference to nonexperimental data—data that exists as we find them and cannot be experimentally manipulated by the investigator.

The vague nature of theories about human behavior makes it very difficult to evaluate whether or not the conditions, the causes, and the alternatives actually have been duplicated in an experimental situation. Moreover, these theories are plagued by weak transformation rules relating the terms of the theory to observations of the real world. Taking our model of Caesar's murder, the historian would be hard pressed to state the degree of dedication required for a man to murder someone who thwarted his objectives. He would also have great difficulty proposing transformation rules that relate this condition to reports about actual behavior. How do we know when a man is *that* dedicated to achieving a particular objective? At best the historian could offer only a rough approximation of his explanatory model.

A possible solution to this problem might be to perform the experiment in a large number of situations, all of which approximate the conditions under which the covering law is supposed to apply. This strategy would not yield a "yes/no" answer as to whether the model is correct. By examining a large number of situations, the researcher can determine the probabilities that each one of the four cases portrayed in Figure IV would actually occur: the probability that the effect (A murders B) follows the cause (A is certain that B blocks an objective of A); the probability that the contrasting event (A takes action short of murder) follows the alternative to the cause (A is uncertain as to whether B blocks an objective of A); the probability that the effect follows the alternative to the cause; and the probability that the contrasting event follows the cause. The higher the first two probabilities and the lower the second two probabilities, the greater the support for the model in question.

These four probabilities are calculated as follows:

1. probability that the effect follows the cause:

$$\frac{\text{number of times that the effect and the cause both occur}}{\text{number of times that the cause occurs}}$$

2. probability that contrasting event follows the alternative to the cause:

$$\frac{\text{number of times that the contrasting event and the alternative to the cause both occur}}{\text{number of times that the alternative to the cause occurs}}$$

3. probability that effect follows the alternative to the cause:

$$\frac{\text{number of times that effect and alternative to the cause both occur}}{\text{number of times that alternative to the cause occurs}}$$

4. probability that contrasting event follows the cause:

$$\frac{\text{number of times that both contrasting event and the cause both occur}}{\text{number of times that the cause occurs}}$$

Even this strategy will not suffice for most of the models that interest historians. It may be impossible to duplicate even well specified models in an experimental context. For example, the conditions under which laws of human behavior are said to apply may relate to an individual's life history or to a cultural milieu. Even a most resourceful experimenter could scarcely be expected to reproduce such conditions. Moreover, the very performance of an experiment with human subjects also may become part of the conditions relevant to the behavior being considered. And it is very difficult to predict how the reactions of people to being part of an experiment will affect the relationships being tested. Finally, experimentation with human subjects often raises grave ethical questions.

Generally, to evaluate the models that sustain his explanations, the historian must search for examples from actual experiences rather than recreating experiences in a laboratory setting. Instead of repeatedly performing an experiment, the historian tries to find a large number of actual situations that approximate the conditions stated in the model. He would then determine the probability of obtaining each of the four results portrayed in Figure IV.

The most serious problem facing the historian who seeks to evaluate a causal model is the difficulty of finding cases that approximate the conditions under which the model is supposed to hold. Since each case only approximates these conditions, reliable evaluation of the model requires consideration of large numbers of cases. Errors produced by variations from stated conditions tend to even out as additional cases are added to the analysis. The reliability of the analysis thus increases as the number of cases increases.

The time dependence of historical explanations often makes it very difficult to find similar cases for analysis. We know that human behavior is vitally affected by the time and place in which it occurs. Yet we cannot fully state what it is about time and place that influences behavior. As a result, the relationships between events will vary in unpredictable ways depending upon time and place. Indeed, the very act that an historian seeks to explain may have influenced the behavior of people in similar situations at later times. People's perceptions of Brutus' actions and its consequences may have affected their willingness to murder in order to advance moral objectives.

One way of dealing with problems of time and place is to limit the testing of a model to particular times and places. In principle, the historian could express in general terms the circumstances associated with these times and places that affect relationships among the events being considered. In practice, though, the historian usually knows only that time and place influence these relationships without knowing the exact nature of this influence.

This strategy is effective whenever the historian studies behavior that is repeated a large number of times at a particular time and place. A historian of twentieth–century America, for example, might suggest that in the presidential election of 1928, Protestants were motivated by anti-Catholic sentiment to vote against Governor Alfred E. Smith of New York—the first Catholic nominated for President by a major party. The historian would also know that it would be difficult to evaluate this explanation by examining the behavior of Protestants and non-Protestants in other cultures and time periods. He knows that different conditions in these disparate situations would affect the relationship he wishes to investigate, but he cannot specify the factors necessary for recognizing those situations that would be comparable to the situation prevailing in the United States in 1928. However, because large numbers of individuals participated in the presidential election of 1928, the historian can legitimately limit his investigation to behavior in this one election and examine the influence of religion on voting decisions.

Often historians will not be able to test their models by reference to repeated events within a given culture and time period. For example, a historian seeking to explain Brutus' murder of Caesar could not employ the same strategy as the historian seeking to explain a voter's response to the presidential election of 1928. There were not millions of other individuals in Rome of the first century B.C. faced with the same decision that confronted Brutus. Rather, the historian would be forced to set forth a general statement of the conditions relevant to Brutus' action and search for situations that fulfill these conditions. He would also have to formulate a general statement of the cause and effect included in his explanation of Brutus' behavior so that these causes and effects could be identified in the comparable situations isolated by the historian.

One problem with this strategy is that as statements of conditions, causes, and effects become more general, the historian becomes less certain that the details of his case actually fulfill the requirements of the general categories he has employed. Moreover, the connections between very general statements about the world are usually problematic; it may be very difficult either to accept or reject an explanation founded on broad generalizations. Historians must forthrightly admit that they often cannot decide among competing explanations of a particular event. There are still many mysteries of the past whose solutions await new evidence or more refined methods of inquiry.

Irrespective of the problem of finding a large number of comparable cases, what appears to be a causal relationship between events may be nothing more than a correlation produced by common causes of the two events. When two events have common causes, they will regularly occur together, even though they have nothing to do with the occurrence of each other. Relationships of this type are known as spurious relationships and are the bane of those who try to solve puzzles of causality. For instance, sailors warn us that on the open sea, a red sky in the morning means bad weather in the afternoon. Whether the relationship between the color of the sky and the conditions of the weather is causal or spurious would be a matter of indifference to the practical minded sailor. Concerned about the safety of his ship, the sailor probably would care only that observations of sky color could be used to predict reliably the likelihood of foul weather. But the scientist who wanted to discover the causes of the weather would have to consider the nature of the relationship between sky color and weather conditions. Most likely he would suggest that red skies in the morning and storms in the afternoon are not causally related to each other, but are both produced by certain atmospheric conditions.

As the distinguished statistical theorist Hubert Blalock points out, a researcher might find a correlation showing that teenagers who eat a lot of ice cream are much less likely to be juvenile delinquents than teenagers who do not eat much ice cream. This correlation might enable him to infer with reasonable accuracy the likelihood that an individual actually is a juvenile delinquent. But it may signify a spurious rather than a causal relationship between ice cream consumption and juvenile crime. Upon being informed of the correlation, would a policymaker recommend solving the juvenile delinquency problem by dosing all teenagers with large quantities of ice cream? No. He would see that this correlation is spurious—that some third factor, probably economic status, influences both the consumption of ice cream and the likelihood of juvenile delinquency.

The following diagram illustrates spurious relationships between events. The direction of the single–headed arrows in the diagram represent the flow of cause and effect. The broken, double–headed arrow represents the spurious correlation.

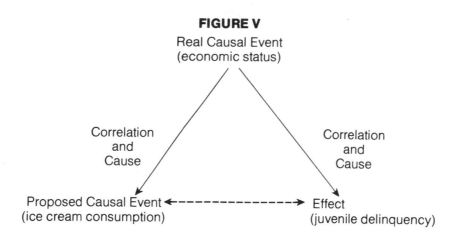

FIGURE V

Real Causal Event
(economic status)

Correlation
and
Cause

Correlation
and
Cause

Proposed Causal Event
(ice cream consumption)

Effect
(juvenile delinquency)

Spurious correlations that masquerade as cause-and-effect relationships are not always so easy to detect. For example, some authorities have argued that the nation's birth rate has declined because more women are employed outside the home. But is it true that women are having fewer babies because they have jobs? Might not both the birth rate and the employment rate of women be dependent on some other factor such as economic conditions, later age at marriage, male attitudes about family size, or the availability of contraception and abortion? If a historian suspects that the relationship between two events is spurious rather than causal, he must formulate two models portraying both a causal and spurious relationship between the events.

To discriminate between two conflicting models of cause and effect, the historian must identify the contrary expectations of the two models and see which of these expectations is better sustained by the available information. A model linking ice cream consumption and juvenile delinquency as cause and effect and a model portraying these two events as common effects of economic status would lead us to expect very different relationships between the consumption of ice cream and the commission of juvenile crime when we look at teenagers only from the *same* economic class. By considering only individuals from the same economic class we can, in effect, hold economic status constant (or in statistical parlance, "control for" the influence of economic status), and explore the relationship between ice cream consumption and juvenile delinquency without worrying about the spurious effects of this factor. If the first model is correct, we would expect the correlation between ice cream consumption and juvenile delinquency to persist, even when we consider only rich teenagers or only poor teenagers. If the second model is correct, we would expect this correlation to disappear when we look at only rich or only poor individuals. According to this second model, variations in the consumption of ice cream should be unrelated to the commission of juvenile crime when economic status is held constant.

No matter how refined his analysis, the historian can never rule out the possibility that an apparent causal relationship actually is a spurious correlation. He cannot be certain that he has taken into account all the factors that could produce a spurious relationship between the events being considered. He may simply be unaware of relevant factors. Causal explanation is necessarily indeterminate. The historian can never rule out the possibility that a proposed causal relationship may be generated by the influence of some factor he has not considered.

A historian can further check the plausibility of an explanation by thinking about the consequences that would follow if the explanation actually was correct. A historian's explanation of a particular event is itself a statement about the past upon which he can base inferences about later events. A historian who claims that a voter supported Herbert Hoover in 1928 because the voter objected to Al Smith's religion is claiming that things actually happened this way. If the voter in question converted to Catholicism a week after the election, the historian might suspect that his explanation is not correct, that things actually did not happen the way he thinks they did. Thus, the examination of events following the event to be explained can serve as another means of evaluating the relative credibility of competing explanations. The historian can evaluate the probability of obtaining subsequent events, given the truth of these alternative explanations.

We are now in a position to explain how historians can solve the puzzle within the puzzle and evaluate conflicting explanations of the same event. Virtually every notable historical event has generated disputes over its explanations. Anthologies that present competing explanations are standard fare in many history courses. To evaluate competing explanations, historians must consider both the reports of causes and effects included in the explanations and the models used to establish a causal connection between these reports. The probable truth of any causal explanation depends upon the probable truth of a causal model linking cause and effect.

Assume that one historian proposes that John Doe voted for Herbert Hoover rather than Al Smith in 1928 because John was a Protestant rather than a Catholic; another historian proposes that John Doe voted for Hoover because John lived in the country rather than the city. To determine the credibility of the first explanation relative to the second, we would evaluate the probability that John Doe was Protestant rather than Catholic and the probability that he lived in the country rather than the city. If the probability that John Doe was Protestant is significantly higher than that he lived in the country, then we have partial grounds for selecting the first explanation; conversely, if the probability that John Doe lived in the country is significantly greater than that he was a Protestant, we would lean towards the second explanation. The larger the difference in probability, the stronger the grounds for preferring one explanation over the other.

To evaluate the two explanations thoroughly, we also would have to examine the models linking the proposed causes and effects. In this case, we have the advantage of explaining behavior that has been repeated by a large number of individuals at the same time. The statement of conditions for the two causal models would refer specifically to the presidential election of 1928 in the United States. To distinguish between the two explanations, the statement of conditions for the first causal model would have to include the residence in city or country and the second model, the individual's religion. Models must be formulated that control for spurious relationships produced either by the influence of religion on both voting and residence or by the influence of residence on both voting and religion. The two models would generate different predictions of voter behavior that could be tested against the actual behavior of large numbers of voters to compare the credibility of the models. If the model linking voting and religion were correct, we would expect Protestant, city dwellers to vote for Hoover rather than Smith and Catholic, country dwellers to vote for Smith rather than Hoover. If the model linking voting and urban rural residence were correct, we would expect Protestant, city dwellers to vote for Smith rather than Hoover, and Catholic, country dwellers to vote for Hoover rather than Smith. The greater the probability that urban Protestant voters supported Hoover and that rural Catholics supported Smith, the stronger the support for the first rather than the second model. The lower these probabilities, the stronger the support for the second rather than the first model.

Of course, a historian could argue that John Doe was not a typical Protestant or country dweller, and that his behavior cannot be explained by looking at differences in the behavior of all Protestants and Catholics, all city dwellers and country folk. To sustain this objection the historian would have to specify the distinguishing features of John Doe (for example, residence in a particular region, membership in a particular Protestant sect), include them as conditions in the model, and see if they affect the relationships considered.

In addition to explaining the occurrence of an event rather than some contrasting event, historians also are interested in explaining variation over time and place in the quantitative or numerical properties of events. Historians can learn a great deal from the consideration of events susceptible to numerical measurement—the political, economic, and social characteristics of geographic units, the income and education of individuals, the price and quantity of manufactured goods, and so on. A historian might want to explain why the fertility rate of American women declined steadily in the nineteenth century; another might want to explain why a greater proportion of male children became clergymen in medieval France than in Renaissance England.

The process used to explain particular events can be adapted readily to the explanation of variation in quantitative measures. In both cases an explanation is dependent upon both reports of causes and effects and the model used to connect these reports. For the units of analysis being considered (individuals, states, or industrial plants), causal events included in a model are designed to account for the quantitative values of the event to be explained. An historian might hypothesize that variation from state to state in Hoover's percentage of the 1928 vote is explained by the variation in the percentage of urban dwellers, Catholics, and supporters of prohibition. This model can be tested by determining how well we can predict Hoover's percentage in each state from knowledge of these three percentages. In addition to testing the credibility of the model, this analysis would also reveal how much of the variation from state to state is accounted for individually by urbanism, religion, and prohibition.

As with explanations of particular events, the historian must be careful that explanations of variation in quantitative events are not tainted by spurious relationships. For example, a correlation from state to state between Hoover's percentage of the presidential vote and the percentage of urban residents may be due to the influence of some other factor, perhaps a state's percentage of Catholics. To guard against spurious relationships, the historian must include in his model as many of the relevant factors as possible.

The analysis of change over time is particularly vexing. Many important factors trace similar patterns across time without being in any way related to one another. Too often, historians have assumed that changes in one factor explain changes in another factor simply because both changes follow roughly similar temporal patterns and because they can think of some substantive connection between the two factors. Throughout nineteenth–century America, for example, industrialization and urbanization steadily increased. Historians have used these two trends to explain virtually every other trend that steadily increased or decreased during the nineteenth century—birth rates, death rates, educational levels, and levels of political participation. Some historians have uncritically assumed that the declining birth rates of nineteenth–century America could be explained by the decreasing economic value of children in a society that was becoming increasingly urban and industrial. However, further analysis has demonstrated that regardless of urban or rural residence, birth rates declined throughout the nineteenth century. Moreover, during the nineteenth century, variations from state to state in fertility rates are not well-explained by differences in the levels of urbanization.

Historians also must be aware that models used to explain variations in a type of event at a particular time cannot be used necessarily to explain variations over time in the same type of event. At any given point of time, a historian of the United States would find that well-educated individuals are more likely than their less educated counterparts to vote in political contests. We must not jump to the conclusion, however, that as our society has become more educated, rates of voter turnout have correspondingly increased. Actually, increases over time in the educational level of the American people generally have been associated with declining rates of voter turnout.

In addition to using explanatory models in the explanation of particular events, we have noted that historians can apply their understanding of particular events to test the applicability of covering laws from the social sciences to various historical situations. This approach is particularly valuable as it liberates the historian from the need to choose a particular model. Instead, the historian's own piece of research becomes part of the testing and evaluation of alternative models.

Research by historians sensitive to the theories being developed in the

·social sciences can help us gain a better understanding of the conditions under which these covering laws can be applied to human behavior. Historians who desire to explore the applicability of social science covering laws would test the laws in particular historical situations. If the details of a situation do not conform to the expectations of the model, it will be necessary to reconsider the conditions under which the covering law applies. Historical work has suggested, for example, that covering laws of individual psychology drawn from the observations of Americans and Europeans in the twentieth century may be inapplicable to earlier periods of time. In a more positive vein, historical research may also lead to the formulation of new models that can be tested, in turn, in other historical situations. In Chapter VI, on new approaches to history, we will further explore the interactions between historical research and social science theory.

Moral Judgments

There remains one more important question confronting all who either personally undertake or read history—making moral judgments about the past. Many philosophers believe that we can make two kinds of statements about the real world—empirical statements or moral statements. Empirical statements express our beliefs about the way the world is; moral statements express our beliefs about the way the world ought to be. Moral statements apply only to morally responsible agents (most human beings), whereas empirical statements may apply to any aspect of the real world. Moral statements express our system of values or our judgments about the way people ought to think and behave. Whether people actually think and behave in this fashion is irrelevant to our belief in these statements. We either accept or reject moral statements; they cannot be tested by reference to observations of the real world.

A famous example of a moral statement is the golden rule—"Do unto others as you would have others do unto you." Other examples include such statements as "Thou shalt not kill," "Men should follow their own self-interests," and "Treat people as ends in themselves rather than as means to ends." These moral statements are usually applied to all morally responsible agents, independent of time and place.

From one perspective, moral judgments are inseparable from historical study. The very decision to study the past, to ask particular questions, and to adopt a given methodology are moral decisions made by individuals who must live with the consequences of their actions. Ever since philosophers disposed of the notion of self-evident truths, they have realized that such basic decisions cannot be justified objectively by pointing to something that lies completely outside the subjective world of the decision maker. These decisions represent value judgments by the historian about how he should spend his time, what is worthy of study, and how he should proceed to learn about the world.

From the time of Thucydides in the fifth century B.C., to the nineteenth century A.D., many historians have gone beyond this recognition and viewed their work as part of moral philosophy. In the eighteenth century, Viscount Bolingbroke wrote in *On the Study and Use of History,* "I have read somewhere or other, in Dionysius Halicarnassus, I think, that History is Philosophy teaching by examples." By studying the past, men hoped to derive general moral principles that could guide the conduct of human affairs. Today, most professional historians would disclaim any attempt to deduce moral precepts from study of the past. Indeed, most historians would deny that principles of morality could be inferred from knowledge of the world. Nonetheless, many historians believe that their work has moral implications, and there is considerable controversy over the place of moral judgments in historical study.

Historical study not only requires moral decisions on the part of the historian, but also necessarily raises moral questions that historians should be free to explore. Neither historians nor their readers can close their minds to thought about the morality and immorality of what men and women have done in the past. Moreover, historians often choose to study particular issues precisely because they raise significant moral questions. Once a historian decides how to approach the study of history, however, he must not allow moral judgements to intrude upon his empirical work. Historians must be careful not to confuse investigation of what happened with moral judgments about what ought to have been.

Like all other aspects of historical inquiry, the process of reaching judgments about events in the past has a definite structure. Just as a historian cannot infer an empirical statement about the past from another empirical statement (for example, inferring that Piers Plowman was illiterate from knowledge that he was a medieval peasant), without a connecting generalization (for example, that 90 percent of all medieval peasants were illiterate), a historian cannot infer a moral judgment from an empirical statement without an intervening moral principle. This principle is a generalization about the way morally responsible agents should think and act. It thus sets forth the moral implications of an empirical statement. The process of inferring moral judgments is set forth in Figure VI below.

Figure VI demonstrates that different moral judgments may be derived

FIGURE VI

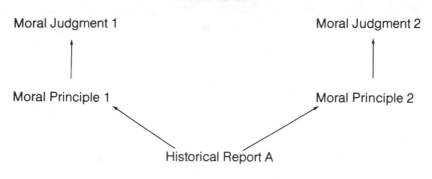

Moral Judgment 1   Moral Judgment 2

Moral Principle 1   Moral Principle 2

Historical Report A

from the same historical report if different moral principles are invoked. Assume that historical report A represents the view that Brutus killed Caesar in order to preserve the Roman Republic. If moral principle 1 expresses the belief that it is wrong to kill under any circumstances, then moral judgment 1 will condemn Brutus' act. If, however, moral principle 2 expresses the belief that murder is morally justified to protect a republic from the ambitions of a dictator, then moral judgment 2 will exonerate Brutus.

One could criticize a given moral judgment either by proposing an alternative moral principle or questioning the applicability of a particular principle to the case being considered. The application of moral principles to historical conclusions is not always straightforward. Like covering laws, moral principles include terms whose application to actual situations is not always clear. Even if a historian believes that murder is morally justified to protect a republic from the ambitions of a dictator, it may be very difficult for him to demonstrate that Caesar actually posed such a threat.

If historians are to render moral judgments about past events, they should do so explicitly and not insinuate value judgments into their empirical analysis. To separate the process of forming moral judgments about historical events from the process of learning about those events is vital. Those who study the past must not allow their beliefs about what ought to be influence their analysis of what was. Just as moral principles cannot be derived from empirical knowledge, empirical knowledge cannot be derived from moral principles. To allow empirical conclusions to be influenced by moral considerations is to risk grave errors of analysis. For example, a historian eager to demonstrate the virtues of democracy might be tempted to overstate the quality of life in ancient Greece. Or a historian intent upon illustrating the evils of slavery in the United States might exaggerate the hardships and deprivations suffered by the slave population. Or a historian evaluating the authenticity of three different accounts of the First Crusade might choose the one that seems most morally instructive.

Moral judgments about the past should be clearly labeled as such and not smuggled into what seems to be a discussion of empirical issues. Historians often influence their readers by inserting into their discussion words and phrases with value connotations. A given action, for example, may be called "needed," "beneficial," "salutory," "reprehensible," "misguided," or "nonfunctional." The problem with insinuating moral judgments in this fashion is that the reader may be influenced by the author's judgments without ever realizing that the author has invoked moral principles to reach moral judgments about past events. The value judgments of the historian take on the coloration of his special expertise and knowledge and may be accorded undue authority by unwary readers. The empirical conclusions of a historical study reflect the author's training and research. But no special weight should be accorded the moral principles that are applied to these conclusions in order to render moral judgments. Historians have a responsibility to set forth their values, and readers a responsibility to evaluate and criticize these values.

Some critics have given historians leeway to analyze the moral implications of past events, but have admonished historians to be moderate and balanced in their judgments or to judge only public affairs, not private lives. In this view, historians should not become crusaders for particular moral causes and should not rigidly or dogmatically impose standards of the present on events of the past. Obviously, critics of this persuasion are concerned that overzealous or present minded historians will distort what actually happened in the past. Yet they impose upon the writing of history moral strictures as rigid and dogmatic as any other. Their warnings imply that historians venturing to judge the past should use an eclectic or relativistic standard of morality that recognizes a plurality of moral positions and gives due weight to a historical actor's own judgments as well as the "moral climate" of the times.

Questions pertaining to an individual's own perceptions and evaluations and to the moral values of different societies are empirical questions that can be answered perfectly well without embracing a position of moral relativism or indeed rendering moral judgments at all. If, however, a historian is to judge the actions of men in past time, he should be free to apply whatever moral values he feels are appropriate and to defend them as vigorously as he sees fit. So long as the historian is aware of what he is doing and carefully maintains the distinction between empirical and moral analysis, the moral values he chooses are a matter between himself and his conscience. Since no external or objective standards govern the choice of moral values, no critic can do more than try to persuade others to adopt his own set of values.

In another sense, historians should be aware of the need for balance in their moral judgments. Historians sometimes confuse judgments about an individual or group with judgments about particular actions they have taken. While deploring individual acts, a historian still might refrain from blanket condemnation of the persons performing these acts. For example, a historian observing that Marcus Brutus had lived an honest and upright life apart from his participation in Julius Caesar's assassination might refuse to damn Brutus because of this single act of murder. Assuming that what Brutus actually did is not in question, a critic disputing this judgment would either have to challenge the balancing of murder against Brutus' other commendable behavior or advance another moral standard that condemns Brutus irrespective of his actions other than murder. A moral covering law could well be proposed that condemns someone as evil for a single heinous act like murder. But unless the historian is prepared to advance and defend such a moral standard, he must weigh all relevant actions against one another to reach a balanced moral judgment about an individual or group.

"Conclusions"

Historians assign heavy burdens to such words as "because" and "since," "factor" and "force." These words signify that a historian is offering an explanation of why something happened in the past. But in most historical works there is far more to these explanations than meets the eye. We have tried to show that the probability that the conclusion of a causal argument identifies an actual cause of an actual event depends on several things: (1) the probable truth of the reports about the causes and the effects; (2) the determination not only of the event and its cause but also of a contrasting event and an alternative to the cause; and (3) the applicability of the covering law or laws to the actual historical situation being considered. We have indicated some of the most dangerous traps that lurk, waiting to ensnare the unwary puzzle solver—spurious correlation, time and place dependency, imprecise or vague theories, and indeterminate conditions.

Finally, we have argued that historians are free to render moral judgments on the past, but that they should exercise special care to separate moral and empirical statements. In Lewis Carroll's poem, *The Jabberwocky,* a concerned father offers his adventurous son the following words of advice:

> Beware the Jabberwock, my son!
> The jaws that bite, the claws that catch!
> Beware the Jubjub bird, and shun
> The frumious Bandersnatch!

In the same spirit, we offer you the following advice:

> Beware, my friend, the clause "because"
> The cause that lurks, the morals that hide!
> Beware such terms as "factor" and "force," and shun
> Spurious correlation, of course!

IV

Myth, Force, and Man:
Approaches to the Past

In the last chapter we sought to show how historians explain events and test competing explanations against one another. Yet historians bring a host of prior notions to the task of explaining the past. Obviously we cannot test these broad views of the world every time we try to explain particular events or trends. Rather, these prior ideas suggest which historical puzzles to explain, what kinds of solutions to seek, and when a puzzle is satisfactorily solved. Our model of explanation itself includes some fundamental assumptions about how to account for what we believe happened in our past. We assume, for instance, that we can explain human affairs by combining the application of reason with the careful observation of historical evidence. We assume that the theories sustaining competing explanations can be stated and tested against one another by reference to verifiable data. For most of man's past, however, very different ideas directed efforts to comprehend his heritage. And, even today, not all historians would accept our basic assumptions. Distinct approaches to historical explanation reflect different ideas about how to acquire knowledge and different conceptions of man and his place in his universe.

All of us have assumptions about how the world is organized. We acquire these guiding assumptions from our religion, culture, family, teachers, friends, and sometimes—but rarely—we create them for ourselves. We may presume that men act primarily out of greed and self-interest, or that people are normally generous and cooperative. We may believe that there is a divine being who created and directs the world, or we may deny the existence of supernatural forces. We may assume that groups of people will always wage war, or we may believe in the possibility of ending organized hostility. We may believe that men act unwittingly upon subconscious fears and desires, or that their actions are primarily responses to outside stimuli. Whatever our notions about the organization of the world, we use them to explain, order, and unify our experience. Our minds do not passively receive and record information, but rather attempt to make sense out of it.

The same assumptions or principles that give meaning to our immediate experience also guide our interpretation of events in the past. The patterns of thought that we impose upon the past reflect our general view of the world. Likewise, what we believe about the past profoundly affects the ways in which we order and interpret information about the present world. We cannot think clearly about the present or the future unless we consciously examine our assumptions about the past.

In general, men have followed three broad approaches to historical explanation in the four millenia since the Sumerians and Egyptians first created stories to account for their past. We call these routes to the past myth, force, and man. Myth does not recognize change over time; everything is explained by the repetition of the events with which the world began. To tell stories or myths about these events is to explain man's past, present, and future. Thus myth explains *why* something happened by describing *what* happened. Historical explanations that rest primarily on the idea of force assume that powers external to man—a deity, climate, and geography—control the course of human affairs. Thirdly, explanations that center on man account for experience by exploring the nature of man himself and the institutions he constructs. Each of these approaches to historical explanations at one time has dominated western thought; they all continue to guide the ways in which we interpret human experience.

These three modes of explanation are founded on two distinct forms of thinking. Explanations that focus on external forces or on man himself rest primarily on scientific thought, employing abstract systems of logic and formal procedures for evaluating conclusions by reference to empirical observation. Mythic explanation, on the contrary, does not recognize formal rules of logic or any requirement that speculation be verified by factual material. Mythic thought explains the world through the free creation of images inseparable from reality.

Although most historians in the last three centuries have sought to explain the past by references to man and society, many of their explanations lack the scope and power offered by myth or historical explanations conceived as the unfolding of God's plan. These forms of explanation, which dominated earlier ages, integrated all of man's experience into a single, unified vision. Overarching theories of history have been proposed by modern thinkers, too, including Karl Marx and Sigmund Freud; but most historians insist that no preconceived theory can account for the rich variety of the past, even if it is centered on man rather than myth or force. They maintain that the historian must approach events with an open mind and apply whatever explanation seems best to fit each particular case. These scholars are willing to sacrifice the unity, simplicity, and firm guidance that a general theory provides for what they see as the greater accuracy of an essentially eclectic approach to explanation. The eclectic credo that experience does not conform to the principles of any single theory has led to specialization on chronological periods, geographic regions, and the study of such themes as politics, social relations, economics, and intellectual life.

However varied, all forms of explanation since the end of the mythic era have had to struggle with the dilemma of explaining man's actions without seeming to eliminate his freedom of choice. No approach to historical explanation has yet resolved this contradiction—asserting, on the one hand, that events can be explained by pointing to the causes required for them to have happened, and, on the other, affirming that man is free to act according to his own will. As we noted in the last chapter, no matter how clever their terminology, historians cannot circumvent the intellectual or philosophical commitments they make whenever they try to explain why things happened as they did.

A brief survey, of course, cannot do justice to the full range of historical literature. Although we discuss many historical works, we have not tried to write a systematic or general overview of western historiography. Rather, we have attempted to delineate and then exemplify the basic ways in which men have sought to comprehend their past. Our discussion of these three basic approaches to historical understanding will begin with myth—the form of thought and mode of historical explanation that prevailed in the ancient Near East from c. 3000 to 600 B.C. During the first millenium B.C., two groups of people—the Hebrews and Greeks—began the movement away from myth to new forms of thought and to new kinds of historical explanation. The Hebrews first grasped the idea of change and development over time, and the Greeks created a rational and empirical form of thought that depended on logic and verifiable observation. These new ideas had a profound effect on the way that men understood their world and explained their past. Out of Hebraic and Greek thinking emerged the other two major approaches historians have followed to account for their past—force and man.

Myth: A Distinctive Form of Thought and Approach to the Past

Mythopoeism,* or a mythic approach to historical understanding, was man's first way of trying to comprehend the world. Through the mists that shroud the formative periods of Sumerian and Egyptian civilizations, historians can discern the outlines of those ancient people's attempts to understand where they came from and why they existed. Their earliest mythologies sought to explain their world by reference to the past. While few of us are acquainted with the Sumero-Babylonian epic of Gilgamesh, most of us are familiar with the biblical accounts of creation and the Greek stories about such heroes as Odysseus and Oedipus.

Mythic thought satisfied ancient man's urge to explain his surroundings and to understand why his world was the way it was. Today, philosophy, history, science, literature, and religion perform these same tasks. Unlike scientific explanations, myth functions at the level of human experience, explaining events by telling stories about how something came about rather than by invoking theories to connect cause and effect. These stories may explain a ritual followed by a people, a taboo or rule of behavior, a form of organization, or a phenomenon of nature. According to Babylonian mythology, for instance, the earth is separated from the sky because the wind god, Marduk, cut the goddess Tiamat in half, producing the sky from her upper half and the earth from her lower half. In mythopoeic thought, explanation is provided by the stories recounted in the myths. For mythopoeic man, description served as explanation.

Myths developed and grew in an oral tradition. Transmitted by word of mouth, myths were flexible enough to allow for adjustments in content and form to meet the needs of successive generations. Indeed, the word "myth" comes from the Greek word, "muthos," whose basic meaning is "what they say." Thus, the word itself emphasizes oral transmission.

As the great orientalist Henri Frankfort has persuasively argued, mythic thought presumes an orientation to the world fundamentally different from

---

*Mythopoeism means literally "myth-making."

our own. Myth does not distinguish between explanation in the realm of nature and in the realm of man. Myth explains events of all kinds, including such natural phenomena as earthquakes, floods, planetary movements, and even the creation of the world, in the same way that we normally account for ordinary human actions. Whatever happens in the world is the result of purpose and will. Myth recognizes no other way to explain things. In Greek mythology, a storm destroys Odysseus' ship because Poseidon, the sea god, is angry with Odysseus and causes the waters to rise. In mythic thought, objects are not inanimate or lifeless. The ocean, the desert, the sky, rocks, trees, and animals all have wills of their own. Just as human actions are the expression of man's will, so the actions of everything else spring from the exercise of will.

Those who created myths believed in their literal truth; to people of the ancient Near East, myths were not mere fairy tales or entertaining fantasies. Because mythopoeic people accepted the imagery of myth as real, they did not compare and contrast the contents of their myths in search of contradiction. They could accept different and contradictory myths as being equally true. For example, if while walking along the Nile river we met an ancient Egyptian and said to him, "How is the sky held up? Is it on posts? Is it held up by a god? Is it the underbelly of a cow goddess? Or is it a tin dome with holes poked in it to allow the celestial light through?" The Egyptian would smile and say, "Yes." And we would say, "Yes? But which one of these four things is it?" The ancient Egyptian would be unable to comprehend our difficulty. To him, all those myths were acceptable because he regarded the contents of each as literally true. Thus, the mythopoeic mind can admit the validity of several explanations at one and the same time, even if those explanations seem mutually exclusive to us.

By way of contrast, later commentators have suggested that although the contents of myth—sea gods, unicorns, winged chariots, and many headed monsters—may not be real, they stand for or represent something we consider to be true. This is an allegorical or symbolic interpretation of myth. The Genesis myth, for example, has been interpreted to mean, not literally that God created the world in six days, but that He created it in successive stages over long periods of time.

Some modern scholars of myth have adopted yet another way of interpreting the contents of these accounts. Claude Lévi-Strauss, a leading exponent of what scholars call "structuralism," has argued that myths can be understood as a means of mediating contradictions in our view of the world, for instance, to resolve contradictions between nature and culture and life and death. Differing with those who focus on the contents of myths, Lévi-Strauss stresses that myths are best understood by reference to their structure, to the set of relationships prevailing among the elements of myth—gods, goddesses, animals, plants, men, and women. According to Lévi-Strauss, the particular elements found within any myth can be replaced by others according to definite rules without changing the message of a myth, which is conveyed by its structure. Mythic structures, he contends, reflect structures latent in the minds of all men, whether ancient or contemporary, primitive or civilized. Thus the study of myth is also the study of inherent characteristics of the human mind.

Probably because modern man has so much trouble understanding and interpreting the contents of myth with its—to us—fanciful creatures and improbable events, the word myth has now come to mean "false belief." For example, today's professional historians often use the term to describe mistaken or distorted interpretations of the past. But to grasp what myth was in archaic societies and how it still influences our thinking, we must realize that myth is a distinct form of thought for which scientific standards of "truth" and "falsehood" have no meaning. Indeed, myth does not recognize the distinction—essential to modern science—between a subjective world of personal experience and an objective world to be explored through formal systems of logic and verified observations. Myths are accepted because of the thoughts and emotions they stimulate and because of their ability to help make sense of what could not be explained otherwise.

In contrast to myths that focus on the unique details of events, such as gods and goddesses feasting merrily on Mount Olympus, abstract theories of science organize events into general categories for purposes of explanation. Scientific theories also express relationships among events according to theoretical terms—concepts that we cannot perceive in everyday life, such as molecule, atom, supply, or demand. As we noted in the previous chapter, transformation rules are required to relate the terms of theory to observations of the world. Unlike myth, science cannot convey the richness and particularity of what we actually perceive.

Despite the great differences between mythic and scientific forms of explanation, mythic forms infiltrate scientific explanation. The theories that guide modern science (for example, the theory of relativity or the germ theory of disease) are not accepted or rejected solely on the basis of their logical correspondence with observed fact. Other standards, reflecting mythic thought, influence the process of theory formation. These include the simplicity of the theory, its eloquence and symmetry, and its power to evoke new ideas as well as to satisfy man's need for unity in the natural world. As the distinguished philosopher of science Abraham Kaplan has noted: "God is an artist as well as a mathematician and engineer. . . .It has happened more than once that a theory was adhered to because of its simplicity and symmetry in spite of its disagreement with fact, then later observations and intrepretations removed the disagreement. A scientist sometimes needs the courage not only of his convictions, but also of his esthetic sensibilities."

From one perspective, science itself is a form of modern mythic thought. We may believe that scientific thought reveals literal truths about the universe. But men have believed with equal conviction in the literal truth of the stories related in myths. Indeed, all of science builds upon certain assumptions about the world that are simply accepted as true. These assumptions or *axioms,* as they are technically called, cannot themselves be tested by scientific methods, because they are the starting points or the building blocks of all scientific inquiry. A fundamental axiom of standard arithmetic, for example, is that $X + Y = Y + X$. Axioms are structurally similar to myths. Like myths they are not proved to be true, but are accepted as true. Like some myths, axioms are adopted because they prove to be especially useful ways of viewing the world. As we noted in the previous chapter, the axioms of theory are useful because they offer a means for explaining the events we experience.

Modern man still thinks mythopoeically when he tolerates mutually exclusive or logically contradictory elements in his thinking. Many people today believe in both free will and some kind of divine power. Indeed, our major religions simultaneously posit an omniscient (all knowing) God and human beings with free will. These are logically contradictory propositions. If God is omniscient, our futures are already known and therefore we cannot have free choice. In accepting these mutually exclusive ideas, modern man is employing at least quasi-mythopoeic modes of thought, thinking in a manner not much different from ancient near eastern man. Mythic thought still pervades our thinking because contemporary thought, resting upon the formal logical systems originally laid down by the Greek philosopher Aristotle, does not fully express how we understand our world. Indeed, the great philosopher and mathematician Kurt Gödel has shown that formal logic cannot demonstrate the internal consistency even of purely mathematical systems like ordinary arithmetic. In the words of philosophers Ernest Nagel and James R. Newman, Gödel's arguments show that "the resources of the human intellect have not been, and cannot be, fully formalized" by any system of logic yet known.

There is another level, perhaps more profound, on which myth expresses something we regard as true. Like great fiction and drama, myth expresses the ineffable qualities of the human condition. As the philosopher Roberto

Unger has noted, science accounts only for partial aspects of the total individual. Neither physiology, nor chemistry, nor anatomy, nor psychology accounts for a person as a whole. Thus Unger concludes, "The ineffability of the individual is the necessary consequence of the modern view of science," because science cannot express what a man is like as a complete human being. Though we no longer accept its literal truth, the story of Adam and Eve still has meaning for us. We can recognize in ourselves the dilemma of being tempted to do something we want to do even when we are sure it is wrong. The approach of analytic science to the problems posed by choices between good and evil would not evoke the same kind of response as the biblical story. Far more than science, myth expands our intuition, fires our imagination, and taps the wellsprings of our emotions.

Mythopoeic man did not produce what we would recognize today as history. He kept extensive records he could consult. He knew that his own civilization had a past; he remembered great rulers from previous dynasties, important treaties, and heroic battles. But he lacked the idea of development or change over time that is central to historical study. Ancient man believed that the events described in his myths took place eons ago, often at the dawn of creation. These original events recounted in the myths served to fix all that came afterward. Mythic thought does not recognize a continuing process of change over time. Mythic man viewed the world as a unified creation whose characteristic patterns did not vary through time. He often depicted time by drawing a serpent, stretched out in a circle, swallowing its own tail. This picture seems to reflect mythic man's notion that real time is projected into mythic time, and that the world's recurring patterns—changes in the seasons, successions of dynasties, and birth and death—were all part of a grand design established at creation. Mircea Eliade, a seminal theorist of myth and ancient religion, observes that for mythopoeic man: "Everything in a certain sense coincided with the beginning of the world, with the cosmogony. Everything had taken place and had been revealed at that moment. . . , the creation of the world, and that of man, and man's establishment in the situation provided for him in the cosmos."

Mythopoeic thought continues to have profound influence on the study of history. The most common form of historical writing is the narrative or the story; and many historians would contend that storytelling is the proper form of historical explanation. Like mythopoeic man, they would recognize no distinction between description and explanation; the story is the explanation. To explain, for example, why the Giants won the National League pennant in 1951 would be to tell the story of the final playoff game with the Dodgers and Bobby Thomson's two-out, game winning home run in the ninth inning. Although such stories must be faithful to historical evidence, their truth value does not depend solely upon the logical analysis of historical records. The graceful telling of the story itself assumes great importance.

The most eloquent proponent of a mythopoeic approach to historical explanation is J. H. Hexter of Yale University. Hexter rails against attempts to equate history and science, claiming that answers to "why" questions in history are essentially narrative in form, not analytic as in scientific explanation. Historical truth for Hexter depends not only upon "fidelity to the record of the past," and "simple, formal logic," but also upon the way in which historical stories are told. Hexter most clearly relates myth and history when he concludes that "historical truth is not illogical or antilogical; it is translogical. For its maximization the rhetoric of history is not irrelevent; it is indispensible."

From Myth To Rational, Empirical Thought: The Hebrews, Greeks, and New Approaches to Historical Explanation

Even before the philosophers of classical Greece began to fashion modern forms of scientific thought, the ancient Hebrews transcended mythopoeic notions of time and historical explanation. The Hebrews conceived the past as a flow of events through time, propeled primarily by a force external to man and not subject to his control. They created an inclusive system of historical explanation that accounts for human affairs from the creation to the end of history. Both Hebrew and later Christian theology assumes that God directs the historical process, a form of historical explanation called "theocratic history."*

Unlike their near eastern neighbors, the Hebrews had a sense of change and development over time. Possibly because they saw their lives as having been radically altered by such events as the Covenant and the Exodus—events that occurred long after the creation of the world—they discarded the dominant near eastern idea of a static world, one that had remained relatively unchanged since creation. Instead of viewing time as the image of the serpent coiled back on itself, the Hebrews developed a concept of linear time. For them, time proceeded in a straight line, with both a definite beginning (the

---

*"Theocratic" means literally that the power ("cratos") is wielded by God ("theos").

creation) and a predetermined end (the coming of the Messiah). If we portray their idea of time as an arrow pointed in one direction, then the Hebrews sought to describe and account for their heritage by placing historical events along this arrow in a series of before-and-after and cause-and-effect relationships.

For the Hebrews, the major cause of the unfolding of their past was their god, Yahweh, in one sense a force over whom they had no control, but in another sense a personal god to whom they could appeal. Man was seen partly as an instrument and partly as a patient sufferer of the actions ordained by God. The Old Testament can be read as a record of the actions of the Hebrew people; but God is the propelling force. It is Yahweh who led and directed His people, nurtured them, punished and finally coerced them into His design. It is Yahweh who directed the Exodus, who intervened in the human affairs not only of the Hebrews but also of their neighbors as well; the prophets asserted that Yahweh used the Assyrians and Babylonians to smite the Israelites for their faithlessness. Yet Yahweh did not predetermine every event, certainly not the Hebrews' recurrent acts of apostasy. Jews chased after other gods out of their own free choice. Whenever Israelite faithlessness became too prevalent, Yahweh intervened, sending prophets or punishments to His people, redirecting them toward His predetermined destination.

The Hebrews also broke with another facet of mythopoeic explanation. While in ancient near eastern myths, only heroic kings and gods have identifiable personalities, the Old Testament considers the impact of differences in human personality on the past. The Hebrew historians may have had several reasons for looking at how individual men influenced the events in which they participated. First, Hebrew thought allowed for some measure of free choice. Just as the Covenant required Yahweh's direct intervention, so also it required Abraham's agreement. Abraham's decision to bind himself and his tribe to Yahweh showed Hebrew historians that individual men could influence their own destiny. Second, during the period of the monarchy, Israel saw three extraordinarily different and strong rulers—Saul, David, and Solomon—each of whom exerted considerable influence on Hebraic history. When Hebrew historians came to write about their past, these observations and experiences were too powerful to ignore.

Shortly after the Hebrews had begun to develop theocratic history, Greek philosophers of the sixth century B.C., began a full-scale assault on mythopoeic thinking. Over several generations, the Greeks fashioned a new form of thought founded on formal systems of logic and systematic observation of both an animate and an inanimate world. With the birth of philosophy, men had new tools enabling them to analyze what they observed, to fashion abstract theories, to test the validity of generalizations, and to decide between contradictory conclusions about the world.

Using the new methods of reasoning, the classical Greek historians Herodotus (c. 484–425 B.C.) and Thucydides (c. 455–400 B.C.) consciously investigated the past in order to discover what actually happened and to seek explanations that were not mythic in form. Unlike the Hebrews, The Greek historians did not explain the past primarily by references to forces external to man. Both Herodotus and Thucydides believed that the world could be understood and explained mainly by examining human action and motivation. For the Greeks, the familiar dictum of Protagoras that "man is the measure of all things, of those that are and of those that are not," succinctly expressed this idea.

Herodotus, regarded even in antiquity as the father of history, clearly expressed this new purpose and outlook in the preface to his history of the Persian Wars: "In this book, the result of my inquiries into history, I hope to do two things: to preserve the memory of the past by putting on record the astonishing achievements both of our own and of the Asiatic peoples; secondly, and, and more particularly, to show how the two races came into conflict" (de Sélincourt translation).

To show how the great struggle for mastery of the Aegean came about, Herodotus begins by recounting a long series of acts of aggression and reprisal between the Greeks and Asiatics. First some Phoenicians on a trading expedition snatched the Argive king's daughter, Io. Next some Greeks, in retaliation, stole Europa, daughter of the king of Tyre, and Medea, daughter of the king of Colchis. Later Paris of Troy seduced and abducted Helen of Sparta, thus setting off the Trojan War.

Thucydides, the fifth–century Athenian who wrote a superlative history of the Peloponnesian Wars fought between Athens and Sparta, was concerned chiefly with understanding those aspects of human behavior that accounted for the events he observed. In commenting on a revolution that took place on the island of Corcyra (modern Corfu), Thucydides wrote: "There was no length to which violence did not go, sons were killed by their fathers, and suppliants were dragged from the altar or slain upon it. . . . The sufferings which revolution entailed upon the cities were many and terrible, such as have occurred and always will occur, as long as the nature of mankind remains the same; though in severer or milder form, and varying in their symptoms, according to the variety of the particular cases. . . . The cause of all these evils was the lust for power arising from greed and ambition and from these passions proceeded the violence of the parties once engaged in contention" (Crawley translation).

This passage reveals Thucydides' assumption that the psychology of man is basically unchanging and not subject to conscious control by the exercise of will. And, as the analogy to disease indicates, Thucydides' search for psychological laws may have been influenced by the newly developed medical theories of Hippocrates, who argued that disease was not caused by divine action but by a naturally occurring condition of the human body.

The history written by the Hebrews and Greeks reflects the change from a mythopoeic to a rational and empirical form of thought. Moreover, Hebraic and Greek historical literature provides our earliest examples of the two approaches to the past that have dominated western thought since classical antiquity—force and man. During classical antiquity, historians followed the path marked out by Herodotus and Thucydides, one that focused on man. With the triumph of Christianity, however, historians returned to the Hebraic concept of theocratic history, seeing God as the guiding hand behind the unfolding of the past.

Force: Supernatural and Natural

Since the time of the Hebrews, some historians have sought to explain the historical process by arguing that divine power or the natural environment control human affairs. Christian historians, following the lead of Eusebius of Caesarea (260–340) and Saint Augustine of Hippo (354–430), coupled the Hebrew idea of a divinely directed historical process with the Greek notion that man could arrive at an understanding of this process through use of his intellect. In the *City of God,* Augustine contrasted the secular state—evil and transitory—with the kingdom of God—serene and eternal. He notes that "the two Cities . . . , the earthly and the heavenly, are inextricably enwound and intermingled with each other." It is this interaction between the two cities that actually produces history. The City of Man and the City of God will not be separated until "the Last Judgment." The task of historical study "is to trace the steps by which one is slowly replaced by, or transformed into the other." For Augustine, as for the Hebrews, time is an arrow pointed in a particular direction set by God.

The ideas expressed by Eusebius and Saint Augustine shaped the course of Christian historical thought through the Middle Ages and influences those Christians who still analyze history as the unfolding of divine providence. This distinctive approach to the past rests on seven key premises or assumptions:

1. History has a purpose.

2. History proceeds in straight-line fashion towards a specific end point (the Day of Judgment).
3. The end point of the historical process is good, a process equated with progress.
4. God is the external force propelling the historical process.
5. Man can discern aspects of this process by using his intellect.
6. To understand history, man must comprehend the divine revelation of scripture.
7. Man is an active agent, although often an unwitting one, in the development of history.

Although the divine plan of Christian history culminates in a predetermined end, many theologians of early and medieval Christianity, including Saint Augustine and Saint Thomas Aquinas, did not assume that God determines all of man's actions. Instead they allowed some latitude for the free choice of individuals; God uses the choices made by men as part of His plan. According to Saint Augustine, the very notion of the "two cities" depends, in part, on how men choose to live: "there are but two sorts of men that do properly make the two cities we speak of: the one is of men that live according to the flesh, and the other of those who live according to the spirit."

Christian theocratic history reigned supreme in Europe for more than 1,500 years. It unified and ordered all of man's experience, integrating past, present, and future into a single system of explanation. Christian history explained the strivings of men and the seeming chaos and brutality of the world as part of the Creator's grand design.

Thinkers of the Renaissance were not content to accept the dominant Christian explanation of human existence. Among their many challenges to medieval thought, Renaissance scholars assailed the prevailing notion that history was the unfolding of God's plan and that historical study was but an aspect of theology. Reflecting Greek notions of historical study, such Renaissance thinkers as Niccolo Machiavelli (1469–1527) and Francis Bacon (1561–1626) sought to develop a rational, secular approach to historical study, insisting that students of the past must both seek accurate descriptions of what happened by studying the source material and provide explanations without invoking divine providence.

In the eighteenth century's Age of Enlightenment, thinkers intensified the attack on theocratic history, establishing the foundation for the secular historical scholarship developed in the nineteenth century. Following the motto, *Écrasez l'infâme*—"Crush superstition"—Voltaire (1694–1778) spent a lifetime crusading against what he believed to be the superstition of religion. Although Voltaire made no advances in historical methodology, he broke new ground in comparing the histories of diverse civilizations and examining economic, social, and cultural issues as well as the activities of secular and religious leaders. A younger contemporary of Voltaire, the Englishman Edward Gibbon (1737–1794), also sought to secularize the study of history. In his monumental *Decline and Fall of the Roman Empire,* Gibbon explained the transformation of the western half of the empire from classical to medieval civilization by focusing on causes internal to the nature of the empire. He argued: "The decline of Rome was the natural and inevitable effect of immoderate greatness. Prosperity ripened the principle of decay; the causes of destruction multiplied with the extent of conquest; and, as soon as time or accident had removed the artificial supports, the stupendous fabric yielded to the pressure of its own weight."

Rejecting theocratic history did not necessarily mean rejecting efforts to explain the past by looking to forces beyond man's control. Beginning with Louis de Montesquieu's classic *L'Esprit des lois* (1748) and Johann Gottfried von Herder's *Ideen zur Philosophie der menschen Geschichte* (1784–1791), some historians have argued that such environmental factors as climate and geography decisively shape human affairs. Although never a dominant motif of modern historiography, environmental determinism has been a persistent mode of explanation, particularly during the late nineteenth and early twentieth centuries, when scholars struggled to make history scientific and to link the development of human experience with the natural world in which it occurred. John William Draper, for example, looked to the American environment to explain the Civil War. In his three-volume *History of the American Civil War* (1867–1870), Draper maintained that the sectional differences that led to war were ultimately attributable to the difference in the climate of the North and the South. This notion that climate determines culture and character led many Americans to despair of establishing republican forms of government in the tropics. Carl Schurz, although not himself a historian, reflected a common view in an article published in *Harper's Magazine* in 1893. He wrote: "It is a matter of universal experience that democratic institutions have never on a large scale prospered in the tropical latitudes. . . . Such a state of society is not found where, on the one hand, nature is so bountiful as to render steady work unnecessary, and where, on the other hand, the climatic conditions are such as to render steady work especially burdensome and distasteful. This is the case in the tropics."

Ellsworth Huntington, in *Civilization and Climate,* 3rd edition (1924), and in an article published in 1917, attempted a far more ambitious account of how climate determined human events. He argued that climate, including such factors as mean temperature and humidity and variations in temperature from day to night, day to day, and season to season, determine the sophistication and quality of a civilization because they largely govern the energy and productivity of people, regardless of race or ethnic background. Alterations in climate over long periods of time have produced corresponding changes in civilizations. Huntington writes: "On the basis of the actual achievements of thousands of people under different conditions of climate, it is possible to make a map showing the amount of energy which different races would have in different parts of the world on the basis of climate alone. This map is strikingly like a map of civilization." Huntington used this general theory to explain the decline of the Roman empire. He argued that a rather rapid climatic change in the Mediterranean world from 300 to 200 B.C., and a more gradual one through the first to seventh centuries A.D., "had an appreciable effect upon the energy and ability of the Roman people" and thus played a highly significant role in the decline of their civilization.

Another group of scholars followed Herder's dictum that "History is geography set in motion." In the first half of this century, so-called geopoliticians, such as Sir Halford J. Mackinder and James Fairgrieve, argued that geography is the crucial factor determining the relative power of nations. In a paper delivered in 1904 entitled, "The Geographical Pivot of History," Mackinder identified the vast area of Euro-Asia, stretching from the Volga to the Yangtze and from the Himalayas to the Arctic Ocean, as the "Heartland" of the world, the "pivot area" of history. Surrounding the "pivot area" is the "World-Island," the continents of Europe, Asia, and Africa; and around the "World-Island" are grouped the other areas of the world. From this model of world geography, Mackinder concluded that "Who rules east Europe commands the Heartland; who rules the Heartland commands the World-Island; who rules the World-Island commands the World." While few historians have been prepared to accept the claims of the geopoliticians, many have acknowledged the importance of geography for historical explanation. Max Cary clearly described the connections between geography and history in his *The Geographic Background of Greek and Roman History* (1949). And Ellen C. Semple's *American History and Its Geographic Conditions* (1933) discussed not only the importance of America's coastal rivers and interior mountain ranges but also the influence of the geography of western Europe on American history.

One of the most respected historical works of this century, Fernand Braudel's *The Mediterranean and the Mediterranean World in the Age of Phillip II* (first edition, 1949, second revised edition, 1966) relies heavily on analysis of climate and geography to understand life in the Mediterranean world of the sixteenth century. Braudel divides history into several different levels of understanding, one of which is study of man's environment. He explores climate and geography to grasp the long-term realities of the past—"those local, permanent, unchanging and much repeated features which are the 'constants' of Mediterranean history." Braudel maintains that environmental forces must be studied along with other factors in an effort to write a "total history" of man's experience. He argues that "Human life responds to the commands of the environment, but also seeks to evade and overcome them, only to be caught in other toils, which as historians, we can reconstruct more or less accurately."

Few historians have concentrated on the "commands of the environment." Despite these efforts to locate causes of historical development in the natural setting of civilization, most modern historians explain events by focusing on the nature of man himself rather than the operation of external forces, either natural or supernatural.

Man: The Protagonist of History

Historians who place man at the center of historical inquiry and explanation must wrestle with the problem of reconciling their traditional Judaeo-Christian belief in man's freedom of will and their desire to explain human action without invoking either environmental or supernatural forces. To many thinkers, both historians and philosophers, the contradiction between the belief in free will and the belief that events have causes—that a particular event could not have happened differently unless its causes were also changed—is unresolvable. This tension between the effort to explain events and to preserve free will is reflected in much modern historical explanation.

In general, modern historians (from the Age of Englightenment to our own day) have followed one of two approaches in their struggle both to concentrate on man as the principal actor in the drama of the past and to offer causal explanations of his behavior. The first of these approaches seeks to develop an overarching theory of history that offers a means of accounting for all important aspects of human affairs. The theories of such system builders as Georg Wilhelm Friedrich Hegel (1770–1831), Karl Marx (1818–1883), Sigmund Freud (1856–1939), Oswald Spengler (1880–1936), and Arnold Toynbee (1889–1976) deal with the general unfolding of human history rather than the details of day-to-day or even year-to-year events. Advocates of the second of these approaches disdain the search for overarching theories, arguing instead that the causes of events must be sought in the particular circumstances in which those events occurred, that no general theory can account for the tremendous diversity of human experience. We call this second approach eclectic, for it recognizes that the historian can choose among many different and competing causal models to explain the events of human history.

Some might object that both of these approaches are essentially deterministic. If all events have causes, the notion arises that somehow man is not really in control of himself but is manipulated either by forces within himself or by those emanating from the social institutions he has constructed. Thinkers long have searched for a way to resolve this puzzle, but none has yet proposed a solution widely accepted by others. Man today still thinks mythopoeically in accepting positions that cannot be reconciled by the use of formal logic. Indeed, in his stimulating book *What is History?* E. H. Carr asserts that to perform his function properly, the historian must accept both free will and the causal determination of behavior. He writes: "Now let us look at the historian. Like the ordinary man, he believes human actions have causes which are in principle ascertainable. History, like everyday life, would be impossible if this assumption were not made. It is the special function of the historian to investigate these causes. This may be thought to give him a special interest in the determined aspect of human behavior; but he does not reject free will—except on the untenable hypothesis that voluntary actions have no cause."

Rather than continue the debate over free will and determinism, we propose to recast the focus of the discussion, looking not solely at the question of free will versus determinism, but at the kinds of causal explanations based on the nature of man that modern historians offer. By framing the question in this manner, we relegate the age-old conflicts between humanistic and deterministic explanation in history to the background and place in the foreground man, who has indeed been the main character in almost all modern historical explanation.

A philosopher of history rather than an historian, Georg Wilhelm Friedrich Hegel was the first modern thinker to fashion a comprehensive theory for explaining the past that did not subject man's actions to natural or supernatural force. Hegel believed that human affairs followed a process that man could understand through the use of his reason. But he rejected the systems of explanation put forth by traditional Christian historians and the environmental determinists of his time. To Hegel, the invocation of divine providence by Christian historians was too vague; it could not explain the concrete events of the historical process. "We cannot," Hegel wrote, "be satisfied with ... the merely abstract, undetermined faith in the universal statement that there is a Providence, without determining its definite acts." Moreover, Hegel believed that environmental conditions could not explain the dynamism of history; he knew that such conditions had remained relatively constant at times when great changes were occurring in the world.

Hegel abandoned the traditional logic of Renaissance and Enlightenment science for a method of reasoning called the *dialectical* method. Like myth, the dialectical method of reasoning is a means of coping with contradiction. One way of expressing the process of dialectical reasoning is that ideas give rise to opposing or contrary ideas; for example, the idea of white gives rise to the idea of black, the idea of good to the idea of evil. These opposing ideas then combine to form new ideas that include aspects of both the original ideas. This dialectical method of reasoning is often simplified into the following formula: thesis (original idea) + antithesis (opposing idea) = synthesis (new idea). Dialectical reasoning can be applied to more than ideas. Nations, social groups, and institutions may also generate dialectical tensions that are resolved through the formation of new syntheses.

Although Hegel's dialectical approach to the whole historical process avoided reference to an intervening God or the forces of environment, a strongly religious tone pervades his discussion of the meaning of history. God for Hegel represents something called the Idea—pure thought unconnected to any material reality and unconscious of itself. Taking the Idea as the thesis of a dialectical process, nature or the material world becomes its antithesis. From this dialectical opposition emerges a synthesis, which Hegel calls Spirit, best regarded as man's reason, that part of him closest to God. At the beginning, man's reasoning capacity was rudimentary. Thus the historical process becomes the developmental progress of reason, or Spirit, toward final perfection.

As men pursue their own self-interests according to their own volition, they advance the development of Spirit or reason. Usually the historical actors are not conscious of the process they are serving. This unknowing service for the development of Spirit Hegel calls the "cunning of reason." According to Hegel, "Human actions produce additional results, beyond their immediate purpose and attainment, beyond their immediate knowledge and desire."

All the actions of men are part of the historical process by which reason or Spirit develops. But the deeds and achievements of "world-historical individuals"—Caesar, Alexander, or Napoleon—propel the historical process toward the perfection of Spirit, ensuring that Spirit keeps advancing to ever higher stages of development. Unique among men, these "heroes" grasp the demands of Spirit in their particular age. Although not necessarily aware that they are serving a process transcending their own interests and ambitions, the "great men" of an age "instinctively" sense what is needed to move Spirit to its next level of development. Only the great man "can put into words the will of his age, tell his age what its will is and accomplish it." Because of their special service to Spirit, they cannot be judged by ordinary standards. "So mighty a figure" as the great man, Hegel wrote, "must trample down many an innocent flower, crush to pieces many things in its path."

Hegel points out that at various stages of the historical process men form cultures that represent a particular expression of reason. Each separate culture in all its manifestations—art, philosophy, law, and religion—is a way station on the road to the final development of reason. Dialectical tensions arise in each culture that eventually lead to its downfall and replacement by a new culture. Thus historical development is not a smooth and gradual, but a discontinuous process generated by the tensions that arise between opposing forces in society. Since each new expression of Spirit represents a more advanced stage of its development, the dialectical process of change—however discontinuous and conflict ridden—is one that leads to continuing progress.

An obvious tension exists within Hegel's own system between the necessary movement of history toward the perfection of reason and the willful actions of the men and women who make history. But Hegel's philosophy is designed precisely to deal with such tensions. "Objectively seen," Hegel notes, "the Idea and the particular individual stand in the great opposition of Necessity and Freedom—the struggle of man against fate." For Hegel, the resolution of the contradiction between fate and human freedom comes about dialectally: the thesis of Necessity and the antithesis of Freedom develop the synthesis of universal Freedom, or Absolute Spirit. Hegel then presses on to argue that universal Freedom will take concrete form in the laws, morals, and philosophy of the nation-state. Thus the development of the state is a dominant theme of history.

In tracing the development of the state, for example, Hegel maintains that the English barons who forced King John to sign the Magna Carta in 1215 merely sought to guarantee their own independence from the monarch in certain spheres of activity. Yet the Magna Carta made it more apparent than before that the bulk of the population had no freedom. The dialectical tension between the universal notion of freedom and the limited scope of freedom in medieval England is resolved only when the monarch grants each group within society—peasants, craftsmen, merchants, etc.—civil rights and responsibilities. This still leaves the position of different groups unequal to one another. Only gradually does the notion of *individual* freedom emerge in the modern state.

Spirit, the divine element within man, reaches its highest stage of development simultaneously with the final perfection of the state. The contradiction between Freedom and Necessity is resolved as all citizens come to realize that the state is the guardian of their interests. Man achieves universal freedom and unity with the divine by consciously and freely submitting to the state, fully understanding that his personal interests are the same as the common interests protected by the state. At this point, the necessity of history and man's capacity for free choice merge into what Hegel considers the highest form of freedom: the freedom to submit to reason. Indeed, "law, morality, the State, and they alone," Hegel declared, "are the positive reality and satisfaction of freedom. . . . Only the will that obeys the law is free, for it obeys itself and, being in itself, is free." In his homeland of Prussia, Hegel claimed, the modern state had attained the highest stage that Spirit had achieved thus far.

Hegel's philosophy of history profoundly affected subsequent studies of the past as well as many other realms of thought. Historians have adapted and applied his idea that history proceeds according to a dialectic and discontinuous process, his notion of progressive stages in the development of reason, his theory of the nation-state and the "world-historical individual," and his concept that each age has a spirit that pervades all spheres of life. Ironically, his thought has probably been most influential as reinterpreted by another German thinker with a radically different temperament and outlook —Karl Marx.

Marx used Hegel's dialectical method of reasoning, but gave it much more specific content and developed a far more concrete theory of historical change. Hegel was a pillar of the Prussian establishment; the government subsidized his lectures in philosophy, hoping to tame the revolutionary spirit of the students. On the other hand, Marx was an outsider, committed to revolutionary change and the liberation of the exploited and oppressed. From the abstract notion of dialectical reason, he fashioned a theory of revolution that has mightily influenced the subsequent course of events.

Marx divided human affairs into distinct eras based on the means that men used for producing and distributing goods and services. He identified social classes, defined according to their place in the process of production, as the contending forces of each era. Members of a social class were bound together in a society because they performed a common economic function. As a result of this common function, they had a common interest, a "class" interest. The nature of man, Marx believed, is such that he will pursue what he believes to be his class interest. Opposing class interests in a particular economic system set in motion the dialectical process that generates historical change. In every era, a ruling class controls the means of production.

When another class with interests opposed to those of the ruling class becomes sufficiently self-aware and sufficiently powerful to contend for supremacy, then it may become the new ruling class, usually through revolution, thus changing the existing economic order in accordance with its own interests. Class conflict was the basis, not only of politics, but also of the cultural, aesthetic, and religious life of men. Marx maintained that man's major ideas, political systems, religions, and artistic enterprises are conditioned by his class interests. In contrast to Hegel, he argued that it was not the spirit of an age that generates its modes of production, but rather its modes of production that generates the spirit of an age—its "superstructure." "It is not the consciousness of men that determines their being, but, on the contrary, their social being that determines their consciousness."

According to Marx, capitalism—the system of economic relations prevailing in his own time—had been created by the bourgeoisie (tradesmen and craftsmen), a class born within feudal society. The bourgeoisie destroyed the once dominant feudal nobility and forged an economic form better suited to its material interests. The capitalistic state, which Hegel had regarded as an impartial arbiter of conflict, became for Marx the means by which the new ruling class promoted and protected its own specific interests. But capitalism also spawned the proletariat, the class consisting of those who labored in the factories but had no control over the means of production. Marx contended that the final stage of the historical process would begin with the triumph of this propertyless class. By overthrowing capitalism and achieving its own freedom, the proletariat would liberate all mankind since it would be the only remaining class. No class below the proletariat would remain to be exploited.

The overthrow of capitalism by the proletariat leads to the final synthesis of Marxist dialectic—the development of socialism, an economic system in which the means of production are collectively owned. Socialism would lead to a classless society, since all individuals would be in the same position with respect to the means of production.

In *Das Kapital,* a massive synthesis of economic theory and practice, Marx sought to demonstrate that socialism had to develop out of capitalism. Although capitalism had brought production to a higher level than previous economic systems, it had also swelled the ranks of the working class and raised its consciousness, while shrinking the number of those in control of production. When the capitalistic system ceased to play a progressive historical role, Marx argued, it would be superceded throughout the world by socialism.

Like Hegel, Marx sees the final stage of historical development as the triumph of man's rationality. What was especially revolutionary in Marx was the theory that creating a classless society would necessarily free the proletariat from exploitation and thus end human struggle and conflict. With the final victory of communism, the highest form of socialism, man would be able to organize his labor rationally and achieve full and harmonious expression of his creative capacities. With the overthrow of capitalism, Marx suggested, social injustice and oppression would come to an end and the history of a free humanity would finally begin.

Marx's utopian outline of the future communist society made him especially vulnerable to critics who thought it unwise to steer history into the perilous waters of future predictions. In addition, Marxist thought exhibits the same tension between a belief in free choice and determinism reflected in Hegel as well as in the work of Hebrew and Christian historians. Although Marx argued that socialism is the final synthesis of the dialectical process, he recognized that in a given historical period, political forces may operate independently of class interests. In Marx's *The Eighteenth Brumaire of Louis Bonaparte,* Louis Bonaparte's triumph represents not simply a stage in the rule of the French bourgeoisie, but a period of transition in which shifting political and social forces created a deadlock that could be exploited by the would-be emperor, an achievement of individual will. Most important, Marx also noted that the speed and efficiency with which socialism is realized depended on the initiative and understanding of both the masses and their leaders. Indeed, he thought of his own scholarship as a form of intellectual labor designed to make men conscious of their historical position and their potential historical role, and thereby to influence the course of human events. Marx wrote what may be taken as an encouraging appeal (to himself?) in his *Theses on Feuerbach:* "Philosophers [up until now] have only interpreted the world in various ways; the point is to change it." In his own time, Marx was a spokesman for the political cause of socialism and for working class movements throughout Europe. Within a Marxist interpretation of history, ideas can represent an active and even independent force.

Underlying both Hegel's and Marx's dialectics is an implicit assumption that the dialectical process would not work out as it does if man's nature was different. Some modern historians have explicitly sought to comprehend the unfolding of the past by focusing on psychological laws that inexorably push the actions of men in certain directions. Such general laws are especially appealing to those wishing to explain what they perceive as recurrent patterns of human activity.

It is in this context that the significance of Sigmund Freud to historians becomes clear. At the beginning of the twentieth century, Freud's studies provided a new and penetrating insight into the psychological nature of man. Rejecting both the Judaeo-Christian view of human nature and John Locke's notion that the mind at birth is a tabula rasa (clean slate), Freud sought to understand the process by which individuals develop distinctive personalities. He investigated primarily the unconscious or nonrational part of the mind. He posited that all people are born with certain instincts, among which the pleasure seeking drive, or libido, is of fundamental importance. Freud argued that by examining the development of the libido, by seeing how it is satisfied and frustrated, we can come to understand how the unconscious mind determines behavior. The following chapter will provide a fuller discussion of the influence of psychoanalytic theories on historical studies; here we must indicate how the work of Freud and his followers offers yet another overarching theory of historical explanation.

A psychoanalytic determinist sees the past as the working out of conflicts existing in the unconscious, and the theory of psychoanalysis as the explanatory key to every major turn in the experience of man. Freud himself wrote a number of historical works addressing the problems of how man moved from a condition of savagery to civilization. He assumes that the evolution of mankind generally parallels the growth of an individual from birth to adulthood, and that, just as an individual carries with him into later life the unconscious conflicts developed during early childhood, so also groups of people carry with them the unresolved conflicts experienced during the formative stages of their development.

Following the suggestions made by Charles Darwin, Freud argued in *Totem and Taboo* (1912) that early man lived in a "father-horde" in which the strongest male ruled with unlimited power, banishing all other males, his offspring, from the group. At some time, these exiled brothers banded together, rebelled, killed their father, and then ate his body. Although each one of the brothers desired to become the new "father," they realized that continuation of the old form of organization was no longer possible. Instead of engaging in futile struggles among themselves, the brothers compromised; each gave up his claim to replace the father, and all agreed not to mate with the father's females, their mothers. Thus a new form of social organization was created, one based on mutual obligations and mating outside the group; thus were established the beginnings of law and morality. To replace the murdered father, the brothers created a totem, usually a sacred animal which no one was allowed to kill. This new form of organization brought with it, however, universal neuroses that correspond to the repressed wishes of the Oedipus complex—the desire to be rid of the father and to have the mother. The sense of guilt caused by the murder of the father was continually expressed and thereby relieved by the worship of the totem (father substitute). In addition, by denying themselves the right to the father's females (their mothers) and by resolving to mate only outside their own group, they created the incest taboo.

Freud's historical explanations have met with resounding criticism, chiefly on the grounds that there is no evidence at all, apart from the contents of ancient myths, to corroborate the story that Freud developed from his general theory of human personality. Nonetheless, historians continue to apply psychoanalytic theories of human personality as definitive theories of explanation, analyzing humanity in the mass according to the principles of individual psychology.

Theories of explanation based on some form of dialectical process or on the inherent nature of man are not the only overarching theories employed by historians. Another is based on an analogy between an individual's life cycle and the development of civilizations, or what historians sometimes call the "biological metaphor." In this view, civilizations go through a natural life cycle of birth, rise, decline, and fall just as an individual is born, matures, and dies. Indeed, the biological metaphor seems to pervade much of the language that we commonly use to describe cultures or societies. When we use such phrases as the growth, height, decay, or death of a civilization, we may be making an implicit comparison between that civilization and an organic life cycle.

Two well-known historians, Oswald Spengler and Arnold Toynbee, have explicitly based their work on the biological metaphor. In his *Decline of the West,* Spengler argues that history is the story of one distinct culture succeeding another. Each of them begins in a state of barbarism; develops primitive forms of political, social, economic, and intellectual institutions; flowers into a period of its own particular classical form; and then begins to wither and die, finally sinking back into barbarism, from which nothing new can grow because the culture's procreative powers have been exhausted by its life cycle. Toynbee follows Spengler's comprehensive theory, identifying in his six-volume *A Study of History* twenty-one separate civilizations in world history. Though critics of Toynbee invariably praise his immense erudition, few professional historians accept the biological scheme that is the organizing and explanatory principle of his work.

Overarching theories of historical explanation like those of Hegel, Marx, Freud, and Toynbee appeal to our yearning for a world that is orderly and comprehensible. Especially when the times seem out of joint and uncertainty prevails, people search for ideas to impose some semblance of regularity on the disorder they see around them. Historians, too, find in these explanatory schemes firm guidance in approaching the vast territory of man's past.

Eclectic Explanation

Most historians reject the comforts of overarching theories. No system ever devised by man, they argue, can account for the entire process of history. The British historian A. L. Rowse forcefully presented this argument in a discussion of Marxist theory: "the Marxist dialectic . . . is an intellectual formula that is applied from outside to the rich diversity, the almost infinite variability of history; it does not arise from the phenomena, the facts themselves. . . . It is far too schematic, too rigid a formula for the sublety of history, where people and causes are not only defeated and fall out of the process, but sometimes suffer, almost inexplicably, a failure of nerve and disappear." Rowse's argument expresses the eclectic approach to historical explanation. According to the eclectics, those who use preconceived theories end up bending their accounts of the past to fit their theories, thereby distorting what they are trying to understand.

Most historians today take this eclectic approach to historical explanation, studying each situation without a prior commitment to a particular type of explanation. Like Rowse, they believe that no single theory will account for the vagaries of human nature, or the ways in which the special conditions of an era influence human thought and action, the role of accident and coincidence in history, or the part played by genius and madness. Eclectic historians do not assume in advance of investigation that important actions of men must be explained by reference to economics, ideology, psychological compulsion, social structure, or any other factor. They recognize instead that any one or more of these factors might be used in explanations of particular events. It is not their purpose to examine broad stretches of the past to extract general laws of behavior.

Eclectic historians maintain that only their approach to historical explanation can account for the influence of the "contingencies" or "accidents" of human affairs. Historical accidents are not events that take place randomly without specific causes. Rather an accident or a contingency refers to the coincidental occurrence of events with unrelated causes. Eclectic historians argue that the simultaneous occurrence of disparate events cannot be included in any preconceived theory, but can influence the course of history. J. B. Bury, for instance, argues that the fall of the Roman Empire "was the consequence of *a series of contingent events.*" The invasion of the barbarian hordes, came at the very time when the Empire was experiencing internal weakness. The invasions and the internal problems were unrelated events arising from separate causes, but their coincidence helps account for the fall of Rome.

Eclectic historians often approach the past and determine what is worthy of study on the basis of their personal experience and understanding of human events. Many focus on the great men and the epic events of history. They concentrate on men who seem to have dominated their times—Caesar, Jesus, Napoleon, Jefferson, and Churchill—and events that seemed to deflect the course of history—the battle of Marathon, the signing of the Magna Carta, and the election of Franklin D. Roosevelt. Indeed, some historians have viewed history as equivalent to biography. The great nineteenth century English historian Thomas Carlyle spoke for others as well when he declared that "No great man lives in vain; history is but the biographies of great men."

An eclectic approach to historical explanation need not be restricted to great men and epic events. Many historians emphasize the study of the common man and woman because they believe that scrutiny of the masses is essential to an understanding of historical continuity and change. Yet, like their eclectic colleagues who investigate watershed events and elite groups, they also reject the notion that any overarching theory can adequately explain the past. Moreover, many historians who explicitly work from theories developed by the social sciences retain an eclectic approach to the past by choosing only the theory that seems best to fit the particular problem or situation that they are exploring.

The eclectic approach of historians to explanations of the past is consistent with what some philosophers of history have argued about the nature of all human decisions. These philosophers contend that historians explain decisions made by individuals and groups by referring to the "logic of the situation," that is, by making "statements about historical agents' intentions, appreciations of their situation, and processes of inference." Robert E. Berkhofer, Jr., an important eclectic, suggests that such a situational approach can encompass whatever causal or covering theories a historian chooses to invoke: "situational analysis combines all the factors that enter into human behavioral activity into one order of analysis, whether these be idiosyncratic, rational, cultural, social, psychological, or biological or physical environmental, and places them in relation to the concrete actions of individuals as perceiving, thinking, feeling, acting, and reacting organisms. On one level it can study the actor's conscious process. . . . On another it can attempt to account for the nature of the actor's situational interpretation in terms of some of the biological, psychological, social and cultural factors that produced a given interpretation and the resultant action."

For some historians, the eclectic approach to explanation shades into the notion that all historical events are unique and thus merit unique explanations. As we argued in the last chapter, however, this view of explanation is not logically tenable. Although all events are unique, they share certain *common* features. Man constructs categories based on his perception of those features. Explanations subject to empirical testing must build upon the common properties of events and use causal generalizations that connect these common properties to one another. A historian who espouses the eclectic approach can work easily with the model of explanation described in Chapter III. He still can accept one of the fundamental assumptions of that model, namely, that the covering laws historians use to connect cause and effect can be validated by testing them in situations similar to those events being studied. The eclectic historian only needs to recognize that he can choose from a number of causal models in his effort to explain particular events.

Leopold von Ranke (1795–1886), the great German historian, who is often regarded as the founder of contemporary historical scholarship, expressed an essentially eclectic credo in the preface to his first book, published in 1824. He writes: "History has had assigned to it the task of judging the past, of instructing the present for the benefit of the ages to come. To such lofty functions this work does not aspire. Its aim is merely to show how things actually were."

This famous passage, one of the most frequently quoted statements of historians, is often misinterpreted to mean that the historian must eschew interpretation for the passive recounting of reports about the past. Ranke never intended history to be only a chronicle of the past. Rather, he believed that the historian should reconstruct *and explain* past events. What he did not want was for the historian to become a moralist, a cynic, or a system builder. Particular events, Ranke believed, must be understood individually, in their own context; and human decisions must not be evaluated morally according to the standards of another age. Above all, Ranke insisted on close and critical attention to primary and secondary sources, on learning about the past from the inside rather than imposing an overarching theory from the outside.

Ranke never developed a general theory for understanding the historical process comparable to that of Hegel, Marx, Freud, or Toynbee. As the historiographer Pieter Geyl has noted: "Hegel subjected history ruthlessly to his general conceptions, to his evolutionary scheme. Ranke, on the contrary, always took care that his general conceptions or his scheme (if even the *word* is applicable to his thought) should remain elastic, or vague."

Yet Ranke does approach the past with prior notions about how events should be explained. Like Hegel, he searches for clues to understanding in the great ideas of a time and in the nation-state, both in its politics and in its relationship with other states. Moreover, despite his rejection of theocratic history, Ranke does see history as the realization of a divine plan. In his view, each state must be accepted on its own terms as a manifestation of divine spirit; and the rise of modern national states is the mark of historical progress.

Ranke's work illustrates the tension inherent in an eclectic approach to historical explanation. Insofar as it is based on a system, history tends to become rigid and mechanical; insofar as it is unsystematic, history risks becoming totally formless. Without a prior notion of what we want to learn about the past, we would not know where to begin an investigation, much less how to proceed. Given the vast number of possible explanatory models available, scholars simply cannot suspend judgment until they have completed a rigorous evaluation of every possibility for every event examined. They must instead restrict their vision to a manageable number of hypotheses. And, as we noted in the last chapter, since an indefinite number of causal explanations reasonably could be offered for the occurrence of any event, the historian must set out with an understanding of what puzzle he is trying to solve with his explanation.

Since its establishment as a recognized academic discipline in the late nineteenth century, the study of history has been subject to increasing specialization. This specialization also exhibits tensions inherent in the eclectic approach to historical explanation, reflecting both the general conviction that no single theory affords a complete vista for human experience and the awareness of how difficult it is to be learned and expert enough to treat adequately even a limited subject or period. Moreover, specialization helps solve the riddle of where to begin and how to proceed. Not only does specialization divide the past into more manageable parts, but also each field of history has characteristic sets of problems and approaches that can guide a historian in his work.

The study of the past often has been divided into fields on the basis of chronology or geography. These divisions are best displayed in such familiar course offerings as "American Civilization," "History of England I," "Renaissance and Reformation," or "The Ancient Near East." Unfortunately, the traditional division of time and space have severe drawbacks. Geographic divisions, especially those based on national states, often promote chauvinism and a parochial view of the past. Chronological divisions raise the problem of how to partition experience into distinct periods. At what point, for example, does the ancient world become the Middle Ages, the Middle Ages the Renaissance? By presenting these periods as wholes, transitions become difficult to define and often appear founded on arbitrary distinctions.

In addition to dividing the past into periods and geographic areas, historians have increasingly carved out for themselves particular aspects of human experience. The most common fields are political, social, economic, and intellectual history. Historians still hold out the ideal of trying to understand society as a whole and often protest the violence allegedly perpetrated on history's "seamless web" by these divisions. Harking back to a virtue of mythopoeic thought, they reject the fragmentation of both science and social science, affirming the special role of history in achieving a unified approach to understanding the life of man. Nonetheless, since most of the history that has been written and continues to be written falls into one of these categories, a fuller understanding of the eclectic approach to history demands some discussion of each of these routes to historical understanding.

Eclectic scholarship not only gives rise to specialized fields, but spawns a variety of questions, assumptions, and methods within each field. For example, specialists in political history, having reached no consensus on how best to grasp the study of political life, might concentrate on political leaders, political institutions, political ideas, or on self-interest as a source of political ideas. Indeed, political history is perhaps the original historical specialization. Until the twentieth century, nearly all written history was a form of political history, and into the early 1960's historical textbooks were overwhelmingly political in content, offering little more than a passing nod to social life, the arts, or philosophy.

In the modern era political history accentuates the quest for power. G. R. Elton, an English historian who holds a chair of constitutional history at Cambridge, is one of the leading advocates of political history. In a book describing the nature and value of political history, Elton writes: "Political history is the study of that dynamic activity in the past . . . which has direct relevance to the organizational aspects of society . . . it is concerned with those activities which arise from the fact that men create, maintain, transform, and destroy social structures in which they live. Dynamic activity depends on the presence of a force—on the employment of energy—and the force applicable to political action is power: the power to do things for, or to, other people. Power constitutes the essential theme of political history."

Modern political history, then, tells the story of how men strive for and use power. Questions asked by political historians concern the acquisition of power and its use both within society and between different societies. Political history, as defined here, subsumes other fields of historical specialization such as diplomatic and military history, as well as administrative, constitutional, and legal history. All of these fields explore how men and institutions acquire and wield power. And with power as its fundamental theme, political history almost inexorably becomes the story of struggle and conflict. Revolutions and elections, as well as battles and wars, provide the motifs for political history.

Modern political history developed in the middle of the nineteenth century, an era of intense nationalism, when new nations were being built and political struggle within and between nations was the order of the day. Political historians swept into their ambit the major forces that directed the destiny of nations and propelled international rivalry and conflict. Their works were far broader than most present-day studies of political history. If historians of the mid nineteenth century stressed the ideas and accomplishments of statesmen, prelates, and diplomats, they also delved into varied aspects of national life to disclose the struggles over such contending ideas as liberty, monarchy, democracy and equality. Nationalist histories of this period verge on describing politics as the inevitable triumph of ideals. Thomas Babbington Macaulay (1800–1859) portrayed British history of the seventeenth and eighteenth century as the victory of the Whig idea of liberty over the despotism of the British crown. Similarly, George Bancroft (1800–1891) described the American past as the necessary flowering of a uniquely virtuous ideal of democracy. Even as the scope of political history has narrowed since the late nineteenth century, a concern with the fate of ideas like liberty and democracy has remained a preoccupation of historians. Among American historians, for example, controversies have continued over just how democratic America really was at various periods of her history.

Other historians, however, have seen the key to politics in the institutions that channel political power—constitutions, legislatures, political parties, and administrative agencies. Influenced by the development of the modern bureaucratic state and its legal apparatus, they have tried to understand how the institutions of politics work and how they affect the struggle for political power and shape the life of a nation. How does a constitution serve to bind a people together and preserve stable government? How do rules for succession affect the authority exercised by rulers? How does the operation of administrative agencies influence the impact of legislation? Institutional histories have tackled some of the large issues of political history, often endeavoring to show how institutions circumscribe the decisions and actions of individuals.

Moreover, political historians of the twentieth century also have supplemented studies of clashing ideas and political forces with new concepts about what motivates behavior and produces political strife. Influenced both by Marxist thought and twentieth–century social science, scholars have sought to penetrate the rhetoric of politicians and discover the "real" mainsprings of political activity. Using techniques called "prosopography" and 'collective biography," historians have examined the familial and social relationships, the material interests, and the psychological motivations of those who contend for political power—members of legislatures and lobby groups, leaders of factions and political parties, diplomats, aristocrats, and clergymen. In *An Economic Interpretation of the Constitution of the United States,* first published in 1913, Charles A. Beard studied the economic interests of the American founding fathers and the means they used to engineer the drafting and ratification of the Constitution. He concluded that the Constitution was forged not to foster freedom and democracy but to advance the immediate economic interests of a small group of property holders. Beard's work sparked decades of heated debate over the origins of the American form of government. In England, Sir Lewis Namier (1888–1960) used the methods of collective biography to reevaluate Macaulay's interpretation of eighteenth century British politics. Rather than looking at the debates of political spokesmen, Namier examined the motives of individual members of Parliament. He suggested that the great ideals presumably reflected in the rhetoric of the times had little impact on the actual process of politics.

Many historians have continued to insist that ideals are not merely the bombast of politicians but must be accorded a central place in the history of political life. While recognizing the achievement of Namier, Sir Herbert Butterfield criticized the tendency of Namier's work both in obscuring the important "idea of freedom" in British politics and in abandoning the narrative in favor of a format resembling that of political science. For British politics of the eighteenth century, Butterfield wrote, "The story must never be cut away from this aspect of the mental life of the time, in which the general idea of freedom loomed large, occupying a significant place even in the political writings of the 'Tory.' " Clearly reflecting an eclectic approach, Butterfield argued that elements of the older and the newer traditions would have to be combined in order to achieve a satisfactory "synthesis" of British politics.

Political historians, especially those writing about the last two centuries of western history, have also sought to introduce the mass of ordinary people into their discussions of past politics. Such historians as George Rudé, Pierre Soboul, Ramsey Macmullen, Jesse Lemisch, and Ernest May have explored the influence of crowds and mobs on revolutions and political protest as well as the political influence of public opinion in general. And they have applied the concept of public opinion in efforts to explain the results of political contests, the policies followed by national leaders, and the outbreak of war and civil conflict.

Despite the recent attention to public opinion, however, political history traditionally has been the story of the elite. As such, political history tele-scopes the affairs of all men and women into the actions of a few, considering the mass of ordinary citizens only as a force to be reckoned with by the movers and shakers of politics. The sources for political history have been produced by the power wielding elite; in turn, the story of political history has focused on these few people.

But the story of the elite is surely not the whole or the only story of a society that can be told. Prehistorians and anthropologists can tell a limited story of Mousterian or Neanderthal man. Archaeologists have reconstructed a rather full picture of Minoan civilization, that apparently peaceful society on Crete that flourished from c. 2000–1400 B.C. In the newest edition of the *Cambridge Ancient History,* 900 pages are devoted to Minoan Crete—900 pages of historical study, rich in detail; and yet not one bit of it is based on written source material, simply because no one yet knows how to read the few scraps of Minoan writing that survive. Since the kinds of evidence necessary for its political history are unavailable, the story of Minoan civiliza-tion does not focus on power, kings (even though the mythical Minos and the legend of the Minotaur are discussed, no real conclusions about Minoan politics can be based on these tales), revolutions, or palace intrigue. Instead, the story of Minoan Crete concentrates on the ways in which people lived and worked, on the social history of that ancient island civilization.

Social history, however, is difficult to define because the concept of a society is sufficiently general to include virtually everything man does, in-cluding his quest for political power. Traditionally, social historians have looked at how men and women live and work together, at the quality of their lives, and at their relationships with one another; and provided descriptions of manners and morals, diet, costume, home life, and entertainment. Social historians look at humanity in general, regardless of social or economic class. They are often especially concerned to examine the experience of the name-less and faceless, or "inarticulate," people usually left out of accounts of struggles for political power—women, children, slaves, and the poor.

A broad view of social history also takes in cultural history—an examina-tion of the ideas, attitudes, values, and beliefs that shape a society's culture. Cultural historians try to reconstruct the pictures and ideas that guide people's interpretation of the world. And in recreating a culture, these his-torians may well examine precisely the kinds of evidence neglected by many political historians—folktales, children's stories, buildings, art, music, and popular crafts.

Social history arose from the effort to understand the distinctive civiliza-tions created by men. In his *Essay on the Manners and Spirit of Nations*

(1756), Voltaire set out on an effort, never completed, to describe the distinctive civilizations of all peoples and periods. Hegel, as we have seen, elaborated upon the idea that each age has a unique spirit expressed in all spheres of life. In his *Civilization of the Renaissance in Italy* (1860), Jakob Burckhardt literally created the Renaissance as a chronological period of historical study, qualitatively different from the medieval era. Although largely based on elitist literary sources, Burckhardt's narrative sharply distinguished the common features of Renaissance life—not only the statecraft, diplomacy, and economics that preoccupied the elite, but also the religion, morality, and social relations that governed the middle class as well as the aristocracy. German historians of the mid and late nineteenth century similarly concentrated on changes in the spirit of the German people through their long and varied history. Karl Lamprecht (1856–1910) strengthened and extended this tradition of German scholarship. Rejecting the stricture that history should fasten on the unique and the particular, Lamprecht sought instead to discover what was representative in each era of German history, a task that led to a monumental history of Germany in twenty-one volumes.

Some social historians of the twentieth century have vigorously objected to the very attempt to generalize about the character or culture of an entire people. They argue that such generalizations create the false impression that nations can be regarded as though they were individual persons, thus obscuring the differences among distinct groups. Instead of trying to grasp a single spirit that characterized an entire society, these historians have sought to fashion a social history that sets forth the distinctive culture and social relations of particular groups within the society and that describes and explains how these groups interact. Historians working within this tradition would partition society according to such variables as social status, race, religion, and economic position.

Attempts to partition society for purposes of analysis often build upon Marx's insight that a group's economic function generates a distinctive class culture and social system as well as particular economic interests. In *The Making of the English Working Class* (1963), E. P. Thompson brilliantly used the Marxist notion of class to analyze the class consciousness or culture of British workers in the eighteenth and nineteenth centuries. Thompson contended that class is not an abstract concept that can be lifted out of context and treated as a static category. If class consciousness is "largely determined by the productive relations into which we are born," he wrote, it still develops over time and is conditioned by particular experiences. Class consciousness cannot be deduced from general principles, but must be studied historically. Thompson insisted that although the rise of class consciousness follows similar patterns in different times and places, it never occurs "in just the same way."

The work of social historians who have been influenced by Marxist thought—such as Thompson, E. J. Hobsbawm, Eugene Genovese, Michael I. Rostovtzeff (1870–1952)—reflects Marx's illuminating discussion of the connections among economic factors, social structure, culture, and politics. The historian who adopts a Marxist approach commits himself perhaps not to specific findings, but at least to a specific focus and to the use of certain concepts, most notably to Marx's definition of class. Sophisticated Marxist historians know how to adapt Marxist concepts to different historical periods and conditions, but the concepts of analysis that they use may become unwieldy. It seems almost as if such historians are straining to see the past through a heavy set of binoculars, wearying to hold, whereas others do just as well or better with a lighter (non-Marxist) set. On the other hand, the lighter binoculars sometimes may lack the power to transmit a clear image, in contrast to the sharply defined images available through Marxist lenses.

In recent times social historians have also emphasized the dynamic character of their field, focusing on both social and geographic mobility of peoples. They have explored what opportunities and options were available to people in different societies, and sought to define the degree and direction of changes within one generation or over many, in occupation, income, education, and political and social status. Historians of both France and England, for example, have generated a large scholarly controversy over whether the economic, political, and social position of the nobility was rising, falling, or remaining stable in the early modern period. Whatever changes occurred in the status of the nobility, these scholars have argued, are linked to even broader developments such as the French Revolution and the growth of parliamentary power in modern Europe. Similarly, other social historians have studied the geographic migration of peoples and their assimilation into new lands. Two such landmarks in American social history are Oscar Handlin's *The Uprooted* (1951), which seeks to calculate the impact of movement from the Old to the New World on immigrants to the United States, and John Higham's *Strangers in the Land* (1955), which conversely attempts to relate the history of immigration to the ebb and flow of nativist agitation against alien peoples and culture.

Social history has been a valuable corrective to the predominantly elitist thrust of political history. By reconstructing the lives and sometimes the thoughts and feelings of ordinary people, social historians demonstrate how life has changed over time and at the same time deepen our understanding of the common humanity of people in all ages. Moreover, focusing on how the commonality have lived has increased our understanding of the distribution of power within societies. How elites act cannot be fully understood in isolation from how societies as a whole have acted. Here is the most significant potential contribution of social history—providing an understanding of the relationship between how ordinary peoples have lived and how societies as a whole have been organized and functioned.

Most social history has usually stopped well short of illuminating social structures and explaining social change over time. Part of the problem is a lack of adequate theory to link together the reports of social history with reports of substantial historical change. We do not know yet how to connect reports about particular social systems with the general phenomena of historical change. We cannot even explain very well why such common social institutions as marriage, child rearing practices, or religions vary so markedly from culture to culture.

The work of the *Annales* school of historians represents the most ambitious and significant effort to address these problems. The French historians Lucien Febvre (1878–1956) and Marc Bloch (1886–1944) founded the journal, *Annales d'histoire economique et sociale,* in 1929 to advance their notion of a "total" history of society. Anticipating later trends in historical scholarship, Bloch and Febvre insisted that the historian should explain, not merely describe; that he should exploit nondocumentary sources and the theories of social science; and that he should focus on the structures of different societies rather than on the flow of historical events. In his classic work on medieval civilization, *Feudal Society,* Marc Bloch describes and explains feudalism as a complex system of relationships among people from all orders of society. In order to show how this complex system functioned in theory and practice, Bloch not only treats the familiar topics of vassalage, fealty, and chivalry, but also illumines how feudal society generally was related to agriculture, commerce, village life, family and tribal systems, military practices, technology, and law. Historians of the *Annales* school institutionalized their approach to history through their journal and their association with the Sixth Section of the École Pratique des Hautes Études.

A spirit similar to that of the *Annales* school had animated the movement for a new history that began in the United States shortly after the turn of the twentieth century. The new history movement in America arose as a loose association among like-minded historians, rather than an organized school of scholarly endeavor. Although its stated program was less influential than that of the *Annales* school, the new history movement attracted some of America's most notable historians of the early twentieth century—Charles A. Beard

(1874–1948), James Harvey Robinson (1863–1936), Carl Becker (1873–
1954), and Arthur M. Schlesinger, Sr. (1888–1965). The new historians
rejected the idea that history should be isolated from either the learning of
other disciplines or the contemporary preoccupation with public affairs.
They advocated a form of history integrated with the social sciences and
capable of functioning as an instrument of social reform. Like Bloch and
Febvre, they advocated a history that was comprehensive rather than specialized, explanatory rather than descriptive, and analytic rather than episodic.

A third traditional specialization among approaches to historical understanding—economic history—employs yet another theme and set of questions. At its most basic level, economic history is devoted to how men have
produced, organized, and distributed the wealth of societies. Reflecting the
dominance of the eclectic approach to history, few economic historians today
would assert that all human actions spring ultimately from man's material
circumstances. Even fewer would hold that greed or acquisitiveness are the
mainsprings of human action. Yet economic history does permit the historian
to focus on an aspect of human life in which all members of a society
inevitably participate, as producers or consumers, or both.

Theory has been especially important for the study of economic history.
This is partly because the issues of economic life—the productivity of
agriculture, the financing of international trade, and the development of
industry—do not seem readily susceptible to a commonsense understanding.
Yet, until the advent of the new economic history (which we will discuss more
fully in the following chapter), those economic historians who did draw upon
economic theory usually did so, not to construct general models for the
explanation of economic phenomena, but to find categories helpful in integrating information and suggesting specific reasons for economic change.

Since the nineteenth century, economic history has flowed in two parallel
streams. First, scholars have sought simply to compile reliable reports about
economic life in the past. Economic historians have frequently asked basic
reportorial questions, such as what goods and services were produced and
consumed? How were they produced? How much did they cost? Who controlled the means of production? How much income did people have? How
were goods distributed? What role did government play in the economy?
Some of the classic work in economic history is primarily descriptive, aimed
at dispelling legends or opening up new areas of knowledge. For example, J.
H. Clapham, regarded as a titan of modern economic history, dedicated his
three-volume *Economic History of Modern Britain* (1926–1938) to more
accurate, detailed, and quantitative reports of British economic life. Simon

Kuznets, also a pioneer in economic analysis, advanced our knowledge of American economic history through his reconstructions of data on income and wealth.

Second, economic historians have sought to provide explanations of important events and processes in economic history. They have explored the origins of different economic systems, the process of economic growth, the role of technology in economic change, the changes in the economic well-being of individuals and groups, the role of the state in economic life, and the effects of economics on ideas, politics, and social relations. Not surprisingly, historians from industrial states of the West have long been concerned with the process of industrialization itself, identifying stages in the development of industrial economies and seeking to explain how societies proceed from one stage to the next. Debates on these issues are obviously relevant at a time when a large number of nations is striving for the first time to industrialize and the industrial powers are vying with one another to influence such developing countries.

Early in this century, the remarkable, path breaking work of Max Weber (1864–1930) sparked a debate that still continues over the origins of the capitalist system of economic exchange that preceded western industrialization. Weber, combining cultural and economic history, argued that the Protestant Reformation of the sixteenth and seventeenth centuries created a new spirit that was a precondition for the development of capitalism. In particular, he argued, the teachings of John Calvin fostered a "Protestant ethic" peculiar to capitalist enterprise. "In fact, the *summum bonum* of this ethic" Weber wrote, is "the earning of more and more money, combined with the strict avoidance of all spontaneous enjoyment." In *Religion and the Rise of Capitalism* (1926), R. H. Tawney reexamined the same problem and, instead of emphasizing only the Calvinist ideal, pointed out the importance of the Protestant Reformation in general. Offering a much more eclectic explanation than Weber's, Tawney also stressed the significance of other social, economic, and political forces in sixteenth and seventeenth–century Europe that stimulated the rise of capitalism.

A more recent effort by W. W. Rostow to set forth specific stages of industrialization and to explain their relationships to one another has also provoked lively debate. Rostow's theory, first developed in the 1950's and most fully elaborated in *The Stages of Economic Growth* (subtitled, "A Non-Communist Manifesto"), posits that once the preconditions for industrialization emerge within a society, economic life moves into a period of "take–off" to steady growth and mature enterprise. The take-off rapidly leads to a qualitative leap forward in economic life. Rostow contends: "In a decade or two both the basic structure of the economy and the social and political structure of the society are transformed in such a way that a steady rate of growth can be, thereafter, regularly sustained." Turning from theoretician to historian, Rostow sought to apply his ideas to the experience of such nations as Britain, France, the United States, Germany, and even India and China. Not only did his specific predictions for developing countries fail to materialize, but also his general historical analysis provoked devastating criticisms from both economists and historians who suggest the futility of trying to apply a single theory to the process of development in all societies and time periods.

Just as political and social historians study the institutions that channel political power and shape social relations, economic historians study the institutions that order economic life. Institutional history crosscuts all historical areas. Economic historians have explored the ancient slave trade, the medieval guild, and the modern corporation. The relationship between the government and the economy is a major theme in any period of economic history. Glenn Porter, an institutionalist himself, has nicely described the workings and ramifications of this approach to understanding economic life. He writes: "Drawing on sociology, organization theory, and (to a lesser extent) economics, [historians] have attempted to analyze process and structure without passing explicit moral judgments on the men and institutions of the past. This kind of work in institutional economic and business history . . . has pointed to the relationships between the functions of an organization and its structures."

A dialectical tension characterizes the work of many economic historians. On the one hand, scholars look to ideology, politics, and social structure to explain economic change. On the other, they also look to economic changes to explain changes in man's consciousness, his political struggles, and his life within society. Not only Marxist historians travel the route from economics to these other features of human experience. In *Mohammed and Charlemagne* (1939), Henri Pirenne, the great Belgian historian, argued that "the whole course of European history" after the seventh century was transformed by Moslem control of the Mediterranean trade routes. During the seventh century, the Mediterranean became a "Moslem Lake," a barrier rather than a conduit between West and East. Forced to abandon the southern sea, the "Christians of the West" were compelled to redirect the traditional southern focus of their politics and commerce to the north; this change in orientation, according to Pirenne, produced "a new economic order," which in turn changed the nature of western civilization. While other scholars have disputed the validity of the Pirenne thesis, most notably his contention that after

c. 800, trade between northern Europe and the East ceased, all have lauded Pirenne's attempt to show how economic changes can influence other aspects of historical change. In this respect, Pirenne's work exemplifies the best of economic history, which is sensitive to the interactions between the economy and other phases of life.

Economic historians seem to face especially formidable obstacles in securing readers for their works. Although these scholars deal with fundamental issues affecting the quality of life, their work often seems devoid of human drama. Trade routes, materials manufactured and sold, and mechanisms of finance seem to be the dramatis personnae of much economic history; such lifeless characters fail to ignite much sympathy and interest among readers. The most popular economic history is often cast in biographical modes or subtly altered into "political" history by focusing on the struggle for power, with man in the spotlight. Influenced by Joseph Schumpeter's (1883–1950) ideas about the importance of the entrepreneur in fostering the growth and development of economies, so-called "entrepreneurial" historians have stressed the creative, farsighted accomplishments of such titans of business as Alfred Krupp, John Jacob Astor, and J. P. Morgan. Others, also adopting the biographical approach to economic history, have piqued readers' interests through stressing the opportunism and financial peculations of "Robber Barons" grown powerful at the expense of ordinary people.

We have seen that whatever their major interest, no historian can safely ignore how ideas, behavior, and institutions are related to one another. Intellectual history, defined as the investigation of ideas in their own right, is the most abstract of the four traditional approaches to historical study. It is also a recent field of specialization, whose boundaries are not yet clearly marked. Most intellectual historians have studied the ideas of the articulate and the influential—novelists, scientists, philosophers, and statesmen. Intellectual history begins to shade into cultural history when it explores the ideas held by all members of a society or by large groups within the society.

Intellectual historians have sought to examine the ideas prevailing in societies at particular points in time. Some ambitious scholars have even tried to integrate the ideas of a people into a complete system of thought, a distinctive way of viewing the world. Perry Miller's classic study, *The New England Mind* (1939–1953), seeks to recreate the thinking of American Puritans in the seventeenth and eighteenth centuries. Rather than focusing on the ideas of individual New Englanders or what New Englanders thought about particular issues, Miller tries to grasp the Puritan mentality as a whole. Like studies of national character, the work of Miller and like-minded scholars assumes that the thought of a people can be recreated as though it were the thought of a single individual. Other historians working within a period do not attempt to weave ideas into complete systems but instead study particular slices of ideology—ideas about progress, religion, morality, politics, justice or love. Some historians combine the study of ideas in different realms to characterize the major ideological themes of an entire historical era.

Historians have made the same kinds of criticisms of attempts to personify the thought of a whole people as those levelled against studies of national character. They have also noted the dubious assumption of intellectual historians that elite sources can accurately reflect the mind set of an entire society. Miller, for instance, reconstructs the Puritan mind from a remarkably small number of sermons and writings, showing little sensitivity to problems of inferring accurate reports from this limited sample of material. Attempting an even more daring leap of inference, Henry Steele Commager in *The American Mind* (1950) transmutes the ideas of notable thinkers into a personification of a common American mind. Those departing from this broad approach seek, more modestly, to portray the ideology of particular groups within a society. Fairly recent work in the intellectual history of the United States accentuates the distinctive ideology of groups defined according to the function they perform—educators, doctors, lawyers, ministers, social workers, business leaders, and politicians.

Intellectual historians also trace the development of ideas over time, considering both the logical relationship among ideas arising at different times and the origins of intellectual change. Historians of ideas taking this longitudinal approach may seek to describe and explain changes in the ideas alleged to characterize an era, looking both at the fashioning of new ideas and the alterations in previous modes of thought. Often this process involved a necessary simplification of the intellectual currents running through a period. For example, Will Durant divides the past according to his understanding of main currents in ideology. His multivolume study of western history is based on such periods as "The Age of Faith," "The Age of Reason," and "The Reformation."

Some historians have also sought to trace modifications in a complete system of ideas or follow the development of a single idea or theme over a span of time. Perry Miller's work on the New England mind includes a dynamic element. Miller relates the transformation of ideas within the Puritan world view and demonstrates how these changes reoriented Puritan ideology considered as a complete system. Looking at a key theme in the thought of Europeans and Americans, Winthrop Jordan in *White Over Black* (1968) focuses on the development of white ideas about black people during "the first two centuries of European and American settlement in what became the United States of America." Studies like J. B. Bury's *The Idea of Progress* (1932), R. G. Collingwood's *The Idea of History* (1946), or Stephen

Toulmin and June Goodfield's *The Discovery of Time* (1965) explore how people in different ages and societies have wrestled with some of our basic categories of thought. Histories of historical writing, law, music, philosophy, and scientific thought are all part of intellectual history. Indeed, this chapter is itself a brief intellectual history of historical explanation.

Historians generally have looked at intellectual change from two radically different perspectives. Implicit in much intellectual history is the assumption of positive development in the precision and power of man's thought. Like Hegel, intellectual historians have been inclined to believe that man becomes ever more rational with the passage of time. As history progresses, man comes to learn far more about the world, and about his own reasoning powers. He clears up misconceptions of fact, devises more penetrating theory, and develops new and more sophisticated approaches to reasoning and observation.

Those identified with another outlook maintain that the development of thought has not been a continuous progression from error and superstition to knowledge and rationality. According to this relatively new viewpoint, western civilization has seen a series of patterns (called "paradigms") of thought that have defined the "real" world and the nature of "truth." We have moved from one definition of truth to another. Thomas Kuhn has forcefully argued for this vision of intellectual change in his history of scientific thought, *The Structure of Scientific Revolutions*, 2d edition (1970). A few other historians have applied Kuhn's "paradigm theory" to other aspects of man's past. The notion has emerged from these studies that a person's view of the world is conditioned by an entire constellation of beliefs, values, techniques, axioms, and theories, shared by his community at any particular time in history. One paradigm does not slowly or continuously evolve into a new one. Instead, Kuhn and others contend that paradigms succeed one another rather abruptly and the period of transition from an older to a newer paradigm sees a revolution in fundamental ways of thinking about the world. For example, the Greek Intellectual Revolution, the shift from a purely mythopoeic to a predominately rational/empirical mode of thought, is, perhaps, the most dramatic example of paradigmatic change in western civilization. Our own century has witnessed another revolutionary change in scientific thought, the change from the Newtonian to the Einsteinian conception of the universe, from a universe seen as governed by absolute dimensions of time and space to one in which those basic dimensions are viewed as relative. The passage from the Newtonian to the Einsteinian paradigm was not a gradual evolution of thought, based on increments of ever increasing sophistication in scientific technique and knowledge. Instead, the movement was an abrupt break in man's conception of how his universe is structured.

Specialization in history has enriched our understanding of the past. By applying the microscope to experience, historians have cleared up misconceptions and identified significant areas of controversy and debate. Working on narrowly defined questions, they have attained a depth and detail of knowledge that cannot be matched by more sweeping studies. Although historians continue to insist that their discipline rejects the fragmentation of man and society, the eclectic approach to historical study has encouraged specialization and probably will continue to do so. Some historians devote their lives to a single individual or decade or to an individual thread in the broader fabric of political, social, economic, or intellectual history. Diplomatic, legal, and military history have now come to be regarded as distinct specialties themselves.

Yet historians pay a price for specialized study. As research in history becomes more specialized, scholars tend to work in greater isolation from one another, following their own separate paths and sometimes developing their own distinctive methodologies and language. Specialized studies do not foster an understanding of society as a whole or portray historical development as an integrated process. Even the historian seeking to unify specialized knowledge will discover that the parts he finds to work with will not fit neatly together to form a coherent whole. Neither historians nor scholars in other disciplines have yet found a way to harness and unify the explosion of knowledge that specialized study has produced.

Conclusion

Our attempt to explain the past cannot be separated from efforts to explain events of contemporary life and form expectations for the future. The various forms of historical explanation described under the categories of myth, force, and man are each distinct ways of viewing the world, of making sense out of experience. For example, if we are Marxist in our politics, we usually will be Marxist in our interpretation of history as well. If we believe that major events of the past can be explained best by reference to man's environment, we are likely to look for the influence of environment in such current issues as the energy crisis, the conflict in the Middle East, and the arms race between Russia and the United States. Shifts in our broad approach to history may trigger changes in our outlook on life today and, conversely, changes in our view of the contemporary world may produce new visions of the past.

Despite the differences among the various approaches to explanation described in this chapter, elements of each approach are often blended together in historical explanation. Various forms of explanation, for instance, appear in the work of George F. Will and George E. Kennan recounted in Chapter I. Both reflect aspects of mythopoeic thought in describing how something occurred in order to provide an explanation of why it occurred. Both concentrate, however, primarily on man as the motive force in historical development, taking a fundamentally eclectic stance; neither the journalist nor the historian begins with an overarching theory, be it Marxian, Hegelian, Freudian, or environmental. Yet both authors resort on occasion to sweeping generalizations. Will invokes the "iron law of politics," asserting that "when a politician intones support for a principle, he is about to make an exception to that principle for the benefit of a friend." Kennan maintains that democracies are "peace-loving" and "slow to rise to provocation"; but once aroused, they fight "to punish the power that was rash enough and hostile enough to provoke it—to teach that power a lesson it will not forget." Moreover, although Kennan focuses on man, he occasionally echoes Old Testament prophets by suggesting that God intervenes in the historical process. Kennan concludes his essay on "The Sources of Soviet Conduct" with an affirmation that somehow Providence is using the confrontation between American and Soviet societies to test America's commitment to her cause. "Providence," he wrote, has provided "the American people with this implacable challenge, has made their entire security dependent on their pulling themselves together and accepting the responsibilities of moral and political leadership that history plainly intended them to bear."

Although historians may still express explanations in mythopoeic form, they now separate man and nature, reject the circular notion of time, and demand the logical analysis of information that can be verified by observation. These modern standards of rationality create tensions that were not present in mythopoeic explanations of the world. The historical literature of our own time reflects conflicts between a commitment to causal explanation and a belief in free will, between ordering the past through overarching theory and understanding events individually, and between treating the past as a whole and dividing it into separate parts. Few historians, however, seem fully committed to one side or another of these various conflicts. Historians who affirm that man is able to shape his own destiny argue nonetheless that historical circumstances significantly narrow the range in which free will can operate. Historians who advance overarching theories leave room, in explaining particular events, for the influence of factors outside the scope of their theory. Historians who concentrate on politics, social relations, economics, or ideology know that no one field can be isolated rigidly from the rest of experience. Tensions visible in historical explanation today reflect much about the intellectual temper of our times—its complexity, its struggle to identify basic themes and questions in the study of man, and its delight in experimentation and technology.

To understand any historical work, the reader, whose own thinking about the past reflects various approaches to explanation, should try to determine the extent to which different forms of explanation influence the author's understanding of the past. A reader's doubts about the validity of a historical work may derive from his preference for explanatory forms that differ from the author's. A reader also should observe how the author copes with the tensions arising from attempts to explain why things happened as they did. A critical reading of any historical work requires a conscious interplay between the forms of explanation that we impose on the past and those imposed by the author. Such an interplay should expand our self-knowledge by enhancing awareness of the assumptions that shape our own interpretation of experience.

Over the past two decades, efforts to fashion new approaches to history have produced another crop of specialists. In many cases, the expertise of these historians cuts across the traditional thematic divisions of history. We now have specialists in women's history, black history, psychohistory, quantitative history, and family history. The next two chapters will explore some of the approaches that have developed in recent years.

V

The New History

Periodically, groups of professional historians declare themselves to be exponents of a new history. Indeed, there has been a parade of "new" historians since the turn of the century, and the current crop is merely the latest group to appropriate that title for themselves. Happily, each group has been content to call themselves simply "new" historians; otherwise we might be confronted by such ungainly nomenclature as neo-new history or even new history III.

The current new history is far easier to describe than to define. Although devotees of the new history follow the paths of eclecticism and specialization described in the last chapter, they explore the past in a distinctive way. Using instruments fashioned from the theories and methodologies of the social sciences—psychology, sociology, economics, political science, and anthropology—new historians ask questions that reflect the theoretical concerns of social science, as well as the social scientists' emphasis on groups and recurring events, rather than on individuals and particular events. Moreover, the new historians are especially concerned with analyzing the generalizations used to link evidence to historical reports, the covering laws required to explain what happened in the past, and the concepts, logic, and methods of historical study.

If we cannot define precisely what the new history is, we can list its common features. Historians are likely to classify as new history any work that exhibits more than one of these features.

1. Emphasis on the study of groups of ordinary people and the realities they confront in daily life. The new historians, like those who pioneered in the development of social history, are convinced that history must consider the masses as well as the elite, day-to-day events as well as dramatic episodes.

2. Emphasis on temporal and cross-cultural comparison. The new historians are interested in establishing generalizations about human behavior that apply to different times and places. They believe that we cannot appreciate what is distinctive about a particular event without comparing it to similar events in other times and places. Some new historians even share Lee Benson's hope "to participate in the overall scholarly enterprise of discovering and developing general laws of human behavior."

3. Explicit use of social science theories and scientific methods of proof. No self-respecting new historian would rely on an impressionistic, intuitive, or "seat of the pants" approach to historical study. The new historians use social science theory in several different ways. They may set out to test the applicability of a theory to historical situations or may use this theory either to fill gaps in their knowledge of what happened or to explain what happened in the past. The use of social science theory also has turned the attention of historians away from the headline events of an era and toward events that are latent rather than manifest in the experience of individuals. These latent events of the past may be accorded great significance in a theory of behavior, but may not even have been recognized as events by people at the time. People of the sixteenth century, for instance, may never have thought about whether families were nuclear or extended in form or whether childhood was identified as a distant stage of personal development. Yet these are among the major issues that have been addressed by new historians steeped in the work of sociologists and psychologists. As yet, however, historians have not effectively integrated study of the latent and the headline events of human experience.

Since new historians are especially sensitive to methodology, they are also likely to describe and defend the logic used to infer historical reports and explain historical events. New historians are more inclined than traditional scholars to believe that the arguments sustaining historical conclusions can explicitly be set forth. Often they will attempt to supply the reader with the information needed to follow the historical argument as it moves from evidence to conclusion.

4. Emphasis on quantifiable data and statistical methods of analysis. The last feature of the new history is closely related to its other characteristics.

Generalizations about groups of people are inherently quantitative in character (even if stated verbally) and can be solidly verified only by systematic analysis of large quantities of data. To make statements about groups, the new historians try to examine the entire group or a sample drawn from the group. They try not to depend on the study of so-called "typical" or "representative" individuals. The testing of theories taken from social science often requires the analysis of data that can be organized in quantitative form. In recent years, the development of high-speed computers and refined quantitative techniques has greatly increased our capacity for the statistical analysis of historical evidence.

Although the new history has its own distinctive features, it has also affected, in different ways, the fields of political, social, economic, and intellectual history.

The new historians of politics have concentrated their attention on recurring events and groups of leaders and followers. A new historian interested in Congress, for example, would probably not write the biography of a notable legislator like Daniel Webster or Sam Rayburn. He would be more likely to attempt a collective biography of congressional leaders or a statistical analysis of roll call votes to see how all members of Congress aligned themselves on various issues. Similarly, a new historian interested in presidential elections would probably not focus on the political strategies of different candidates but would attempt to describe and explain the voting behavior of voters in different political systems. He might even use his findings as a springboard to revise relevant political theory.

Social history has always focused on the lives of ordinary people and has pursued themes suggested by "common sense"—how people have dressed and housed themselves, the type of work they have done, and their attitudes toward strangers and outsiders. The new social history also relies heavily on sociology and psychology. Its topics of interest read like entries in the new *Encyclopedia of Social Science*—family structure, sex roles, socialization, social control, deviancy, and aging. Rather than learning about different groups from the study of typical or representative individuals, the new social historians have used quantitative procedures to form aggregate profiles of group behavior. And they have been especially interested in such exploited and disadvantaged groups as women, peasants, industrial workers, and ethnic minorities.

The new historians also seek to make social history less descriptive and more explanatory. Instead of confining themselves to descriptions of how men and women lived in past societies, the new social historians are attempting to explain not only why groups of people lived as they did, but also how and why groups changed their styles of life. Like their compatriots in the new political and economic history, the new social historians explain behavior with covering laws taken from social science. Indeed, their work is already contributing to the shaping of social theory itself.

The practice of economic history has been most affected by the new history. Most of the work now being done in economic history reflects the interests and methods of the new historians. Economic historians have been most successful in uniting the study of history with theoretical principles and have employed the most sophisticated methods of quantitative analysis. Every issue of *The Journal of Economic History* bristles with equations, statistics, and the jargon of economic theory; many of today's most renowned economic historians were actually trained as economists rather than as historians.

Economic theory suggests the very categories new economic historians use to describe and explain the past—productivity, capital, supply, demand, social savings, economies of scale, and rate of return. Specifically, the new economic history has been most concerned with broad problems of growth and development. Its practitioners have, for example, explored the influence of railroads on American economic growth, the role of technological change in England's industrial revolution, or the effects of the debasement of coinage on the economy of the Roman Empire.

The new economic historians formulate hypotheses with the aid of economic theory and frequently employ statistical methods of verification. They have avoided questions for which theory is poorly developed or for which quantitative analysis is not appropriate. The new economic historians have not paid much attention to the biographies of business leaders, the strategies that particular business firms employ, the interactions between workers and employers, or the relationship between business interests and economic imperialism.

The new economic history also emphasizes the analysis of counterfactual hypotheses. In their quest to determine the influences on economic growth and development, historians and economists sometimes ask the question: "What would have happened if some significant event had not happened?" The historian attempting to answer such a counterfactual question may replace the event that actually happened with a specific alternative event— for example, what would have happened if Stephen Douglas rather than Abraham Lincoln had been elected president in 1860? Or he might try to ascertain what would have been the most likely alternative to the event in question—for example, what would have happened if there had been no railroads and Americans in the nineteenth century had had to rely on other modes of transportation? The first type of counterfactual situation is "closed," the second type "open." One of the best-known (perhaps notorious) attempts to apply counterfactual analysis to historical study is Robert W. Fogel's *Railroads and American Economic Growth: Essays in Econometric History* (1964). Fogel wanted to determine the importance of railroads in the economic growth of nineteenth–century America. To answer this question, he constructed a model of the American economy in which there were no railroads. His counterfactual model was closed to the extent that it included no technological innovations other than those that actually occurred in nineteenth–century America, and open to the extent that he imposed no limits on the use of available technology (other than the railroads, of course). He concluded from his model that the American economy would have performed almost as well without railroads as it did with them; and, therefore, that railroads were not "indispensable" for American economic growth.

Fogel's work has been criticized justly for lack of rigor in both theory and use of historical evidence. But his work has also provided sharp criticism of the counterfactual method itself. Some critics have argued that the historian cannot use evidence from what actually happened to infer what might have happened if things were different. As we indicated in our discussion of historical explanation, however, all causal explanations implicity depend upon a counterfactual analysis of past events. To assert that one event influences a later event is the same thing as saying that the later event would have been different if a different earlier event had preceded it. If we did not believe that altering a cause would also alter the effect, we would have no grounds for asserting in the first place that any event was a cause of any other event. In short, the new economic historians' emphasis on counterfactual analysis makes explicit what is already implicit in all causal explanations of past events.

We must, however, be careful to specify exactly what counterfactual analysis can and cannot demonstrate. Although any explanatory model includes both causal events and their alternatives, in practice we cannot investigate all possible alternative events. Even if Fogel's analysis were as flawless as the Mona Lisa, his counterfactual argument could demonstrate only that railroads were not essential in his particular counterfactual world. In other counterfactual worlds, the railroads might well appear to be indispensable to American economic growth. Fogel cannot show that without railroads nineteenth–century America would have conformed to his description; thus he cannot prove that railroads were unimportant in the actual course of events. Perhaps the railroads' stimulus to the American economy produced many other technological innovations without which Fogel's counterfactual world would not have worked.

Many aspects of the new history—its focus on ordinary people and common experience, its use of quantification—are tangential to the study of intellectual history. Psychologists and sociologists still do not know very much about how advances in understanding are achieved. But some historians have begun to draw upon the insights of cognitive psychology and the sociology of knowledge to shape a new intellectual history. Instead of investigating the contents of ideas, these historians are exploring how ideas are shaped and the functions they serve. Michel Foucault's seminal explorations of medicine, science, penology, economics, and grammar have virtually created a new genre of intellectual history. In his quest to ascertain underlying structures of thought, Foucault probes for the rules governing what can be thought, said, and done in each field. He argues, for example, that the development of clinical medicine in Europe meant fundamental changes in views of life and death, in notions of disease and treatment, in the position of the doctor and the patient, and in the relationships between medical practice and the institutions of society.

We cannot hope to detail all the varieties of the new history in so cursory a survey. Although this brief discussion of the new history does pinpoint a few of its major features, achievements, and weaknesses, it has not yet allowed us to focus on two important examples of the new history that deserve considerably more elaboration—psychohistory and quantification.

Psychohistory

It is some measure of the newness of this field that neither Webster's latest edition, the *American Heritage,* the *New American,* nor the *Oxford English Dictionary* has an entry for "psychohistory." Failing a dictionary definition, we shall have to supply our own. Broadly speaking, psychohistory is the attempt to apply the understandings of psychology and psychiatry to historical analysis. Even though the general field is comparatively new, two broad subfields have already emerged: psychohistory that treats the individual and psychohistory that treats the group or society.

There is an obvious affinity between the kinds of questions that the psychologist and the historian ask. Both want to understand why people think, feel, and act as they do. The prospects for a mutually beneficial marriage between history and psychology would seem to be bright. The theories of psychology offer the historian new covering laws for the explanation of both group and individual behavior. Historians no longer need to rely solely on their intuitions about human behavior, but can also draw upon the insights psychologists and psychiatrists have achieved. Psychological theory is especially useful for explaining irrational or contradictory behavior. Too often, historians have simply thrown up their hands and labeled such behavior insane or aberrant. Psychological theory also suggests new issues for historians to consider. Psychologists have argued, for example, that the care afforded children in the first three years of life exerts an important influence on the development of adult personalities. Even those historians unwilling to venture upon full explanations of individual personality development may be prepared to see the importance of reporting the early-childrearing practices of whole societies.

Historians may also be interested in testing the applicability of psychological theories to different cultures and time periods. Psychohistorians can make significant contributions to our understanding of human behavior by trying to determine which theories apply best to past societies. By discovering the time dependent conditions that influence the application of psychological theories to actual behavior, historians may even foster the development of dynamic theories that explain how different historical circumstances affect the growth and development of human personality.

Yet psychology has proved to be a most troublesome partner of history despite the obvious advantages of the match. Historians often quarrel over different approaches to the past, but the struggles of psychologists over theory are far more bitter and intense. If a Freudian will not lie down with a Skinnerian, what place is there for history in the bedchamber of psychology? However much historians may disagree with one another, no political historian would categorically deny the value of economic history. Historians may disagree, but their positions are not irreconcilable.

The situation in the discipline of psychology is different. The major theories of personality seem to be mutually exclusive, and psychologists often identify more with the particular theory they espouse than with their general discipline. Moreover, although data exists to support each of the theories, no one of them has yet been validated scientifically in competition with the others. No theory has been firmly established by scientific methods of experimentation or by the systematic observation of large numbers of actual cases. Neither has any one theory proved to be an effective tool for prediction.

What general theories of human behavior are applicable to historical study? The theory developed by Sigmund Freud is by far the best known. Although a detailed description of Freudian psychology is unnecessary here, we should consider those features that are pertinent to history. Freud focused intensively on the early years of development, and particularly on the relationship between the child and its mother. Unfortunately, for most historical periods, evidence about early childhood is almost impossible to find. As Lawrence Stone has remarked, "Freudian psychology has not been much use to the historian, who is usually unable to penetrate the bedroom, the bathroom, or the nursery." A theory of personality development that accords primary importance to the very early years will hardly benefit the historian who cannot reconstruct this period of life, even for the great figures of the past.

Paucity of evidence, however, has not deterred some psychologists from deductively reconstructing a particular person's childhood from what they have discovered about him as an adult. With good cause, historians are extremely reluctant to employ such reasoning. If we think back to the model of historical inquiry, we will see immediately why. The evidence that the psychologist uses describes the effect (adult behavior). From that effect, he infers the causes (childhood experiences). The probability that his inference is right, assuming his historical reports of adult behavior are valid (and too many psychologists have proved to be woefully slipshod in their handling of historical evidence), depends upon the probable truth of the generalizations linking effect to a specific set of causes. Thus the psychohistorian rests his inference on the claim that Freudian theory shows that, given certain adult behavior, certain childhood experiences must have occurred. Since Freudian theory is by no means scientifically validated, the probability that such an inference is correct will be very difficult to determine.

Moreover, after using psychological theory to infer reports of what must have happened in early life, these same psychologists then use these reports as causes for explaining the same adult experiences from which the reports were inferred in the first place! Their theory does double duty; it infers the events of childhood from the experiences of later life and explains these adult experiences from what was inferred about childhood.

Good psychohistory requires good history as well as good psychology. Unfortunately, theories of behavior have so fascinated some psychohistorians that they have paid little attention to the reliability of their reporting of either the causes or the events to be explained.

Several psychologists have developed more elaborate thories of personality based on an essentially Freudian model. Perhaps the theory most adaptable to historical inquiry is that of Erik Erikson. While not denying the importance of early childhood experience, Erikson has posited that the individual personality proceeds through eight stages of development in the course of life. Since we are likely to have far more evidence about a person's life after the age of ten or so, we can check the inferences made from Erikson's theory against tangible historical evidence. Erikson's theory can be applied to the explanation of particular personalities, and the theory can be tested in different historical contexts. Erikson himself shows an exceptionally keen awareness of the natural affinities between psychological and historical study. He views psychoanalytic methods as essentially historical methods, arguing that the individual at any point in life is influenced by past experiences. Moreover, Erikson sees the individual human being as an organism—as a growing rather than a static being. This vision of man as developing and changing over time is crucial for historians. Specifically, Erikson posits that the individual can be analyzed as a triad of processes intimately interconnected with one another— the somatic (physiological), the ego (psychological), and the societal. To understand the whole person, we must understand each of these processes. Although the historian is usually more interested in the third (societal) and the psychologist in the second (ego), neither can fully understand an individual by considering one of these processes in isolation from the other two.

The following chart summarizes the eight stages of development and their corresponding "crises" that Erikson sees in the growth of an adult personality. The chart is fully discussed and explained in his important work, *Childhood and Society,* 2nd edition (1963). The important thing to note here is that the growth of an individual's ego is related to both physiological and societal processes but is more closely tied to physiology in the early years and to society in the later years.

Erikson's theory has great inherent appeal for historians. First, the broadly developmental scheme corresponds to the historian's predisposition to examine change and process over time. Second, according to Erikson, important stages of growth occur in late childhood and early adulthood; historians are much more likely to have data from the second decade of a person's life than from the first. Third, Erikson's theory takes into account conscious as well as subconscious conflicts within the person. Erikson sees the individual not as a victim of his early life, but as an active and conscious participant in his own growth; this view corresponds with the assumptions of most historians. Finally, Erikson's theory provides a way to link up the societal to the physiological and ego processes. Historians seek to understand the individual in relation to the particular society in which he or she lived. Erikson's model of development provides a theoretical construct for these interactions. For example, in his book *Childhood and Society,* Erikson discusses the plight of a young man who had served in World War II as a medic and had been discharged from the marines as a "psychoneurotic casualty." Many young men had suffered from "war neuroses," but why? Was it simply the trauma of combat that provoked their illnesses? The historical circumstances alone

FIGURE VII

	1	2	3	4	5	6	7	8
VIII Maturity								Ego Integrity vs. Despair
VII Adulthood							Generativity vs. Stagnation	
VI Young Adulthood						Intimacy vs. Isolation		
V Puberty and Adolescence					Identity vs. Role Confusion			
IV Latency				Industry vs. Inferiority				
III Locomotor-Genital			Initiative vs. Guilt					
II Muscular-Anal		Autonomy vs. Shame, Doubt						
I Oral Sensory	Basic Trust vs. Mistrust							

From Childhood and Society, 2d. ed., by Erik H. Erikson, with the permission of W.W. Norton & Company, Inc., New York, N.Y., Copyright 1950, © 1963 by W.W. Norton & Company, Inc.

would not provide an adequate explanation, for the war did not cripple all men emotionally. By examining this particular individual's past, Erikson was able to show how the historical circumstances, the war, and the individual's own history combined to destroy his sense of identity.

Perhaps the school of psychology that most closely matches Freud's in scope and influence is behaviorism. Behaviorism emphasizes the influence of the environment over the individual; it assumes that our actions are essentially responses to outside stimuli. Behaviorists see man as a fundamentally "reactive" being.

The most important difference between behaviorism and Freudian theory lies in their divergent views of motivation. Freudians see motivation as emanating mostly from within the psyche; behaviorists see motivation as learned elaborations on responses to a few drives that are primarily biological. The baby learns which behaviors are likely to produce parental approval and which will elicit disapproval. The baby then acts in such a way as to encourage approval. Behaviorists assume that people choose to do those things that bring pleasure (e.g., rewards or approval) and avoid those things that bring pain or discomfort (e.g., punishment or disapproval). Thus, positive reinforcement or pleasure encourages some activities, and negative reinforcement or pain discourages others. Behaviorism posits that our repertoire of behaviors consists of learned responses to our environment and that, to explain human behavior, we should study the environment, particularly its positive and negative reinforcements.

While few historians have tried explicitly to apply behaviorists theory to historical analysis, there are similarities between the approaches taken by many historians and behaviorists in explaining human action. Historians often point to external events, to the historical situation, when they try to explain why someone or some group took some action. They try to discover what changed in the environment in order to understand why people altered their behavior. For example, in assessing the causes of the Red Scare of 1919–1920, a wave of nearly hysterical anticommunism that swept over the United States, historians have pointed to such things as the Russian Revolution of 1917 and the bombings commonly attributed to left-wing American radicals. A historian might argue that these events caused such anxiety, fear, and pain that people reacted with wild fury in an effort to eliminate the forces that they believed were responsible for the threat to their way of life. American people changed their behavior. They had been reasonably calm and confident of their security; they became hysterical and aggressive, acting in response to the environmental stimuli that produced feelings of fear and terror.

However, this explanation would not satisfy all historians, for it does not explain why the Russian Revolution and some hundred bombings around the nation produced hysteria rather than some milder reaction. A few historians seeking an answer to this question have another level of motivation to understand why the Americans found the revolutionary activities so threatening, and why they reacted with such frenzy. To penetrate this level of understanding, the historian must employ depth psychology, theories that explain why people find some experiences pleasurable and others painful; why some ideas and goals are pursued, even in the face of adversity; and why some things are more frightening than others.

In recent years, behaviorists have become increasingly aware of factors in human motivation that are not well accounted for by simple stimulus/response models of behavior. For example, Albert Bandura has developed a considerably more sophisticated explanatory model that takes into account man's ability to learn through observation, to think through the possible consequences of various actions, to defer gratification, and to act in a way that maintains his sense of self-esteem, even if he believes that his actions will produce painful consequences. In contrast to many behaviorial models, Bandura's social learning theory stresses man's capacity for vicarious experience, anticipation, imagination, and foresight as important determinants in his behavior. Despite its greater detail and sophistication, however, Bandura's model still does not provide the same level of explanation that theories of depth psychology do. For instance, it could not thoroughly explain why Americans generally became hysterical during the Red Scare or why two people of very similar background and experience would have had different kinds of reactions to these same events. Nonetheless, explanatory theories like Bandura's do provide potentially useful models for the historian, particularly when he is working with the kinds of behavior that the model was explicitly designed to explain.

Over the past two decades another approach to understanding human behavior has been mapped out in the work of Ludwig von Bertalanffy, Jean Piaget, Noam Chomsky, Robert White, and others. These scholars not only reject the behaviorist view that people are molded primarily by outside stimuli, but they also reject the notion of Freudians and neo-Freudians that only non-rational instincts and drives inhabit man's unconscious mind. Instead, these scholars argue that our psyche also includes rational ordering principles that enable us to organize information received from the outside world and develop capacities to interact creatively with our environment. In this view, man is a prisoner neither of external conditions nor of instincts and drives. Rather, he explores and interprets the world for himself; he decides what part of society's values he will accept, what he will reject, and what he will transform.

Robert White has supplemented the Eriksonian model of psychosexual development with a "competence model" with stages parallel to those that Erikson proposes. According to White and others, the developing person needs to do more than resolve instinctual conflicts to become an adult capable of coping with adversity and complexity. He needs to master certain skills—walking, talking, getting along with others, and learning to work—to achieve "competence" in the activities that will allow him to deal successfully with his environment. The innate capacities for learning within each individual enable that person to develop capabilities on his own, rather than to be molded by either instinct or environment. The work that White and like-minded theorists have accomplished has not yet been exploited effectively by historians. Aside from the unfamiliarity of most historians with competence psychology, we do not have sufficient understanding yet of man's innate "competence" to explore its development in different historical circumstances.

The Gestalt school of psychology offers yet another approach to understanding individuals. Based initially on Max Wertheimer's explorations of how we perceive "apparent" as opposed to "real" motion (for example, why we see letters and words moving across a signboard when stationary lights flash in specific sequences), Gestalt pscyhology concentrates on the study of perception and the comprehension of conscious experience. Gestaltists maintain that to understand *what* a person perceives, we must consider the total pattern or configuration of the person's environment (i.e., the *Gestalt,* a German word meaning pattern, shape, or structure), the relationships among elements of the pattern, and the way people impose their own interpretations on the information gained through their senses. Moreover, Gestaltists insist that our perception of any one part of a situation is influenced by how we understand the whole situation.

There is much in Gestalt psychology that should prove attractive to historians. First, its emphasis on the person's whole environment and the person's own interpretation of his entire situation corresponds to many historians' views of how human activity should be understood. Gestalt psychology rejects both psychoanalytic and behaviorist concentration on a single or limited facet of man's mental and emotional life. Second, it focuses on man's conscious experiences, the kinds of experiences most readily documentable in historical evidence. Third, Gestaltists believe in letting an individual tell his own story without superimposing a theory on his account. They also engage in the kind of rigorous questioning of individuals that historians bring to their study of historical evidence. They try to understand how well a person perceives the totality of his environment, including his own feelings and attitudes. They try to find out what he is aware of and primarily what he avoids noticing—his "blind spots." There are limitations, however, to the applicability of Gestalt psychology to historical explanation. The most obvious, is that historians rarely have their subjects available for personal interviews. But just as important is the very elasticity of the psychology itself. With no detailed theory to tell us what aspects of our total environment to be aware of, historians have no guide for assessing whether a person's "blind spots" (assuming he can identify them) were significant determinants of the behavior the historian is trying to explain.

Finally, there is the eclectic school of psychology. Here is probably the most comfortable home for the historian who wishes to work in psychohistory. The eclectic psychologist uses whatever theory seems best to explain the actions and thoughts of the people he is studying. The eclectic faces squarely the reality of modern psychology—no one theory of personality has been demonstrated so far to be correct or applicable to all human thought and action. Although a distinct minority in their discipline, eclectics enjoy the freedom to pick and choose that theory which offers the best explanation of particular observed behavior. The posture of the eclectic also enables the historian to test the applicability of various theories to different historical situations. He need not assume that any one theory best explains human behavior in all times and places. The historian following the example of the eclectic psychologist is also less likely to commit the sins of the true believer, biasing his reports of past events in order to make them fit a particular theory.

The value of such flexibility for the historian hardly needs comment. But there are concomitant dangers. First, whatever model of personality the historian chooses, proponents of competing schools will reject his work out of hand. Second, he may be hard pressed to justify choosing one theory over another. His argument that the theory fits the evidence and the historical reports inferred from that evidence probably will not convince many of his fellow historians that his theory is therefore credible. Third, the historian will have to become thoroughly familiar with all the competing schools of psychological thought. Few historians are likely to achieve this level of expertise.

Beyond general theories of personality development, historians may also draw upon the work that psychologists have done in abnormal or deviant psychology. As H. Stuart Hughes remarked, "Where to date history has notably failed is in its explanation of the 'irrational.' " Usually historians have been content to say simply that someone was mad or disturbed, with no further explanation. Such an explanation is fundamentally mythopoeic; the historian has provided a description of behavior, labeled it "insane," and offered that label as explanation. In short, historians have normally dealt with the "irrational" by merely acknowledging its presence. This is no better than dismissing it. We can and should do better.

The experience of Hitler and World War II has perhaps spurred many historians to seek more rigorous explanations of manifestly "irrational" behavior and thought. We cannot explain adequately either Hitler himself or the German acceptance of him without recourse to abnormal psychology. No treatment of Hitler or his rise to power that follows a purely economic, political, social, or intellectual approach can be sufficient. Unfortunately, the same problems that have plagued historical studies in normal personality development—conflicting theories and slipshod use of evidence—have bedeviled attempts to employ theories of abnormal psychology. Nonetheless, we cannot achieve the quality and depth of understanding we seek without attempting to assess the sources of bizarre behavior and attitudes. Throughout, historians working on such problems should remain constantly aware that their explanations can be only as credible as their covering laws (in this case, laws based on theories of abnormal psychology).

Although practitioners of psychohistory cannot claim yet that they have solved the many problems attendant upon this approach, they can claim that their line of inquiry provides a promising way to deal with "irrational" and "contradictory" behavior. The concept of "contradictory" behavior warrants fuller comment. Too often historians have posed dichotomous questions about individuals. Was Martin Luther a revolutionary or reactionary? Did Alexander the Great seek to rule the world as god or did he want a world united in brotherhood? Was Abraham Lincoln a racist or a true emancipator? Historians have usually assumed that we must argue one side or the other but not both. They have not been able to deal successfully with people whose words often contradict their behavior or whose actions reflect ambivalent thoughts and feelings. On the other hand, psychologists accept such contradictions as a regular part of human personality. They assume that an individual can perform a single act out of mutually exclusive motives. In his psychobiography of Martin Luther, Erikson pointed out: "Historical dialectics refuses to acknowledge the principle that a great revolutionary's psyche may also harbor a great reactionary; but psychological dialectics must assume it to be possible, and even probable."

Psychology offers insights to historians engaged in studying groups as well as individuals, but the problems here are even more difficult and vexing than for individual psychohistory. At the outset, the historian is confronted with an enormous conceptual hurdle—the relationship between the individual and the group. Psychologists have not been able yet to explain how the dynamics of this relationship works. Moreover, the historian has at his disposal two different kinds of data—individually generated and aggregate. We may have for example, diaries and letters from individual members of a group that we wish to study. Also we may have data that describe how that group as a whole behaved. What we do not have is a set of covering laws that will enable us to move back and forth between these two kinds of data. The behavior of a group is not necessarily the sum of the behavior of individual members. Taken individually, every member of a wild and frenzied lynch mob may be as meek and quiet as the legendary Mr. Milquetoast. Describing and explaining group behavior solely on the basis of data pertaining to individuals is often termed the "individualistic fallacy"

Another significant problem of group level psychohistory is that too often historians and psychologists have personified the group. They have constructed a profile of group behavior, feelings, and attitudes, and then tried to explain that group profile by employing personality theories for individuals. This is akin to explaining an orchard by calling it an apple. The group and the individual are as different as an orchard and an apple; they ought not to be equated.

Obviously, historians interested in psychohistory at the group level must use aggregate data and refrain from employing personality theories that properly apply only to individuals in order to avoid the individualistic fallacy or the mistaken personification of groups. It might seem that little latitude is left for group level psychohistory. Fortunately, the confines are not so narrow as they might appear. First, there is a wealth of aggregate data available, especially for the more recent periods of our past. Census statistics, voting returns, public opinion polls, and records of purchases—the list is enormous. Second, social psychologists have developed a significant number of concepts designed specifically for the study of group behavior. Thus the historian has at his disposal both the kinds of data and the conceptual tools requisite for group level psychohistory.

We can discuss here only a few of the sociopsychological concepts available to historians, though enough to indicate how the historian can work with such models for some aspects of group behavior. However, two important points should be noted. First, in dealing with psychohistory at the group level, the historian (as well as the social psychologist) has to work with behavior. There is no way to ascertain directly what the group feels or thinks. All we can see by direct observation is what the group does. We must infer what the group feels and thinks from its behavior. This problem becomes even more complex when the group is treated historically. Unlike the social psychologist, the historian cannot observe directly the behavior of the group he studies; he must infer that past behavior from surviving evidence.

Second, most of the sociopsychological constructs so far developed have been aimed at explaining what many psychologists call maladaptive group behavior, probably because such behavior causes problems for our society and hence attracts the attention of social psychologists. Concepts such as prejudice, status anxiety, revolution of rising expectations, negative reference groups, relative deprivation, alienation, group aggression, and even "Future Shock" focus on group behaviors that are seen as damaging to the whole society. Psychologists have developed only a handful of constructs that treat the day-to-day behaviors of groups or behaviors that are perceived as nourishing, or at least not harmful to society. Among these few, historians have worked with "cultural perceptual fields," insanity as a cultural definition, community cooperative responses to disaster, group dynamics, and child-rearing patterns. Obviously, we need concepts and models that explain why groups act in ways perceived as both detrimental and beneficial to society; we also need ways to explain group behaviors that have no apparently positive or negative effect on society at all.

For the purposes of illustration, let us single out one of these sociopsychological constructs for further consideration, the notion of status anxiety.

Historians have relied on the concept of status anxiety to explain some of the most notable social movements of nineteenth and twentieth–century America. In his seminal study of American reform movements, *The Age of Reform* (1955), Richard Hofstadter has argued that the declining status and prestige of middle-class Americans at the turn of the twentieth century motivated them to become leaders of the progressive movement. As newly rich industrialists and seemingly corrupt political bosses became dominant forces in American society, the scions of older middle-class families turned to reform as a means of relieving their anxiety about their status and prestige. Similarly, in a highly influential study of the prohibition movement, Joseph Gusfield has argued that the conflict over liquor control was a struggle for prestige between an "old" America that was largely "rural, middle-class, native-stock and Protestant" and a "new" America that was largely "urban, working-class, foreign-stock and Catholic." According to Gusfield, legislation outlawing the manufacture and sale of liquor enhanced the prestige of the old America, since it indorsed its values and condemned the life-style of the new America. For this reason, Gusfield argues, it did not matter very much to supporters of liquor control that prohibition laws were not effectively enforced. They were seeking symbolic affirmation of their way of life, not actual control of drinking practices. The concept of status anxiety has enriched the study of American politics and reform movements. Historians have used this notion to explain such diverse forms of group behavior as the abolition movement of the antebellum period, agrarian protest in the late nineteenth century, and right-wing extremism in the 1950's. Nonetheless, critics have argued that historians cannot reliably establish historical reports showing that people actually suffered from status anxiety, and that the theory itself does not persuasively explain why people behaved as they did. Few historians would now subscribe to Hofstadter's account of the progressive movement.

Quantitative History

History used to be a refuge for mathematical illiterates. Any one put off by the equations of physics or the statistical tables of psychology could study history without having to add up a column of figures or find the square root of twenty-five. Since the mid 1960's, however, quantifiers have infiltrated history. Historical works now regularly include charts and graphs, tables of percentages, computations of means and medians, and perhaps even such bizarre intruders as Chi-square statistics and regression coefficients. Textbooks have appeared on "Quantitative History" and graduate courses in the field are popping up at universities all over the country. History students accustomed to skipping tables and even page numbers are now being asked to solve simultaneous equations.

The ubiquitous computer is in part responsible for this revolution in historical study. But historians are also becoming aware that statistical methods are the most reliable means of verifying any statement about a group or aggregate. Essentially, quantitative history is the application of statistical procedures to the analysis of historical evidence.

Professional reactions to quantitative history have ranged from bitter denunciation to uncritical acclaim. Some die-hard traditionalists have thundered against subjugation to the "bitch goddess of quantification," warning that quantification destroys the literary value of history and distorts our vision of the past. Some zealous converts have hailed quantification as the new messiah that will rescue history from ignorance and superstition. Most practitioners, however, view quantification as yet another way of helping scholars explore the past; they see it neither as a panacea nor as a substitute for traditional methods. Most professional historians who have not themselves been trained in statistics maintain a respectful but skeptical attitude toward quantification.

Obviously we cannot present here a detailed description of the methods and procedures that quantifiers use. But we will describe briefly what quantifiers do and examine both the benefits and pitfalls of this approach to historical understanding. Anyone interested in studying the past ought to cultivate at least a nodding acquaintance with quantitative history. Quantification is undoubtedly here to stay.

All of us are always counting things. Statements using such terms as more, less, usually, rarely, typical, many, intense, few, probably, or scarcely reflect at least a rough type of counting operation. Most quantifiers only profess to make such essentially numerical judgments more explicit and precise. Quantifiers seek both to verify statements of numerical assessment and to refine these statements as much as possible, given the limitations of historical information.

Statistical procedures can be applied to all data that can be organized into a statistical series. To construct a series one simply divides a collection of items (individuals, families, countries, ships, houses, automobiles, etc.) into different divisions or categories and counts the number of items that fall into each category. The categories of a statistical series may be based on qualitative as well as quantitative distinctions. For example, a historian could categorize individuals according to a qualitative distinction such as religion (Protestants, Catholics, and Jews) or ethnic origin (native-born and foreign-born). Or he may categorize the same individuals according to a quantitative distinction such as age, number of years of education, or income. The historian can then describe, compare, and analyze these statistical series.

A "time–series" is a type of statistical series of particular interest to historians. A time–series counts the quantity of some item at different points of time or different intervals of time. For example, a time–series might count the number of individuals graduating from Oxford College each year between 1600 and 1770, or the tons of steel the United States exported each year between 1900 and 1970. Through the analysis of time–series, the historian can gain a better understanding of amounts and rates of change over time. He can also compare time–series for two or more items to see how they change, relative to one another. In this way, the historian can find correlations that may signify causal connections.

Historians can learn a great deal about the past simply by doing the counting and sorting necessary to organize items into statistical series and by using a few basic tools like ratios and percentages. Percentages can indicate the proportion of items in each category of a series (for example, the percentage of individuals that are Protestant rather than Jewish or Catholic). And percentages can be used to compare different series by disclosing the proportion of items from a particular category of one series that fall into a particular category of another series (for example, the percentage of Protestants that live in the city rather than the country). Historians could have done this kind of work long ago; the data were available. Without the aid of computers, however, the sorting and counting of large quantities of data is tedious and time-consuming.

Through the use of very simple counting and sorting procedures, Richard McCormick has revised our understanding of Andrew Jackson's influence on popular participation in national elections. Prior to McCormick's work, the conventional view was that General Jackson, candidate and President of the common people, had stimulated an enormous upsurge in the percentage of eligible voters who cast ballots in the presidential elections. Simply by tabulating on a state by state basis the percentage of adult white males who participated in the presidential elections of 1828 and 1832, McCormick was able to show that increases in voter turnout did not coincide with the candidacies of Andrew Jackson. His work forced historians to reconsider one of their most commonly held notions about Jackson's influence on American politics.

The potential benefits of simple counting and sorting are not limited to electoral data. Information from such diverse sources as census reports, tax lists, probate records, records of births, deaths, marriages, church records, ship manifests, and even entries in telephone books can be organized into statistical series that indicate where people lived, how long they lived, who they lived with, how much they earned, where they were born, and where they worshipped. Simple counting and sorting—a technique within the grasp of all historians—can assist scholars to portray more completely and reliably the activities and movements of the people they study.

Counting and sorting techniques can also be applied to the study of historical documents. At its most elementary level, "content analysis" of documents allows historians to determine more precisely and reliably than by a simple reading of written materials the attitudes, beliefs, values, and interests of their authors. Suppose, for instance, that a historian wanted to know what Cicero really thought about Caesar. Traditionally, he would read through the corpus of Cicero's work and choose what seemed to him to be representative passages indicating Cicero's real feelings. Even this traditional procedure involves counting; implicitly the historian divides Cicero's comments into categories that reveal his attitudes toward Caesar, and roughly counts the number of statements in each category. But the historian might unwittingly revise his criteria for categorizing Cicero's statements as he reads through the work, or unconsciously focus on passages that fit some preconceived idea. Moreover, the reader has no way of knowing the assumptions on which the historian based his counting and categorizing.

A quantifier would supplement—not replace—his reading of Cicero with content analysis. He would set up a list of key words and phrases that indicated both positive and negative feelings about Caesar. Perhaps with the aid of a computer, he would then count the number of times Cicero used each type of word or phrase. Content analysis generates a statistical series that provides a useful check on the historian's own reading of the documents. The analysis is founded on assumptions that are explicit rather than implicit; it considers all words and phrases in the material; it consistently applies the same criteria to all the documents; and it guards against distortion due to preconceived ideas. Despite these virtues, content analysis cannot elicit the emotional overtones, the intricate connections and comparisons that a sensitive reader often picks up. Reading and content analysis complement, but do not substitute for each other.

Some critics might object that this simple content analysis ignores changes over time in Cicero's feelings about Caesar. The historian could formulate a more sophisticated program for analysis that would reveal temporal changes in the balance between positive and negative feelings. But even this more sophisticated analysis does little more than generate statistical series which the historian can look at and compare.

As useful as simple counting and sorting techniques are, historians often encounter statistical series that demand a more complicated analysis. For example, historians are interested in the distribution of income within a society and want to know whether patterns of income distribution change over time. To answer these questions, historians must employ some statistical measures that summarize aspects of the series.

The most important summary measures of quantitative series are familiar to us from grade school arithmetic. If a historian mastered sixth grade math, he can compute these summary measures even though the terminology that statisticians employ differs somewhat from that of elementary school teachers. Quantifiers talk about central tendency, dispersion, and skewness. These terms simply denote measures of what is representative of the series as a whole (central tendency), the extent to which the individual values in a series are dispersed rather than clustered together around a central value (dispersion), and the extent to which a series is pulled to the high side or to the low side by extremely high or extremely low values (skewness).

To get at the central tendency of a series, we can compute the mean or arithmetic average of the series and the median or middle value. The mean is determined by adding up all the individual values of a series and dividing that sum by the number of items in the whole series. The median of a series is reckoned by arranging all the items of a series in ascending order and then determining the value at which there are an equal number of items above and below.

The most important measure of dispersion is the standard deviation; this statistic indicates the extent to which the values in a series differ from the mean value. Measures of skewness are a bit more difficult to compute. If a series has in it a few very high values, the mean or arithmetic average will be skewed to the high side; conversely, if the series has a few very low values, the mean will be skewed to the low side. The simplest way to measure the direction and extent of skewness is to compare the mean and the median. Since the mean includes all values in the series, it is sensitive to either extremely high or low values. If the mean is higher than the median, the distribution of the series has been skewed to the high side by some extremely high values; if the mean is lower than the median, the series has been skewed to the low side by extremely low values. In a series with a relatively few items we can detect skewness by simple inspection. However, since quantitative studies may use series with hundreds or even thousands of individual items, more formal measurement of skewness is necessary.

Historians have used these summary measures to examine the distribution of such measurable characteristics as income, wealth, land holdings, age, education, and family size in all kinds of communities. For example, a historian studying the distribution of wealth in a New England town of the seventeenth century might construct a statistical series from probate records and tax lists. The mean value of this series would tell him how wealthy the town as a whole was (per capita wealth). The median value would disclose approximately how much wealth had been amassed by those who were neither rich nor poor, but somewhere in the middle. The standard deviation would reveal the extent to which the wealth that individuals hold deviates from the average wealth of the town. A comparison of the mean and median would disclose whether or not the series was skewed by a few individuals, either much poorer or much richer than the rest. In addition, the historian might use percentage computations to determine how evenly the wealth was distributed among town residents. For example, what percentage of the total wealth was held by the wealthiest 1 percent? The wealthiest 10 percent? The poorest 30 percent?

The historian could compare the statistics generated for this town with statistics from other towns or from the same town at different times. The comparisons would help him to answer many questions of historical interest. What kinds of towns were the wealthiest or had the most even distribution of wealth? Was the particular town becoming wealthier or less wealthy over time? Were wealthy individuals becoming relatively more wealthy? Were the poor becoming relatively poorer? Did wealth become dispersed or more clustered about the mean value?

Quantitative studies of wealth distribution have been conducted for cities, towns, and counties in colonial America. These studies have shown that wealth was generally far less evenly distributed than impressionistic work had suggested. They have shown that over time wealth was becoming more and more concentrated and that, contrary to the conventional wisdom, the American Revolution did not produce a more uniform distribution of wealth. The quantitative studies have also disclosed important differences in the distribution of wealth in different types of communities.

Some quantifiers have pressed beyond this level of statistical work to use more complex techniques in investigating the relationship between two or more statistical series. For purposes of convenience, we can use the technical term "variable" to signify the individual series being considered. Virtually any historian interested in group behavior must explore the relationships among variables. Political historians, for example, are interested in the relationship between voting behavior and religious affiliation, social historians in the relationship between race and family structure, and economic historians in the relationship between productivity and wages. Traditional historians often infer the nature of the relationship between variables from such literary sources as newspapers, letters, and diaries. But statistical information, when available, permits more precise and reliable inferences.

The relationship of variables to each other can be determined by organizing data into tables and graphs. But the visual inspection of data does not reveal very much about a relationship. First of all, the historian would want to assess the strength of the correlation between variables. Measures of correlation tell the investigator how well he can predict the values of one variable from knowledge of the values of another variable. Since historians, however they phrase it, often describe events in terms of correlations between variables of interest, statistical measures of correlation are important for historical study. If two variables were perfectly correlated, then knowing the values of one would enable a historian to predict without error the values of the other. Conversely, if two variables were not at all correlated, then knowing the values of one would not help at all to predict the values of the other. For example, a variable categorizing individuals as urban or rural dwellers would be perfectly correlated with a variable categorizing individuals as Republicans or Democrats if all urbanites belonged to one party and all rural folk to the other. Statistical measures of correlation have been developed for both qualitative and quantitative series. Most familiar is the linear correlation coefficient (represented by the symbol r), which is applicable to quantitative series.

Louise A. Tilly, for example, used correlation coefficients to study the development of a national market for grain in postmedieval France. Tilly used these coefficients to measure the strength of the correlation among grain prices in Paris and in the distant market of Toulouse and in the nearby market of Beauvais. The higher the correlation between prices in the capital and prices in these markets (she reasoned), the greater the correspondence between the Paris market and markets in the nation as a whole. By examining both a distant and a nearby market, Tilly also expected to gauge the geographic scope of a possible correspondence in grain prices. Overall, Tilly's statistics indicated that "by the end of the eighteenth century, Paris was a price making center for a large area, but that movements in this direction had begun one hundred years before in the case of the distant market, Toulouse, and long before that for the neighboring market, Beauvais."

Often historians are confronted with the problem of trying to assess the strength of the correlation between two variables when they suspect that this correlation is a result of the influence of yet another variable. For example, a historian might find a correlation between land-holding and educational level, but he might suspect that the educational level of individuals helps predict the amount of land they own only because well-educated people tend to be wealthier than poorly educated people. To test this hypothesis, the historian must measure the correlation between education and land-holding while controlling for the influence of wealth. In effect, this control is achieved by statistically manipulating the education and land-holding variables, while holding the wealth variable constant. If the correlation between education and land-holding remains high when wealth is held constant, the investigator knows that the educational level of individuals helps predict their land-holding, even when their wealth is also known. If the correlation disappears when wealth is held constant, the investigator knows that the educational level of individuals does not help predict the amount of land they own when their wealth is also known.

Sheldon Hackney has used these methods to evaluate the notion that a tendency toward violence is a special character trait of white southerners in the United States. Hackney reasoned that this hypothesis could not be tested merely by examining statistics of violent crime and suicide for the South and the rest of the nation. Differences in crime and suicide rates might result from differences in the demographic composition of the South and other regions. Using state level data from the Census of 1940, Hackney studied differences in rates of violent crime and suicide (white) for the South and the rest of the nation when controlling for such factors as education, income, unemployment, wealth, age, and urban/rural residence. Finding that southern states had significantly higher rates of violent crime and suicide even when controlling for these factors, Hackney concluded that a world view unique to white Southerners made the South "the nation's most violent region."

If a historian wants to determine the influence of one variable on another, he will investigate the form rather than the strength of the relationship between the variables, for the form of the relationship measures the extent to which the values of one variable change in response to changes in the values of another variable. "Change" in this context does not necessarily imply the passage of time. In statistics, "change" often means the differences observed between similar situations at a specific point in time. Assume, for example, that the percentage of skilled workers in a sample of towns is influenced by the percentage of high school graduates in the towns. To express the form of this relationship, a historian might state that a 10 percent change in the percentage of high school graduates produces a 5 percent change in the percentage of skilled workers. Change here shows variation from one situation to another. Variation over time also may be implied, but not necessarily.

In discussing the form of the relationship between statistical series, the variable to be explained is called the response or dependent variable; the variable used to explain (the variable that influences) is called the explanatory or independent variable. In the example above, the percentage of high school graduates would be the independent or explanatory variable, and the percentage of skilled workers would be the response or dependent variable.

To determine the form of the relationship between variables, historians have employed a technique that has a frightening name—multiple regression analysis. Although this is a powerful tool of analysis, its basic idea is not difficult to comprehend. To use this technique, the historian constructs a model including both the dependent variable and one or more explanatory variables. Once the model is constructed, multiple regression analysis enables the historian to determine the extent to which the dependent variable changes in response to changes in each of the explanatory variables, when the values of all other explanatory variables are held constant. The analysis generates statistics known as regression coefficients which measure the influence of each explanatory variable on the dependent variable, while controlling for the influences coming from any other explanatory variable included in the model. Like any statistical technique, multiple regression analysis cannot control for variables not included in the models.

Maris Vinovskis has used multiple regression analysis to reexamine prevailing notions about what caused differences in fertility rates in mid-nineteenth-century America. For states in the East, South, and Midwest, he used this technique to determine the separate influences of five different variables—sex ratio, percentage of foreign born residents, percentage of urban residents, average farm values, and educational level—on state by state differences in fertility. Vinovskis' regression equations revealed educational level to be the most important influence on differences in fertility among the states. Since most previous work on fertility had been limited to an exploration of the effects of urbanization and agricultural opportunity, Vinovskis' study indicates the need for a general reconsideration of the "role of educational and cultural factors" as determinants of "fertility differentials and trends."

Thus far the discussion of quantification has considered only attempts to describe statistical series and the relationships among series. We have not yet considered the problem of drawing inferences that go beyond the information contained in the series being considered. Historians often want to make statements about a whole class of items (for example, the average income of *all* the families in a town or the average number of crewmen on *all* the ships arriving at a port in a particular year), but have information only about a sample of those items. The value of a statistic computed from a sample of the total is only an estimate of the value of that statistic for the entire class of items. The actual statistical value may be very different from the sample value; the problem is to determine the likelihood that the actual value is substantially different from the sample value.

For certain kinds of samples (for example, a randomly selected sample), statisticians have developed methods for estimating how closely the value computed on the basis of the sample will approximate the actual value for the entire class. The methods of inferential statistics enable the investigator to determine the probability that the actual value of a statistical measure (for example, a mean or a correlation coefficient) for the whole class lies within a given range of the value computed for the sample. The wider this range, the greater the probability that the actual value lies within the range.

A historian can mislead his readers badly if he presents only the sample values and does not consider the ranges within which the actual values can be expected to fall. Assume, for example, that a historian is interested in comparing average family income in two cities; and that he has randomly selected a sample of families from each city and computed their average incomes. Let us assume that the sample value for the first city was $9,000 per year and for the second, $9,500. The historian might be tempted to conclude from this analysis that, on the average, families in the second city had incomes $500 higher than families in the first city. But this difference of $500 pertains only to the samples. Because either sample may overestimate or underestimate average income for the entire city, the actual difference for the entire populations may be less or greater than $500. The historian must use the methods of inferential statistics to specify the range within which the actual difference between family incomes is likely to fall. If this range includes zero (for example, the historian may be fairly sure that the actual difference is between $0 and $1,000), the historian could not with confidence claim that there was any difference at all between family incomes in the two cities. Thus, the historian and his reader will want to know not only the statistical value computed from the sample but also the estimate of how much the actual value is likely to differ from the sample value.

Even when the historian is working with the entire population or class of an item, he may still wish to employ the methods of inferential statistics. For classes with a small number of items, the computed values of statistical measures might reflect error in the measurement of items or a violation of the assumptions upon which a particular technique is based. For example, a historian interested in determining the mean values of one family homes in a small town may know the assessed value of every home. But the assessors may have made mistakes in appraising these homes. They may sometimes have underestimated home values and sometimes overestimated them. Unless the number of homes considered was very large, we would not expect these errors to cancel out. They could lead to an estimate of mean home values that was either too high or too low. The safest procedure is to treat the class as if it were a random sample from a much larger population and to report ranges of values rather than single values for statistical measures.

Historians are faced with a particularly difficult problem of inference when they want to study behavior at one level of analysis but are using data collected on another level. Often historians have to infer the behavior of individuals from data about groups. For example, political historians working in periods before the 1930's generally must infer the behavior of individual voters from data collected for such political units as states, boroughs, parishes, cities, towns, wards, and precincts. But the behavior of political units does not necessarily correspond to the behavior of the individuals comprising these units. Social scientists use the term "ecological fallacy" to describe an incorrect inference from the group to the individual level of analysis. The ecological fallacy is an especially important problem for historians and scholars who are trying to determine the best way to make inferences from the group to the individual level.

This brief tour through the world of the quantifier illustrates some of the major advantages of quantitative analysis. Quantitative methods enable historians to exploit vast quantities of new information. They provide a basis for refining and verifying generalizations and for explaining forms of behavior. The very process of explicitly stating a historical hypothesis so that it can be statistically tested may also expose ambiguities and inconsistencies in the historian's own thinking. Moreover, the exploration of quantitative data may suggest a new hypothesis to the historian.

The gains in historical understanding that can be achieved through quantitative analysis are great. But new problems usually accompany advances, and quantification is no exception to this general rule. Most quantifiers are refreshingly candid about the problems inherent in their approach to the past. First, there is the problem of sampling. Usually historians work with samples and infer the characteristics of the entire group from which the sample was drawn. The methods of inferential statistics are designed for samples obtained by some known procedure; for example, forms of random sampling that give each member of the group an equal chance of selection. But most samples that historians study represent information that has survived the ravages of time rather than information that has been gathered by a known method of sampling. An economist interested in the financial status of banks in our contemporary economy, for example, could select systematically a sample of different kinds of banks to study. A historian seeking to study the status of banks in the 1830's, however, would have to examine those few banks about which financial information still exists. Unless the historian knows how the available sample was derived, he cannot determine the probability that the true value of a statistic for the entire group lies within a given range of the value computed for the sample. Without this knowledge, the historian cannot judge the reliability of conclusions based on the examination of samples.

Second, quantitative analysis can convey a false impression of precision. Numbers seem far more precise than words. Our mathematics include an infinite supply of numbers, no two of which duplicate each other. And historians usually express the results of quantitative work as single numbers rather than ranges of numerical values. Yet precision in the numerical presentation of results does not imply equal precision in the historical conclusions that can be drawn from the numbers. If a number is derived from sample data, it represents only an estimate of the true value for the entire group. At best, the historian knows only the probability that the true value lies within a given range of the sample value. Moreover, problems of validity and reliability can distort numerical results. A statistic is valid if it actually represents what it is used to represent. Given the limitations of historical information, problems of validity are a constant plague of historical research. Historians of crime must rely on statistics of reported crime. But what do changes in reported crime represent? Do they represent changes in actual crimes committed? Changes in police practices? Or perhaps some combination of the two? Even if a statistic represents what it is supposed to represent, it may not be a reliable measure. Scholars have found that the United States Bureau of the Census has undercounted the number of minority peoples in the American population. This measurement error obviously will distort statistics on the proportion of minority groups in various communities.

Third, quantifiers must be careful not to dwarf the soft variables that cannot be subjected to analysis by statistical procedures. If some traditional historians seem to take into account only what *cannot* be counted, quantitative historians might be tempted to contend only with what *can* be counted. In explaining behavior or describing an event, quantifiers tend to focus on those aspects of a situation that can be expressed in statistical form. Yet distortions may result from a selection process that emphasizes one variable simply because it can be analyzed statistically and slights another simply because it cannot be quantified readily. It hardly needs to be argued that a soft variable can be just as important an influence on human behavior and attitudes as a variable that can more easily be counted. A historian of the Inquisition, for example, might be able to assess the influence of such variables as economic status, age, and sex on the likelihood that an individual would be hauled before an Inquisition board. But such soft variables as religious fervor and conviction might have been far more important even if they could not be measured and included in the analysis. To dwarf soft variables is to shrink the full range of human experience.

Fourth, it is possible that quantitative historians, whose primary interest lies in history rather than statistics, will not develop the expertise necessary for the quantitative analysis of historical data. The most severe problem is not that historians will incorrectly compute statistical measures, but that historians will misunderstand or ignore the assumptions of statistical techniques and misinterpret the results of quantitative analysis. Most historians using the correlation coefficient mistakenly use this statistic to measure the causal influence one variable has on another, rather than how well the values of one variable can be predicted from the values of another. Regression analysis is the appropriate technique for determining the causal influence of one variable on another.

Fifth, historians face special problems in applying quantitative methods to the study of change over time. A discussion of time–series analysis can quickly become very complex. At best, we can mention a few of the more serious problems that confront students of history. The very meaning of the terms historians use to form statistical series (for example, such terms as peasant, middle-class, family, and wage) may change over time without the historian's being aware of the nature and extent of such changes. Historians who assume that they are analyzing change over time in the same phenomenon might actually be looking at different phenomena. Historians are further constrained by the mathematics of time–series which are best adapted to smooth and continuous changes, whereas the actual pattern of historical change might be abrupt and discontinuous. Moreover, at different points of time, different statistical measures might be appropriate to understanding aspects of a society. But without a model of temporal change in social systems, the historian would not know how to adapt his analysis to this requirement.

Time–series that are valid and reliable may be difficult to construct even when data seem fairly abundant. Consider, for instance, the practical problems of studying social mobility in nineteenth–century America from information contained in the federal manuscript census—the census takers' reports on individual households, closed to public inspection for seventy years. The historian will find that the government conducted the census only once every ten years and frequently changed the questions that it asked. He will find that little information relevant to social mobility is included in the reports prior to 1850 and that fire destroyed most of the material for 1890. And he will find that individuals located in one census are very difficult to find in subsequent census years and that families often cannot be traced across generations.

Sixth, because of its technical nature, the work of quantitative historians may be incomprehensible to all but the trained specialists. Many of the readers interested in the historical problems quantifiers address may be confronted with the maddening choice of accepting on faith or rejecting out of hand conclusions based on statistical procedures. Moreover, the writing of quantifiers may be so involuted, so filled with social science jargon and technical language, that many readers cannot even understand the issues that are being discussed. While the inherent complexity of some forms of statistical analysis precludes a "Dick and Jane" level of discussion, qualifiers should make a special effort to write in common parlance. Tortuous sentences like "The conclusion is obtained from the factor loadings obtained by orthogonal rotation of the varimax factor" simply give readers a headache. No one should have to reach for the aspirin bottle while reading historical literature.

These problems will be disabling only if quantitative historians ignore them; they are not inherently impervious to solution. Quantitative historians should be sensitive to the limitations of statistical methods and respectful of the contributions that traditional forms of inquiry offer. In contrast to the caricatures sketched by the more extreme critics of quantification, the best quantitative historians routinely integrate statistical procedures with other forms of research, supplementing their statistical work with the kinds of research and descriptive analysis typical of traditional history. But they also report the assumptions on which their analyses depend and try to determine the likely extent and direction of errors in statistical estimates. They, more than their critics, are sensitive to the problems of interpreting statistical measures, conversant with the methodological literature, and willing to seek consultation on problems that they do not fully understand.

The best quantitative historians try to incorporate indicators of soft variables into their analyses or, at least, to consider the effects of their exclusion. And they make special efforts to communicate their findings in clear and graceful prose and even may try to explain their methodology in terms of ordinary language. A properly written quantitative study should offer both a readable text and enough information for the specialist to evaluate its results.

Of course, quantifiers cannot shake off all of their problems. But neither can historians using any other methodology. No one has yet unearthed a philosopher's stone for discovering historical truth. Given the limitations of our knowledge, we cannot afford to reject any means for understanding the past. Some questions can be answered reliably by quantitative analysis; others require another approach. Until we discover the royal road to our past, we must keep open every trail and pathway, no matter how narrow and twisting.

VI

Family and Local History

Our most personal link to the past comes not through books or articles but through our families and communities. Our ancestors, both immediate and remote, and the neighborhoods, towns, or cities in which we have lived our lives constitute our most intimate connections with the past. The perceptions of our families, the attitudes and values of our communities, have been transmitted through generations, culminating for the moment in ourselves. For many people, the most interesting history is that closest to home—the family and its community.

Family History

The new social history, as we indicated in the previous chapter, seeks to illuminate the day-to-day experiences of ordinary people in past societies. New historians try to grasp a totality larger than the thoughts and deeds of the aristocratic, the famous, and the infamous. For those seeking such perspectives on the past, families are a natural object of study. The family is the most fundamental and durable of all human institutions. It has the primary responsibility for population replacement; the care, nurture, and socialization

153

of children; the molding of values and attitudes; the transmission of culture; the provision of love and emotional support for both children and adults; and the arrangement of the individual's daily activities. The study of families can add much to the understanding of an entire society, providing insight into such matters as social and geographic mobility, political behavior, sex roles, assimilation, and acculturation. Changes in the nature of family life also influence and are influenced by social, economic, and political change.

The contemporary tradition of family history began with the work of French scholars in the 1950's. Led by Louis Henry, French demographers* interested in historical studies of fertility developed procedures for reconstituting the major demographic characteristics of families through such varied sources as marriage contracts; birth, baptismal, and death records; declarations of illegitimacy; probate records; and lists of census takers. Touched by the hand of the diligent demographer, families long dead suddenly sprang to life again.

In reconstituting a family, the researcher combs through the pertinent records and constructs a statistical picture of that family, usually for a specific and limited period of time. The statistical picture may detail family size and composition, births and deaths, infant mortality, ages at marriage, and age of the head of the household. The detail of the statistical picture will, of course, be determined by the richness of the available data. By combining statistical pictures of many families, the researcher then can obtain aggregate statistics for the community, with proper sensitivity to sampling problems, if he has not reconstructed all families.

In general, historians and demographers have applied this method to samples of families from particular towns or villages. Given the dispersion of relevant evidence and the time consumed in reconstituting families, the method has limited application to large national samples.

Using techniques pioneered by Henry, British historians have launched a major collaborative investigation of the size and composition of households in Britain from the sixteenth to the nineteenth century. Under the leadership of Peter Laslett, the Cambridge Group for the History of Population and Social Structure has gathered and analyzed vast quantities of information relevant to the reconstitution of British families. A major report of their work is *Household and Family in Past Time* (1972), edited by Peter Laslett. Beginning in the mid 1960's, students of American history such as John Demos, Philip Greven, and Richard Sennett began to use the methods of

---

*Demography is the statistical study of population and usually focuses on such things as births, marriages, deaths, and health.

family reconstitution to study families in the colonial period and in the nineteenth century.

The study of families through reconstitution is an example of microsocial history. Microhistory is the detailed, intensive study of the lives of particular individuals and groups. History under the microscope not only achieves unparalleled accuracy, but it also reveals the fine details and rich variety of human experience. Although microanalysis is a useful corrective to the sweeping generalizations that can flatten and distort reality, its results often do not warrant inferences beyond the particular sample being considered. To determine the trends prevailing within a nation, historians must either bring together large numbers of samples or turn to macrosocial history—the analysis of aggregate data pertaining to the population as a whole. A historian of nineteenth or twentieth–century America, for example, might use aggregate census reports and vital records to compute fertility rates, life expectancy, and median family size. In principle, microhistory and macrohistory are complementary ways of penetrating the same social reality. In practice, however, historians have yet to integrate the two approaches.

In addition to work on family reconstitution, yet another product of French scholarship has revived interest in the history of families. In 1960, Philippe Ariès published his now classic work, *Centuries of Childhood: A Social History of Family Life.* Surveying the western family from medieval times through the industrial revolution, Ariès challenged the views of those who lamented the decline of the family in the modern world. Ariès argues that the family has triumphed in the modern era, exercising far greater power and influence than in earlier periods of history. In the medieval era, Ariès contends, the family did not exist as a distinct unit, separate from the rest of society; moreover, roles within the family were not sharply differentiated. Children mingled freely with adults and family members with the rest of society. People felt no need for family privacy; they perceived no gulf between the world of the family and the world of outsiders or between the world of the child and the world of the adult. While the medieval family fulfilled the function of ensuring "the transmission of life, property and names, . . . it did not penetrate very far into human sensibility." Only in the sixteenth and seventeenth centuries, Ariès argues, did the family begin to turn inward and recognize the need for educating children, for sheltering and preparing them for the transition to adult life. These developments tightened the emotional bond uniting family members, isolated people from the broader society, increased hostility and suspicion towards those outside the family, and made the family a central institution for establishing order and discipline. Withdrawing into their family, people no longer rubbed shoulders with those of other classes— "... there came a time when the middle class could no longer bear the pressure of the multitude. ... It seceded; it withdrew from the vast polymorphous society to organize itself separately, in a homogeneous environment, among its families, in homes designed for privacy, in new districts kept free from all lower-class contamination."

Ariès' provocative and controversial ideas brought family history to the forefront of western historiography. He directly linked changes in family life to the development of the modern world and challenged long cherished notions about the meaning of modernity. Ariès' work also pointed to a variety of sources that could be exploited by the family historian, particularly for sparsely documented periods of history. Instead of relying solely on public documents, Ariès also used paintings and drawings, medical treatises, and language itself. For example, he investigated the range of words used to denote family members and stages of development; he examined doctors' advice to parents and prescriptions for child care; and he looked at the way in which artists drew children and their activities. Moreover, Ariès' focus on the emotional texture of life within the family stimulated an interest in applying psychological theories to the study of family history.

Historians have borrowed the insights of psychology to help make the inferential leap from information about the circumstances of family life to reports of how family members felt about their lives and how family life affected the development of individuals. What were the effects of living within a large crowded household or frequently confronting the death of infants and small children? What did it mean to children to be orphaned or apprenticed at an early age? How did different methods of raising children shape the lives of both the parent and the child? As John Demos has noted, the demographic and the psychological approach can effectively complement one another. As he puts it: " 'Quantitative' information . . . provides us—if all goes well—with certain concrete bench-marks: age of weaning, age of marriage, rate of mortality and so forth. . . . Psychological theory cries out for solid evidence on the timing of certain crucial 'life-happenings.' Demographic results, on the other hand, are arid—and sometimes quite meaningless— without a leavening of 'qualitative' insight."

Demos' own work seeks to bridge the gap between the circumstances and psychology of life experience. In *A Little Commonwealth: Family Life in Plymouth Colony* (1970), Demos applies the theories of Erik Erikson to patterns of child rearing in seventeenth–century Plymouth. Drawing on both quantitative and literary sources, Demos describes early childhood in this Puritan colony as marked by "a year or so of general indulgence," followed by "a radical turn towards severe discipline," especially by parental efforts to crush the child's "earliest efforts at self-assertion." According to Demos, Erikson's model of development suggests that if a child's struggles to achieve autonomy, to "stand on his own feet," are "beaten down" rather than supported, a preoccupation with shame and guilt can be expected in later life. Thus, Demos concludes that distinctive patterns for the rearing of children explain why shame, guilt, and the struggle to "save face" loom so large in Puritan culture.

Historians of the family not only have borrowed theories from social science. They also have challenged notions about the past derived from efforts to project generalizations of social scientists backward in time. The massive research of the Cambridge Group has concentrated on challenging the notion, initially put forward by sociologists and anthropologists relying primarily on supposition rather than detailed historical investigation, that a transition from extended families of grandparents, parents, children, and perhaps other relatives to a nuclear family of only parents and children was part of the transition from preindustrial to industrial society. Members of the Group argue that their research shows just the opposite; the nuclear family was the predominant form of family life well before the advent of industrialization. Historians of the United States have likewise challenged the deductions of such social scientists as Daniel Patrick Moynihan that slavery destroyed the black family, creating a "tangle of pathology" that persists to the present era. John Blassingame, Herbert Gutman, Frank Furstenberg, Robert W. Fogel, and Stanley Engerman suggest, on the contrary, that black people maintained a powerful commitment to organized family life and that stable, two parent families predominated in the period following emancipation.

Recently, historians of the family have displayed a special sensitivity to the dynamics of family life. Historians are beginning to portray the family in dynamic rather than static terms, as something that evolves and changes over time. Historians now recognize that families have a life cycle of their own. Thus, critics suggest that the Cambridge Group failed to find more complex family structures because of their failure to consider the changes that families undergo during their life cycle. Lutz Berkner, for example, found that in Austrian villages of the eighteenth–century family form depended upon the age of the family head. The extended family, he discovered, was "a normal phase in the developmental cycle of the peasant household," constituting a majority of families in which the male head was under forty years of age. Thus, Berkner's work challenges the Cambridge Group's thesis that the nuclear family was the predominant form of family life in both preindustrial and industrial Europe.

Historians are also beginning to explore relationships between the family life cycle and particular historical events. This approach liberates historians from attempts to explain patterns of family life solely by references to such stylized, global concepts as urbanization and industrialization. Glen Elder, for example, in *Children of the Great Depression* (1974), shows how economic deprivation affected the family life of those growing up during the 1930's in America.

Historians have also begun to explore how some catastrophic events, such as war, may have affected the children of families who bore the brunt of suffering. Peter Loewenberg has sought to explain the great popularity of the Nazi Party among German youth by examining that particular age group's experiences as children. The Nazi *Jugend* were young children during the First World War and their experiences during those formative years, Lowenberg contends, were marked by extreme malnutrition, high rates of infant and child mortality, chronic illness, and the loss of one or both parents. Their families were simply unable to provide the minimal food and care that most psychologists believe is necessary for reasonably healthy emotional development.

Even with its emphasis on society's primary institution, on ordinary people, and on the everyday realities of life, family history may still fail to close the gap that separates many of us from our own past. The twentieth century, some have suggested, is the age of alienation. Man, it seems, is alienated from himself, his family, his friends, and his work. Yet little attention has been paid to the alienation of man from his past. Only men, the poet Shelley said, "look before and after and pine for what is not." Without looking to our own past, we would have little sense of personal identity. To know who we are we need to know where we came from and how we got to be what we are. Laden with statistics and social science jargon, much of the new family history makes impenetrable reading. We still await a second generation of work that will present the findings of family historians to a general audience. More important, for those seeking clues to their own past, the new family history offers insights into groups, not individuals, and certainly not the particular individuals who happen to have been our own ancestors.

In the wake of American reaction to Alex Haley's *Roots,* it seems that the exploration of one's own family heritage has become a national preoccupation. Yet until very recently, the exploration of one's own family background has been the exclusive preserve of genealogists. The genealogist does not probe the past to comprehend the experience of social classes, to reconstruct a historical era, to describe significant events, or to discern patterns of change and stability. The primary focus of genealogy is the determination of relationships that prevail within a family—often presented in the form of a "family tree."

In a recent series of articles, Samuel P. Hays has noted that genealogy is no longer dominated by those eager to extend their pedigrees to the Revolutionary War or to find a trace of royalty in their bloodline. The "new genealogy" that is becoming popular among many types of Americans has been less involved in a search for notable ancestors. Indeed, many people today delight in discovering a horse thief or pirate among their progenitors. Practitioners of the new genealogy tend to be most interested simply in the reconstruction of their ancestry. If skeletons were hidden in closets, they now come grinning and rattling out to take their place beside all other family members. Thus, the new genealogists are as likely to move forward to the present as backward to some sought after ancestor. The concerns of the new genealogy converge both methodologically and substantively with those of the new social history. The two disciplines not only draw upon the same sources of information, but also share an interest in tracing the flow of events over time.

The new genealogy and the new social history point toward a fusion of the historical and genealogical approaches to our past. Personal family history unites the concerns of academic family history and genealogy. Combined with the study of professional history to afford breadth and perspective, personal family history helps to bridge the gap between us and our past. Personal family history shares the emphasis of genealogy on the background of our own family. But it shares the emphasis of academic history on obtaining a full knowledge of family life and the relationship of the family to the outside world. Personal family history ranges beyond the reconstruction of family trees, no matter how many branches may be filled in. Those who attempt to do a personal family history would ask the same questions of their own family that historians would ask of the family groups they study. They would draw upon both the sources of genealogy and the oral histories that family members carry with them; and they would benefit from an acquaintance with historical studies of the family.

Any individual can become a historian of his own family. The family member can tap a wealth of intimate history that is beyond the reach of the professional historian. In turn, the work of the interested family member can be of great value to the professional historian. It explores a level of private experience that cannot be found in most historical sources.

To achieve maximum coverage, the family historian should consider his immediate family and the families of any grown children as well as the families of parents, grandparents, and even more remote ancestors. Just as professional historians reconstitute groups of families, so also the family member can construct his family tree and report basic information about the life of each family member. Such information might include: date and place of birth, places of residence, occupations, education, religious preference, and date and place of death.

Second, the family historian can delve into the structure and dynamics of the families being considered. As historical scholarship indicates, among the many issues relevant to this area of inquiry are the size and composition of households, methods of child rearing and discipline, courtship practices, use of time, work assignments, sex roles, economic arrangements, and religious practices.

Third, the family historian can explore the attitudes held by family members. Significant categories of research include attitudes toward courtship, sex, morals, prestige within the family, domesticity, motherhood, fatherhood, work, play, children, the elderly, the "old" country, and the "new" country. If, for example, your grandmother emigrated from Russia fifty years ago, how did she feel about the home country before she left? After she had spent some time in America? Did her attitudes toward the old country change substantially over time? Which customs of the new country did she accept? Which did she reject? Did she retain family legends and myths from the old country?

Fourth, the historian of his family can study the social and geographic mobility of families. How often did the family move? How distant were these moves? Why did they move? Did family members emigrate from a foreign nation? Did family members change their place in the social structure during the course of their lives? Did children do better economically? What options were open to family members?

Fifth, the family historian can investigate the interactions between family life and outside events. He can study both the long-term relationships that develop among families in a given community as well as the influence of particular events on family life. Often events of general interest and significance have profound effects on individual families—war, depression, government policy, natural disasters, technological change, and social conflict. Local events, unnoticed by professional historians, may also shape the experience of particular families—the closing or opening of a factory, the drying up of a well, and changes in the ethnic composition of a neighborhood.

Sixth, the family historian can also investigate the life cycles of individual family members. What types of family arrangements marked different stages of the individual's life cycle? Who influenced the individual most at each stage of life? What options seemed open? What options seem irrevocably closed? Did the individual experience discrimination based on age, sex, religion, race, or ethnic background?

Seventh, the interested family member can compare the experiences of ancestors to the group experiences described by historians. Did your great-grandfather travel west in a covered wagon? How did his life compare to the stories told in textbook accounts of the western migration? Did he experience severe hardship crossing the Rocky Mountains or the Great Plains? Did he carry a gun? Join a vigilante group? Or live in a western boom town?

This brief list is only meant to be suggestive of research possibilities. Many other questions can be addressed by the historian to his own background; and all of these questions have a dynamic dimension, as the historian traces the flow of family life over periods of time. Not only do individuals undergo changes during the course of their lives, but changes also may characterize the life cycles of families.

Nonetheless, most of the questions cited here are not susceptible to easy answers. They require information that may be difficult to obtain. It is always difficult to learn about the internal life of a family or the attitudes held by family members. And the research problems become more vexing as the inquiry recedes from the present.

But the historian of his own family need not undertake a full-scale, time-consuming project. There are many things that can be done by those who are interested in learning more about their family, but who lack the time, resources, or inclination to begin a major project. Families can hold reunions at which relatives are encouraged to swap stories about the family. Family members can construct family trees from information that is readily available. They can collect family letters, photographs, and objects long possessed by the family. If family roots run deeply into a community, the family historian can seek traces of his ancestors in town or church records. Any individual can make a special effort to talk informally with parents and grandparents, asking for interesting stories and anecdotes about their lives. No matter how small the project, it will still be worthwhile.

The more ambitious historian of his own family can exploit a wide range of information. Not only written documents, but also artifacts, photographs, movies, and people have interesting stories to tell. The individual and his family may possess unexpectedly rich sources of information—letters, family bibles, diaries, journals, record books, old furniture, family heirlooms, snapshots, home movies, and even the family dwelling. Public and private repositories—libraries, museums, churches, genealogical societies, historical societies, state and local governments, and the federal government—contain much additional information. Useful unpublished sources include records of births, marriages and deaths, land records, probate records, other court records, military records, school records, tax lists, and passenger arrival lists. The family historian may also benefit from such published sources as family histories and genealogies, local histories, biographies, newspapers and periodicals, or genealogical publications.

The most extensive collections of genealogical materials are located at the National Archives of the United States in Washington, and the Library of the Genealogical Society of the Church of Jesus Christ of Latter-day Saints in Salt Lake City. Probably the most important genealogical documents stored in the National Archives are the census reports for individual Americans, sometimes called the "manuscript census." Federal census reports are available through the census of 1900 (although most of the 1890 reports were destroyed by fire), and some reports are available from the census reports of state governments. Other sources of information available at the Archives include naturalization records, lists of passengers arriving from abroad, passport applications, federal personnel records, records about Indians and District of Columbia residents, and a variety of land and military records. In recent years, the Church of Latter-day Saints has become the prime mover in American genealogy. The holdings of the Genealogical Society's Library include family genealogies, genealogical periodicals, and local histories. The library has records of individual families located in a family record group collection that includes tens of millions of name listings. Moreover, the genealogical society is engaged in a massive effort to microfilm primary sources in genealogy. Their microfilm holdings are available at over 200 branch libraries scattered throughout the United States.

Many family historians, of course, will not have the time, resources, or motivation to exploit the holdings of the National Archives or the Genealogical Society of the Latter-day Saints. Fortunately, much can be learned from the records of state and local governments and the records kept by individual churches. State and local governments usually maintain civil records of births, marriages, and deaths; probate records relating to the disposition of estates; records of land transactions; and records of the civil and criminal courts. It also may be possible to obtain from these units of government school records, tax lists, city directories, and registers of voters. Depending upon the type of record and the state involved, records may be kept on file in the state government itself or held by counties, cities, or towns. Churches as well as state governements may maintain records on births, marriages, and deaths. Church records may also include accounts of removal to or arrival from another congregation, membership lists, confirmation records, records of disciplinary actions, and minutes of church meetings. Some church records

have been compiled, collected, and published; others remain in the posses-
sion of individual churches.

The discovery of new information about your own ancestors is an exhilarat-
ing experience. Yet the family historian who seeks to begin documentary
research should be aware of the difficulties involved. The family historian
must know where to look for information and how to use the information
once it is located. He must learn to cope with problems raised by forms of
handwriting, abbreviations, and spelling; naming practices, missing information, use of foreign language terms; and changes in names, boundaries,
currencies, etc. He may have to travel, spend money, and devote many hours
to squinting at musty records. Before beginning documentary research, the
family historian should plan his project, familiarize himself with the localities
and time periods being considered, consult guides to genealogical and historical research, and if possible, even attend a course in genealogy or family
history. Community colleges, local universities, and state and local historical
and genealogical societies are potential sources of information and instruc-
tion.

For the historian of his own family, oral history is an especially productive
and exciting form of inquiry. Oral history is an attempt to elicit and record
people's recollections of their experiences, ideas, and attitudes. Professional
historians are becoming ever more appreciative of this unique source of
information. Not only are historians intensifying their efforts to interview
society's leaders—Supreme Court Justices, corporation presidents, and No-
bel laureates—but also they are beginning to develop projects for obtaining
the oral histories of ordinary Americans. The most ambitious is the Anonymous Family History Project, cosponsored by the Department of History at
Clark University and the Social Welfare Archives at the University of Minnesota, which is designed to assist students with the preparation of their
personal family histories and to provide facilities for the collection and stor-
age of these histories.

All of us are carriers of fascinating historical information. Yet invariably
most of what we know and remember is lost to posterity. By interviewing
members of his family, one can tap this information and apply it to the
reconstruction of the family's history. Parents, grandparents, children, aunts,
uncles, cousins, brothers, and sisters are storehouses of information and
insights that can be obtained from no other sources. Many of the most
interesting questions about one's background can be answered only by talking
to people. If the historian is fortunate, oral history can help him to learn
about four or five generations of family history.

The recovery of information from family members poses special challenges to the family historian. There are many different ways to design and execute an oral history interview. The strategy followed in each case depends upon the type of information being sought, the characteristics of the person being interviewed, and the nature of the relationship between the family historian and his informant. Unlike the proverbial survey taker, the family historian is talking, not to strangers, but to individuals with whom he may have powerful emotional ties. No family historian can afford to ignore the ways in which he interacts with each person he plans to interview.

In planning an interview, the historian must first decide what he wants to find out from the family member. Interviews can be divided roughly into the topical and autobiographical approaches. The topical approach seeks to obtain information about a particular topic or theme—privacy within the family, sex roles, religion, and ethnic allegiances. An autobiographical interview is not focused on a particular theme but tries to trace the flow of significant events in the individual's life. These events would not be restricted to particular occurrences, such as moving or obtaining a job; they could include any aspect of the individual's life, including his attitudes, the attitudes of those around him, or the structural features of his life (for example, the nature of his job, the composition of his family). Both the family historian and the family member being interviewed could participate in the process of deciding which features of the family member's life should be emphasized in the interview.

Once the family historian determines what he is trying to learn in the interview, he must choose between formal and informal approaches. A formal interview is based on preset questions asked in sequential order, with a minimum of probing or explanation. Informal interviews range from completely nondirective conversations, in which the family member guides the discussion, to interviews built around a flexible set of primarily open-ended questions. Most family historians will want to use some variant of the informal interview. The paramount value of the formal interview is that it achieves greater uniformity than informal techniques and enables a researcher to contrast and compare the responses of many individuals. But the family historian usually is most interested in obtaining the richest possible understanding of the family member's life and experiences. Uniformity and comparability are likely to be of secondary importance since interviews generally will not be used for quantitative analysis.

Entirely nondirective interviews are appropriate when the family historian wants to learn what stands out in the individual's own mind, and he has not yet developed a clear focus for his inquiry. Nondirective interviews may also be appropriate for family members who would be affronted or intimidated by a more structured form of interview. More often, the historian will try to plan his interview to reflect some notion of what he is trying to find out from the family member. He should prepare a series of questions, but be willing to add, delete, or modify questions, and to probe for the clarification or expansion of responses.

Regardless of the particular approach adopted for an interview, the family historian must take pains to prepare the family member for the interview process. He should indicate the purpose of the interview, its approximate length, its procedural format, and its general subject matter. The family historian should also try to reach prior agreement with the respondent about the use of the information obtained and should alert him to the kinds of things that could come up in an interview. But the family historian should also strive not to make the experience seem too formal or foreboding. Each person knows best what methods of persuasion should be used to induce family members to provide complete, accurate, and candid information. If at all possible, both the family historian and his informant should look forward to the interview as an exciting and challenging experience.

The family historian must carefully phrase the questions that form the basis of an interview. Usually the historian will want to ask both closed and open-ended questions. A closed question usually gives the respondent a predetermined set of categories from which to choose his answer. Sometimes categories are not presented to the subject, but his responses are coded by the interviewer into predetermined categories. Closed questions are typically used when the possible answers to a question fall into a limited, well-defined range. For example, questions appropriately presented in this format might relate to religious preference of an individual, the languages he speaks, and the number of individuals that reside in his household. Closed questions also may be appropriate when the family historian seeks to rank responses according to some quantitative distinction. He might ask a family member whether his recreational activities always, mostly, rarely, or never include members of his family. When using closed questions the family historian must make sure that the list of responses covers the entire range of possibilities, and that no response can be fitted into more than one category.

If the responses to a question cannot reasonably be limited to preset categories, the interviewer should use the open-ended format. An open-ended question allows the family member to answer a question any way that he sees fit. He can talk as long as he pleases, provide as much detail as he wants to, tell a story, or select some other form of presentation. For example, the family historian might ask a family member how a particular historical event such as World War I or the Great Depression affected life within his family. Open-ended questions generally require far more intervention by the interviewer than do closed questions. The family historian may want to probe for additional information or seek clarification of particular statements. He may wish to redirect respondents who have strayed into irrelevant areas or to determine the respondent's precise role in the events being described. The family historian may want to juxtapose information obtained from other sources to draw out his subject's personal knowledge. Moreover, responses to open-ended questions may suggest to the historian entirely new lines of inquiry.

Intervention in the interview process must be accomplished with tact and care. The historian must carefully balance the gains of intervention against its potential pitfalls. The interviewer must try not to lead the respondent unduly or to introduce his own biases and preconceptions. He must be careful neither to offend nor embarrass the family member, nor to make him flustered and confused, nor to stifle the free flow of his thoughts. The family historian must always keep in mind that he is not engaged in a dialogue with his subject, but rather is seeking to elicit from him as much pertinent and interesting information as possible.

Regardless of the types of questions he plans to ask, the family historian must pay close attention to the way he words each question. Questions generally should be clear, brief, specific, and phrased in simple language. The meaning of a response is no clearer than the meaning of the question on which it is based. Moreover, an individual cannot respond adequately to a query if he is lost in its complex syntax or bewildered by its arcane terminology. Questions should not reveal the biases of the interviewer, render moral judgments, or lead the family member in particular directions. For example, the question "Did you feel stifled to be an ordinary housewife for thirty years?" suggests to the respondent that she actually was stifled, and denigrates the role of the housewife. The questions asked should never presume information that should be provided by the respondent. In framing questions the family historian may be tempted to beg other questions that need to be answered by the informant. For example, the question "How did it feel to leave your loved ones in Russia and journey to a strange lonely land?" presumes that the individual left loved ones behind and regarded America as a "strange, lonely land." Question begging can, of course, be more subtle. A common error is to word a question so that it implies either that surely things have changed from past to present, or that surely things have remained the same.

In deciding the order in which to ask questions, the family historian usually should begin with the simplest, least challenging types of queries and work his way towards more complex and difficult questions. The interviewer should not restrict himself to safe, inoffensive questions; but he should be careful not to shock or embarrass the respondent. Potentially offensive questions should be saved for the end of the interview. The interview should procede logically and should not exhaust either the family historian or his subject. Ordinarily an hour and a half is about the maximum length for an interview. Another appointment can always be made.

After designing his interview, the family historian must decide how to record the responses he receives. Obviously, the greatest accuracy is achieved by recording the entire interview. But people can be distracted by the whirr of spinning tape; moreover, the transcription of recorded material can be extremely costly and time-consuming. Family historians proficient at taking notes may wish to dispense with the recorder or combine the tape recorder and the note pad. If he decides to use a recorder, he should be thoroughly familiar with the operation of his equipment, and be certain that the respondent does not object to its use.

Before interviewing family members, a family historian should try to pretest his interview scheme. He could practice asking questions with friends or perhaps with other individuals who share his interest in family history. Considerable insight can be gained by actually trying out proposed questions and formats. The experience gained from testing an interview design may suggest additional questions, or demonstrate the need to modify or discard proposed questions. This experience may also lead to changes in the type of interview that the family historian had planned to conduct.

Anyone who tries to use oral history should realize that the information obtained represents the family member's perception of reality. These perceptions will be influenced by errors of recollection as well as conscious and unconscious biases in memory and reporting. Sometimes the individual's perceptions, accurate or not, are precisely what the historian is after. If not, the only effective way to control for distortion and mistakes is to use multiple sources of information. The data obtained from a particular family member can sometimes be cross-checked against documentary information or information obtained from other informants.

Oral history and documentary research are complementary ways of explaining a family's history. Each approach can provide different types of information and act as a means of cross-checking information obtained from the other approach. Research in historical sources helps to suggest the kinds of questions that should be asked in an oral interview, and the results of oral history may suggest leads for documentary research. The family historian should be ready to adapt his research plans to the information uncovered along the way. He should not rigidly adhere to a predetermined program.

Local History

Closely akin to studies of family life are studies of the local communities in which people reside. Local history may treat a neighborhood, a village, a city, or a provincial jurisdiction, such as the American or English county, or the French arrondissement. Local historians insist that like the family, the community organizes and shapes experience. The community, they note, has often determined the options available to individuals and families as well as set standards of conduct and belief. It has performed such functions as maintaining law and order, establishing social control, providing education and vocational training, and offering welfare and other public services. The community has served both to unite people and to divide them, both to forge bonds of loyalty, friendship, obligation, and interest, and to foster suspicion, rivalry, and competition. Some local historians claim that by passing over local communities, national histories obscure the forces that shape the quality of people's lives.

Local history has a venerable tradition in western scholarship, extending back at least to the ancient Greeks. In the Greek world, from about 350 to 250 B.C., local history was the predominant form of historical writing. Scholars from Athens, Lesbos, Argos, Chios, and other city-states wrote accounts of their home cities, crafted according to a relatively strict chronological arrangement and stressing local mythology, cults, and political institutions. Similarly, in medieval Europe, scholars produced chronicles of manors, towns, and provinces. Although these local histories usually emphasized the story of noble families, they also included discussions of notable events, laws, settlement patterns, and land transactions.

In the twentieth century, local history has been forced to struggle for intellectual respectability. In the United States historians long considered local history the domain of patriots, seeking to celebrate the heritage of their town or county, and of antiquarians, unconcerned with historical issues, but enraptured by the task of recording community events and collecting local memorabilia. Too often, amateur local historians drone on for hundreds and hundreds of pages, providing neither analysis nor interpretation.

Since the early 1950's, however, local history has experienced a remarkable resurgence, transforming the discipline almost beyond recognition. What was once a historical backwater has become a gushing tributary of professional as well as amateur history. Although local enthusiasts and antiquarians continue to turn out studies of their communities, the academic historian is now firmly entrenched in the domain. Indeed, local history, like family history, has become a part of the effort to produce a new history. This revival of local history has proceeded roughly along three lines. There are local histories conducted for their own sake, local histories conducted to test hypotheses about broader jurisdictions, usually nation states, and local histories that focus on understanding the processes by which communities grow and develop. Although analytically distinct, in actual practice these lines frequently crisscross and run together.

Among the first and most vigorous advocates of local history in the post World War II period were a small band of English scholars, including H. P. R. Finberg, W. G. Hoskins, and Joan Thirsk; they are often called the "Leicester School," because of their association with the University of Leicester. Members of the Leicester School insist that local history is significant in its own right and is not merely an adjunct to more sweeping concerns. The limited geographic scope of such history does not trouble them. They contend that all historical studies are bound by divisions of time and space and that no one division is more legitimate than another. Even the focus on the nation-state, they note, may reflect peculiarities of our own time. Prior to the Renaissance, they claim, the nation had little meaning in western life; and, indeed, it may be yielding already to multinational institutions. Every community, members of the Leicester School argue, has a life history of its own that illumines the hopes, dreams, struggles, accomplishments, and failures of individuals and groups. Finberg eloquently defends this point of view: "Smaller communities than the nation, local communities, have a history which deserves to be studied for its own sake. . . . Thus the subject matter of local history, as understood by the Leicester school, is not identical either in space or time with the subject matter of national history. It follows that these are two different studies: the one is not a part of the other. The history of Mellstock or Barchester is not a mere fragment splintered off from the history of England: it deals with a social entity which has a perfectly good claim to be studied for its own sake."

Interest in using local history to test hypotheses about broader jurisdictions can be traced largely to the same French demographers and quantitative historians who were so influential in the resurrection of family history. French scholars of the 1950's, concerned with the historical study of population trends, turned their attention to particular towns and villages. For these scholars, local history became the case study—a means of gathering data relevant to answering some question about what was happening within the nation as a whole. For the historian, the locality provides a convenient unit of analysis that seems to liberate him from difficult sampling and retrieval problems, and allows him to mine those local repositories with the richest lodes of historical records. The national hypotheses tested by French students of local history ranged beyond the confines of family studies. As the distinguished historian Pierre Goubert has noted in a review of local history, French regional and local studies have challenged the notion that the nobility were divided into "a hereditary nobility" and a "nobility conferred by appointment." These studies have also reexamined French feudal institutions, methods of farming, crop selection, and the attitudes of peasants toward the French clergy.

Historians of the United States have adopted the case study method of local history to test hypotheses about states, regions, and the entire nation. We noted in Chapter V that studies of cities, towns, and counties in the Colonial period suggest that Colonial society was generally less fluid and open than previous investigators had suspected. Similarly, historians have used local case studies of popular voting in the nineteenth and early twentieth century to suggest that it was not economics but rather the ethnic background and religious affiliations of voters that shaped their choices of parties and candidates. Thus local studies have produced a major reinterpretation of national political history.

The third major trend in the revival of local history is marked by a concentration on the formation, growth, and decline of local communities—how and why they began, how and why they changed over time. Those attempting such developmental histories of communities often combine the Leicester School's concern for the integrity of localities with a desire to venture beyond the particular case, but in a special way. They use the locality as a laboratory for testing general theories of community formation and growth and sometimes make inferences about other similar localities.

This type of local history has been most evident in studies of cities and is an important part of what is often called "the new urban history." Students of urban development draw heavily upon models taken from social science and upon quantitative forms of analysis. Kathleen Neils Conzen has tested the applicability of contemporary theories of residential differentiation to patterns of residence in Milwaukee between 1836 and 1860. Like other "new historians," Conzen was interested in finding out whether social science theories and models that describe and explain today's residential patterns also describe and explain residential patterns from a different historical period. If the contemporary theories do not "fit" the evidence from another period, then the historian may be able to suggest to the social scientist the conditions under which the relationships set forth by the theory actually hold.

Conzen focused on "models of urban structure" that describe the city in terms of such spatial patterns as "concentric rings, sectors, or clusters" and that relate residential differentiation to socioeconomic class, family structure, and ethnic heritage. Conzen used the federal manuscript census, city directories, tax assessment rolls, and contemporary maps to reconstruct the neighborhoods of Milwaukee according to such quantitative characteristics as household size, age, the percentage of school age children, the percentage of school age children actually in school, the mean value of real property, the percentage of those in business or in the professions, the percentage of native-born residents, and the percentage of German and Irish Americans. She also used the statistical technique of factor analysis to reduce the total number of variables that she measured to a smaller group of composite variables or factors that represent features of the neighborhoods. One factor, for example, that was used to represent family structure made it possible to use a single statistical measure that combined within it variables expressing the percentage of school age children, the percentage of children in school, household size, and age. By looking at the geographic distribution of the values of the various factors (e.g., which neighborhoods had high values on the family status factor or on a socioeconomic factor), she could further explore the nature and extent of neighborhood differentiation. Conzen concluded that residential location in Milwaukee could not be explained entirely by any of the prevailing contemporary models. Rather, residential location in Milwaukee resulted from "the interaction of such complex forces" as "chance, site characteristics, economic status, and the locational requirements imposed on ethnic groups," family status, and physical boundaries. Moreover, she noted that the impact of various forces tended to shift over time as the city developed. Conzen warns that models of residential differentiation do seem to be dependent on conditions that vary across time and space. "Nonetheless, the case of antebellum Milwaukee has provided both a caution against facile generalizations about urban social-spatial structure drawn from other times or other places, and an illustration of the advantages to be derived from testing such theories in different historical and geographical contexts."

Her findings also seem to contradict the influential "Turner Thesis" of frontier democracy. In 1893, the historian Frederick Jackson Turner argued that because the organizational structures of cities on the frontier were less rigid than in the East, the native Americans and the various ethnic groups in frontier towns were able to mingle more freely and interact more readily. The frontier towns, therefore, promoted more rapid cultural assimilation and abetted the growth of democratic spirit and practice. Conzen found, however, "a high degree of ethnic clustering, probably greater than that of older cities in the East." This finding is contrary to what one would have expected if the Turner thesis were valid. Thus she speculates that if studies of other frontier towns confirm her findings in Milwaukee, the eastern cities may have come "much closer than the frontier city to being the crucible of Americanization." An additional result of Conzen's local history study well may be to force historians to reconsider a long held assumption about the dynamics of immigration and assimilation in America.

Renewed interest in local history has expanded the scope of historical studies, offering opportunities for both the beginner and the master. Yet historians, in their eagerness to go beyond local history for its own sake, must be alert to the problems involved in trying to use local studies as bases for generalizations about larger areas and jurisdictions.

The study of localities does not resolve problems of sampling for the historian. Rather it introduces its own set of problems. Generally, investigators seeking to draw inferences from a sample of items try to achieve random sampling with respect to all variables that influence the form of behavior being considered. That is, they seek a method of sampling in which the probability of obtaining a score on any relevant variable is equal to the proportion of items with that score in the population as a whole. No one, for example, would try to infer the proportions of people in different occupations in a city by considering only the former occupations of residents in nursing homes. Clearly, age and health influence occupation; the choice of nursing home residents as a sample reduces virtually to zero the probability of selecting young and vigorous individuals. Similarly, the selection of local jurisdictions may not meet the criteria of random sampling for a larger unit—a nation-state—and thus may yield biased results. Conclusions about national rates of infant mortality, based solely on studies of small towns, will not be valid if residence in small towns rather than in large towns, in cities or on farms, has an influence on the mortality of infants.

The same error, in less obvious guise, invades the work of historians who stress the centrality of ethnic and religious affiliations for voting in American elections of the nineteenth and early twentieth century. These historians have relied primarily on the examination of such local units as townships and city wards to discern how different groups voted in particular elections. They have generally selected units roughly homogeneous for the group being studied—for example, nearly all black, all German American, or all Catholic townships. From the breakdown of the vote in these localities, they have inferred the behavior of each group. By its very nature this form of sampling selects only those communities with the highest concentration of the group in question. But the clustering of group members in a particular locality itself may be an important influence on how voters behave. Blacks living in segregated black neighborhoods may vote differently from their counterparts residing in integrated neighborhoods. Moreover, individuals from homogeneous and mixed communities may tend to have different scores on other variables that shape the choices of voters. For instance, German Americans living in ethnic enclaves may tend to be less wealthy than those living in mixed neighborhoods. If wealth as well as ethnic heritage affects voter decisions, then the proportion of German Americans from homogeneous communities voting for a candidate will not be equal to the proportion of all German Americans voting for that candidate. To resolve this problem, the historian not only would have to make a systematic examination of German American communities with varying levels of wealth, but also would have to examine those German American communities with different values on all other variables (such as education or occupation) that may influence both ethnic concentration and voter behavior.

Even if appropriate random sampling could be achieved, inadequate sample size may undermine the process of inference. Random samples offer reliable estimates of behavior only when the sample is large enough so that distortions of selection can be expected to cancel out. Yet historians often are tempted to make judgments from but a handful of cases. Too often respected historians have even generalized from a single locality to an entire state, region, province, or nation. One historian uses his study of a single town in colonial Massachusetts to comment on all New England towns and indeed on aspects of the history of colonial America as a whole. The historian justifies this extraordinary leap of inference by claiming "typicality" or "representativeness" for the town he studied.

The notion of typical or representative cases, however, suffers from several disabling defects. First, historians using the case study method usually deal simultaneously with several different dimensions of behavior. But cases typical for one dimension may not be typical for another. A town's procedures for coping with destitution may be typical of those used by other towns in a region, but its procedures for selecting town officials may be atypical. Second, leaving aside the problem of multidimensional analysis and looking at just one characteristic of a case, the notion of typicality is still vague and misleading. Intuitively, typicality implies conformity to the central tendency of a distribution of cases. But which of the various measures of central tendency best captures the concept of typicality—the mode (representing the category with the largest number of cases), the mean (representing the numerical average), or the median (representing the middle case)? No matter which measure is chosen, variation from locality to locality will be obscured. What is learned, for example, from looking at a case allegedly typical of the economic life of a group of communities ranging from shanty towns to gold coast suburbs? Indeed, the scrutiny of typical cases may be more deceptive than informative except in the rare case of a distribution clustered in a single category or around a single numerical value.

Third, the results of different case studies may not be comparable at all. Obviously problems of comparability may arise when investigators use different definitions and different methodologies. For example, a study of social mobility may not be achieved even when historians strive to study the same variables by the same procedures. As Eric Lampard has noted, even studies that rely on similar occupational categories to chart social mobility across generations may not be comparable because these categories have different meanings in different settings. We would not expect a blacksmith in San Francisco in the 1840's to have the same social status as a blacksmith in Baltimore in the 1940's. Even for the professional occupations, social status may vary considerably over time and geographical setting. Not all doctors enjoy the same income or prestige. Finally, even if acceptable criteria for typicality could be set forth, how can the historian determine whether or not a particular case meets these criteria? An investigator would not know the central tendency of a distribution (using either the mode, mean, or median) until he has examined either the entire population of cases or a large enough sample to yield reliable estimates. At best, he could hope to bridge this gap in his knowledge through deductions from extemely powerful models of behavior. In the social sciences, however, such models remain dreams rather than realities. Moreover, having analyzed a distribution or deployed such a model, what additional insights can be gained from studying the typical case? These reflections suggest that the examination of representative cases is either redundant or unreliable. Rather than worrying about the typicality of the communities they study, the historians should be especially sensitive to variations in the histories of different localities. A major task of historical inquiry is to document and explain such variation.

As with family history, local history can be an exciting field of study for the student or amateur historian seeking a richer sense of the past. A local history could fasten on a single block or neighborhood, a town or village, a farm or agricultural community, or even an entire city or county. It might sweep the entire history of the locality from its founding to the present, or it might carve out a small slice of time. It might try to present the history of the locality as a whole, considering the interrelationship of diverse aspects of experience and both conflict and cohesion within the community of interest. It might focus on the process by which the community grew and developed. It might emphasize one of the traditional categories of history— social history, economic history, political history, or intellectual history. It might consider a particular theme within any of these categories—the means by which members of an agricultural community marketed their crops, the relationships between ethnic groups in an urban neighborhood, or the reform of governmental procedures in a small town. A local history might also explore a particular incident or episode in the history of a community—the founding of a factory, the discovery of gold, the outbreak of a race riot, or the devastation of a flood or fire.

Obviously, the history of the families comprising a community is one aspect of the historical experience of that community. Indeed, some historians and anthropologists have recommended that the histories of communities should be written by tracing the life cycles of individuals and families both from their own perspectives and from the perspective of the community as a whole. Moreover, many of the same sources used to illuminate family history can also reveal other features of local history. Details of local history are preserved in such sources as land records, court records, vital records, tax lists, church records, personal manuscripts, records of schools, records of hospitals and fraternal organizations, records of the manuscript census, published local histories and genealogies, maps, atlases, and gazetteers.

The manuscript census, for example, may not only help the historian to reconstruct the lives of past families, but also may be used to reconstruct a town, a section of the countryside, a block, and a city ward. From the manuscript census, the historian may be able to learn how many people lived in the community, the kinds of homes they lived in, the jobs they held, and the places from which they came. He may be able to calculate rates of population growth and decline as well as changes in racial, ethnic, or economic composition. Even for periods when the manuscript census is closed for reasons of confidentiality, the local historian may be able to use aggregate census reports for this purpose. Moreover, as Conzen did for Milwaukee, the local historian interested in reconstructing communities also may draw upon data from city and rural directories, tax lists, and old maps.

Local directories contain a wealth of information about diverse features of community life. Directories include advertisements that offer glimpses of local styles, tastes and customs, medical practices, the availability of goods, services and transportation, the kinds of jobs people held, and the types of businesses located in the community. Directories have drawings, photographs and etchings of factories, stores, depots, local landmarks, machines, clothing, and other consumer products. In addition to the names, addresses, and occupations of individual citizens, they also may contain maps, addresses of public buildings, places of business, churches, and fraternal organizations. Directories often provide descriptions of local government, of the functions performed by various officials, and of procedures for obtaining licenses and other privileges. Supplementing local directories, state governments publish official manuals that may include considerable information about local jurisdictions within the state. Some manuals publish election returns for counties, cities, and even wards and townships.

Local newspapers evoke even more of the flavor of life in a local community. Newspapers have been published for counties, towns, cities, and even neighborhoods; they have appeared daily, weekly, and bimonthly; and they have catered to entire communities or served such specialized audiences as members of political parties, fraternal organizations, or nationality groups. Local newspapers may be found in public libraries, newspaper offices, local and state historical societies, state libraries, university and even public school libraries. Far more is to be garnered from newspapers than from directories about the ebb and flow of community events. Like directories they contain advertisements and various types of pictorial representations. From their news and feature stories a historian can learn what determines social standing within the community, how people are trained and educated, what they do for recreation, and how they choose their political leaders. From obituary columns, he can glean information about individual residents; from real estate reports, fluctuations in the price of land and buildings; from public announcements, the types of people entering the community; and from editorials and letters, sources of controversy and division. The historian who pages through newspapers may also find such tidbits as recipes, cartoons, sermons, political speeches, bankruptcy notices, and advice to the young.

Reading through an old directory or old newspapers offers an opportunity to engage one's mind in what R. G. Collingwood, probably the most influential philosopher of history in our century, has defined as the historical enterprise, "the imaginative recreation of the past." Few historians, however dedicated to rigorous logic and methodology, despise the chance to use their imaginations to visualize "what it was like." The pleasure of such efforts to "see" the past is enormous. And for many historians, that imaginative pleasure provides much of the motivation to persevere in the often gruelling tasks of research and explanation.

The historian alert to written sources of information also might exploit the specialized reports published by city, town, county, and state governments. The reports of a State Department of Agriculture might include analyses of soil quality, climate, crop production, livestock use, mechanization, and farm income. The report of a Department of Taxation might contain property assessments, license fees, expenditures, and debts of local governments. Moreover, governments often publish or at least save in manuscript form records of legislative debate and judicial proceedings.

In addition to written records, the local community itself, both its natural setting and its man-made features, is a document to be read and interpreted by local historians. The local historian, then, can also be an archaeologist, but with a significant advantage. Our local communities do not usually lie buried beneath several feet of dirt! To guide tours of a community, maps available from the United States Geological Survey cover the nation on a scale of 1 inch to 2,000 feet. These maps are comparable to a view from a low flying airplane and reveal such details as homes, barns, factories, railroad stations, street patterns, county roads, highways, railroad tracks, ponds, swamps, fields, and forests. Moreover, the local historian may be able to obtain commercial maps covering the community at various times. The historian also should consult local residents and use the written sources at his disposal. Field work and library work are complementary aspects of the same enterprise.

Today's concern with ecology should highlight the importance of a community's environment. The local historian can learn a great deal simply by going out and looking at the natural setting of a community. He should pay attention to the climate, to the type and quality of the soil, to such sources of transportation as rivers, lakes, and mountain passes, to the availability of water and power, to physical boundaries like seashores, swamps, and hills, to prevailing types of vegetation, to animal life, and to natural resources like timber, silver, and iron. The local historian always must be aware that land and climate as well as buildings and streets change over time. He should be looking for clues about how the environment has changed. What appears to be a treeless plain once may have been covered with forest; what appears to be a dry river bed once may have sustained the livelihood of an entire neighborhood. The quest to understand a changing environment will lead the historian back to the written record—to newspapers, land records, maps, government reports, and the records of extension schools and agricultural colleges.

The layout of a community is also a compelling source of information about local history. The subdivision of land into farms, home plots, streets, residential and commercial districts, and the courses traced by roads and highways reveal much about the form of early settlement and the pace and pattern of later growth. Is agricultural land divided into neat, square lots or into parcels of irregular shape? Is there a boundary line at which the division of land shifts into new configurations? Does the street plan of a city reveal breakpoints or points of transition where one grid of streets collides with another? Does the break signify grids with different functions, areas settled at different times, or perhaps the merger of once separate jurisdictions? How is territory within a town or city partitioned—by wealth, by ethnic background, by race, or by occupation? What provisions have been made by a community for internal transportation and access to the world outside?

No local historian can afford to ignore messages transmitted by the places where people reside, work, play, worship, and bury their dead. Much about how people lived can be learned from looking at their homes. Americans have long been concerned with describing and preserving especially venerable or opulent homes, or the residences of the notable. But the local historian wants to explore the homes of ordinary people as well. In examining a home, the historian will want to ask: When was it constructed? What materials and methods were used? What style of architecture was adopted? How many rooms does it contain? How large are they? How do they connect with each other? What functions do they seem to serve? How much land does the home include, and how is it landscaped? How is the home heated, cooled, and lighted? What kind of furniture does it have? How old is the furniture? What alterations and additions have been made over time? How have the functions of rooms changed over time?

Not to be slighted in surveys of where people lived are apartment houses as well as private homes. The archeologist of the apartment house may add to his inquiry questions about how many floors there are and how much living space each apartment has. If the apartment house has an elevator, when was it installed? Do individual apartments have their own bathrooms? Was this always the case? What provisions are made for ventilation and the disposal of waste? Is there yard space or recreational facilities?

The places where goods and services are produced, bought, sold, and transported also have stories to tell. They can tell us about the conditions under which people worked, the kinds of tools and machinery they used, the routines they followed, the skills they possessed, the items they produced, and the services they offered. They also contain information about the technologies used at different times and varying arrangements for marketing and distributing goods. The historian who prowls through an old cotton mill might be able to see the amount of space allotted to the spinners, the positions in which they worked, and the tasks they had to perform. He might be able even to imagine the noise and smells of the place, its lighting, and ventilation. An old mine or quarry might disclose methods used for extracting minerals or stone and transporting them to the nearest railroad junction or port. A blacksmith's shop or foundry might reveal the tools of the metalworking trade, the products manufactured by the smith, the types of workers he employed, the forge he used, and the fuel by which he kept his fire going. Shops, markets, and offices might indicate specialization in wholesale and retail trade, the internal organization of local firms, and the physical clustering of types of businesses.

From places where people live and work the local historian must turn to the places where they inter their dead. Inscribed on gravestones and monuments are names, dates of birth and death, and statements of relationships. The historian can construct rough mortality tables, family trees, and naming patterns from this data. These inscriptions might also describe notable events in the community or the special achievements of individuals. Moreover, cemetaries are themselves cultural institutions—places for educating and inspiring the living as well as burying the dead. The size and shape of headstones and monuments, the use of tombs and sarcophagi, and the images engraved in stone all reflect people's religious beliefs, their philosophies, and their notions of status and prestige. Aspects of a community's shared culture or that of a group within the community emerge from the layout of a cemetary, the blend of nature and artifacts, the names chosen for the cemetary, its streets and lanes, the use of fencing, ornamentation, and the display of sculpture.

The local historian should not forget that streets, buildings, farms, and even private homes have names. And names offer us quick transportation into the past. The name of a street might reveal how it was settled, the kinds of businesses it once sustained, the social standing of its residents, and its location near landmarks or natural features since obliterated. Changes in names may accompany transitions in the history of a street or neighborhood —political or social strife, new forms of transportation, or a different distribution of population.

Those who explore the city, the town, and the countryside need not rely solely on memory. They can record what they see, hear, touch, and smell through written reports, sketches, rubbings, tape recordings, photographs, even movies. Although photographic reproduction may seem most accurate and striking, the camera may distort perspective, size, shape, and distance, or alter impressions of color, tint, and shading. The historian must be careful to take photographs from different viewpoints and to supplement photography with other forms of record keeping.

We have been describing what is essentially a kind of local archaeological inquiry. Archaeology is regarded by many as a rather romantic pursuit and often conjures up images of temples, pyramids, and lost cities. The romantic quality of archaeology is undeniable, but one need not trek off to distant lands to enjoy its pleasures. The study of a local community offers equal opportunity for the excitement and discovery associated with excavations that explore antiquity. Indeed, the personal pleasure may be enhanced by one's own ties to the community being investigated.

Local historians as well as family historians must tap the history that people carry with them. Many intimate details of community experience can be gleaned only from local residents. People obviously can recount events and episodes they lived through or heard about from friends and relatives. They can relate community legends and gossip, describe what buildings, streets, and factories once looked like. They can report local customs and ways of life since abandoned. They can talk about the work they did, the clothes they wore, the food they ate and prepared, and the stores and shops they visited. Local residents can relate tales about the rise and fall of families within the community, neighborhoods that changed, businesses since discontinued, farms paved over, and mines run out. They can tell how the community responded to the influx of newcomers, to use of the automobile, and to industrial growth. Local informants can also lead the historian to collections of documents or physical remains.

After completing an ambitious program of research, the local historian or the family historian might wonder what in the world to do with all that material. Several options are open. The historian of his community or family simply might decide to organize and maintain the data he has collected as a mini–archive of local or family history. He could try to make this information available to others and to arrange meetings at which his findings were discussed. He might decide to write up his findings in essay or perhaps even book form. The author of such work could distribute it to friends and relatives or seek private, scholarly, or commercial publication.

Those engaged in probing local or family history need not labor in isolation. The American Association for State and Local History disseminates information on state and local historical societies, publishes *History News* (a magazine for local historians), and various technical pamphlets. Through their local historical societies, individuals can set up projects in local and family history. They can share ideas and information and receive encouragement from others engaged in similar enterprises. Local and family history projects also can be integrated with the curricula of schools, or become part of activities organized by social or fraternal organizations.

Those who actually reconstruct their family or local history need not be persuaded that history is relevant to their own lives. History this close to home brings you in touch with your personal heritage. It establishes contact across generations, building respect and tolerance. It transforms ordinary features of the community into exciting historical records. Even without formal academic training, the family or local historian can know firsthand the joy of discovering information long since forgotten, and of transcribing recollections that otherwise would be lost forever. And the subjects of local and family history are connected to the historian by strong bonds of emotion. The process of discovery may help the historian understand his own identity and perhaps even change the way he regards himself and relates to his family, his friends, and his environment.

VII

Historical Research:
The Detective at Work

"In the third week of November, in the year 1895,"
Sherlock Holmes' equally gifted brother Mycroft demanded that the detective drop his "usual petty puzzles of the police-court" to solve a case vital to the nation's security. "Why do you not solve it yourself, Mycroft?" Holmes asked his brother. "You can see as far as I." "Possibly," Mycroft replied. "But it is a question of details. Give me your details, and from an arm-chair I will return you an expert opinion. But to run here and run there, to cross-question railway guards, and lie on my face with a lens to my eye—it is not my métier." Unlike Mycroft, historians do not enjoy the luxury of remaining in armchairs while others supply them with evidence required to solve the puzzles of their discipline. Like Holmes, they must scurry here and there for clues to the mysteries that command their attention.

"The Case": Questions

Without an intriguing case to solve, Holmes' life lacks direction. He scrapes listlessly at his violin, paces his Baker Street rooms, and even reaches for the seven per cent solution. But given a problem with "points of interest," the detective is transformed. The sagging lines disappear from his face; he becomes taut, eager, aware of exactly what he must do, and precisely how he should proceed. The historian who has not defined his problem would be as aimless as the detective without a case. Only after he poses research questions will the historian know where to begin, what to look for, and what to do with what he finds.

Since history includes all experience, researchers can explore virtually any subject of interest. No area of human endeavor is too grand or too mundane. In addition to such familiar topics as political history, historians can concentrate on such themes as family life, race relations, deviance and crime, sports and leisure, sexual practices and mores, science, and technology. Obviously, a researcher cannot simply leap into the middle of subjects as vast as these. Rather, he must channel his interests into a workable and manageable topic.

A topic for a research paper or even a monograph must be narrow enough for the historian to complete the work in a reasonable amount of time and reach specific, detailed, and reliably supported conclusions. Historians should strive to undertake research relevant to answering significant questions about the past. But an excessively broad project is likely to end in highly speculative conclusions or safe generalities. Those who try to say too much often finish by saying little of value.

Excessively broad historical questions can be narrowed chronologically, geographically, thematically, and evidentially. Assume that a historian wants to probe racial attitudes of black Americans. To convert this interest into a successful research project, he might decide to limit his inquiry to the years from the end of Reconstruction (1877) to the turn of the twentieth century. Then he might choose to study only blacks living north of the Mason-Dixon Line and only black leaders. He might further decide to focus specifically on their attitudes toward black separatism. Finally, he might choose to examine only the evidence pertaining to a single black leader or to a small group of black newspapers.

A researcher should be on guard against topics that seem to be well-focused yet contain the seeds for vast expansion. A research proposal might call for background knowledge beyond one's easy grasp or for mastery of sophisticated methodology. For example, a historian seeking to study family life in a small town might find it mandatory to familiarize himself with what sociologists and psychologists have written on the family and with quantitative procedures for collecting and analyzing data on the structure and composition of families. Historians studying sparsely documented societies realize how easy it is to acquire a false sense of security from the small and apparently manageable amount of evidence available to them. For example, the number of references to infanticide in classical antiquity might take only about fifteen or twenty pages to reproduce. But the problem of drawing reliable inferences from ancient sources is so great that a single paper should probably treat either Greek or Roman infanticide, not both.

Historians must also try to make sure that they can find the evidence needed to complete a research project. Evidence crucial to the project may not exist or may be inaccessible. For instance, a historian interested in black attitudes toward separatism might want to investigate what a town's leading black citizens thought about this issue, but discover that these men left no records of their views. If he chooses instead to examine the editorials of black newspapers, again he may be frustrated if the newspapers are located only in the Library of Congress in Washington, D.C. (unless, of course, he lives nearby). If he then decides to investigate the personal papers of an influential leader, he may find that he needs the permission of the man's heirs to use them; or, if he is able to examine them, he may find little discussion of black separatism. Experienced researchers take time at the beginning of their research projects to find out what evidence is available, whether they can gain access to it, and what information it is likely to yield.

Thus the very first steps in formulating a research topic are to ask and answer the following questions. What subject do I find interesting? Why is it worth investigating? Is this subject too broad to be handled in the time and space available? If so, how can I narrow it down to a manageable size—chronologically? geographically? thematically? evidentially? Does research on this topic demand any special expertise such as knowledge of another discipline or another language, or such special tools of research as quantification? Finally, is the available evidence sufficiently abundant and pertinent to explore the topic thoroughly?

Once the historian has chosen a workable topic, he must frame specific questions to guide his research. Topic selection and question framing are distinct activities. Too often, inexperienced researchers believe they are ready to go to work as soon as they have settled on a topic. Not so. The simple decision to work on the marriages of King Henry VIII of England does not tell the researcher what he is looking for. Is he interested in the shoe sizes of Henry's wives? In Henry's battles with the papacy over divorce? Or in the relationship between the King's foreign policy and his marriages? Without specific and well-defined questions to guide him, the researcher would not know whether to pay attention to the feet of Henry's wives, to papal pronouncements, or to diplomatic correspondence.

Even a seasoned researcher must do some preliminary reading in the historical literature on his general topic before he can frame the specific questions he wants to answer. Surveying existing scholarship often will indicate which questions have been satisfactorily answered, and which still demand more thought and work. Irrespective of how much time a historian gives to reading what others have written, he should not plunge into his research before he has framed specific and well-defined questions to guide his inquiry. In specifically phrasing and defining the terms of questions, a historian usually uncovers contradictions and ambiguities in his thinking, and determines more precisely what he wants to learn from the historical evidence. Only by submitting himself to a rigorous session of question framing can the historian guard against: (a) wasting time reading material that is not germane to the topic, and (b) being misled by red herrings.

The first task is to posit a question and then define the terms of the question. For example, an historian interested in the governance of ancient societies might try to decide whether the government of fifth–century Athens was truly democratic. But he ought not to rush over to the library and check out boxloads of books without considering first what he means by "the government of fifth–century Athens" or "truly democratic." If by "government," he means "how major decisions were arrived at," he will be seeking quite different data than if he means "how Athenians accomplished day-to-day administrative tasks." As we argued in Chapter III (Historical Explanation), many problems and disputes can be avoided if historians carefully phrase their questions and define all controversial terms. For historians and their readers, definition of terms is vital. Too often historians have had one definition in mind while their readers have had quite another.

Explicit and precise definitions avoid both confusion and misunderstanding. One person's notion of what "truly democratic" means might be quite different from another's, since there is no one correct way to define this phrase. At the very least, the historian must set forth the criteria that guide his understanding, for the results of the research enterprise can be significantly shaped through manipulation of definitions. When a player makes up the rules of his own game, he usually wins. Readers at least should be informed of the rules before they choose to enter the game. The question "Was the government of fifth–century Athens truly democratic?" could be reworded as, "How often were major questions of foreign and domestic policy decided by majority vote in the popular assembly of fifth–century Athens?" or as, "Were the magistrates of fifth–century Athens held accountable for their actions by the popular assembly?" While these questions reflect particular notions of democracy, they at least specify the criteria used by the historian.

Even though the questions that guide historical research should be precisely worded and carefully defined, they should not predetermine an historian's findings. Every historical question depends on assumptions that are accepted as true and thus are not considered part of the inquiry. Without such assumptions, historians would be forced in every study to reexamine all that they think they already know. Research would grind to a halt. On the other hand, historians should take pains not to dismiss in advance questions that require fresh research and analysis. In framing questions, historians must carefully decide what can be assumed and what should be investigated. Typical assumptions include whatever theory an investigator is applying rather than testing in his work, factual assertions that pose no controversy, and factual assertions assumed to be true in order to focus and sharpen an inquiry.

When an historical question incorporates an unjustified assumption, a critic may claim that the question begs another question that needs to be answered by research. David Hackett Fischer has described one striking form of question begging as "the fallacy of false dichotomous questions." Dichotomous questions limit the results of inquiry to only one of two possible answers; the very wording of the question excludes all other responses. Among the examples of published works that are premised on false dichotomous questions, Fischer cites the following:

> "The Abolitionists: Reformers or Fanatics?"
> "The Robber Barons—Pirates or Pioneers?"
> "Martin Luther—Reformer or Revolutionary?"
> "What is History—Fact or Fancy?"

While dichotomous questions make catchy titles, they often blind us to the more complex character of the real world. The detective's credo, "Suspect everyone," is an apt reminder that if the question asked seems to exclude possible responses, the historian has probably prejudged the case; the innocent may suffer and the real culprit go undiscovered.

Another form of question begging is to assume without good reason the truth of factual statements that may be false or highly questionable. A historian studying the Watergate affair might ask, "Who was it that deliberately erased over eighteen minutes of the tape?" The question itself presumes that the erasure was deliberate. The historian who proceeds according to this assumption might overlook evidence that suggested an accidental erasure. However unintentionally, he may have closed his own path to open inquiry.

Care and foresight in question framing not only will save the historian hours of labor at research, but also will sharpen his nose for the scent of the trail he wants to follow. The questions the researcher sets out to answer should be:

1. Open-ended, so as not to prejudice the conclusion before the research has even begun.
2. Free of potentially false assumptions.
3. Clear and explicit in their definition of important terms.
4. Testable, i.e., able to be answered with empirical data that are available to the researcher.

Although a historian has formulated a feasible research topic, he cannot thereby feel free to pursue his research to completion. He must first ask, "What related information do I need to know before I can answer my major question?" Like a detailed travel itinerary, supplementary questions can guide the historian through the process of research, leading him to sources of information and insight. Framing useful supplementary questions requires attention both to the substance of a historical problem and the generalizations used to infer historical reports and to devise historical explanations.

Thus the historian probing attitudes of black leaders toward racial separatism in late nineteenth–century America might examine such distinct issues as higher education; black migration; the formation of black communities, churches, and fraternal orders; or black emigration to Africa. Analysis of any one of these issues will probably lead to the posing of several supplementary questions. For instance, in considering the issue of higher education, the historian might ask, what did prominent blacks think about separate college education for black people? about emphasizing vocational skills? about white financial contributions to black institutions? about white influence in the administration of black colleges? But to answer these questions, the historian must decide how to infer what black leaders actually thought. Public and private statements about an issue do not always correspond. What inferences could reliably be drawn from personal letters and diaries, as opposed to newspaper editorials, public speeches, statements given at conventions, sermons, and political tracts? Moreover, if the historian ventures to explain differences in the beliefs of the leaders he is studying, he might use models that suggest considering such diverse factors as childhood experience, education, occupation, religious affiliation, or ancestry. Different sources might contain information on each of these separate features of a particular leader's life. The historian should develop a detailed list of supplementary questions and identify the specific sources of historical evidence needed to answer them.

Those unfamiliar with topic selection, question framing, and development of supplementary questions would be well-advised to consult with more experienced researchers at an early stage of the research project. Our own experience has shown that beginners often get themselves in great difficulty precisely because they have not devised clear, open-ended, and testable questions. They have stacks of note cards or pages full of research notes but no way to make any sense of the materials, because only muddled, implicit questions guided their research. Researchers who find themselves in this plight should not only reexamine their questions, but also seek counsel from more seasoned historians.

Modifying and elaborating historical questions is a process that goes through the full life cycle of a research project. No clear boundary line divides the framing of questions from the performance of research. Throughout a project, information and ideas gleaned from other historians' work and from primary and secondary sources should prompt the historian to revise, add to, or even discard questions previously asked, and sometimes to reinterpret information previously gathered. But the historian should take special care to assess his work at the four pivotal stages of a research project: (1) after compiling a bibliography; (2) after examining source material suggested by the original plan of study; (3) after formulating an outline; and (4) after composing a first draft.

Merely compiling a bibliography may alert the historian to a need to modify his research topic. A superabundance of primary, secondary, and tertiary sources may mean that he should pare down his topic. Too little evidence will probably require recasting his research question or searching for another topic.

Research may uncover sources not previously known to historians or produce information that suggests novel interpretations. Assume that a historian began his work with the question, "What happened to gladiators after their days in the Colosseum were over?" Once into the evidence, he might discover that the sources indicated that, like latter-day pitching coaches, ex–gladiators taught new men the skills of their trade. In the light of the evidence, he might then reformulate his question to, "Of those gladiators who survived the dangers of their first career, what proportion carried on in the sport as coaches? Did they have any other sources of livelihood?" Further exploration might indicate that to ascertain what proportion of ex–gladiators became teachers of the sport, he would need to comb such sources as Tacitus, Suetonius, and Petronius, and compile a list of ex–gladiators that divided them into two categories—those who became teachers and those who did something else. Because his main question also asks what other employment options were available, his list of those who did something else should include what else they did. Then he might try to find something about the nature of the alternative occupations ex–gladiators pursued and how these men became engaged in their second jobs. Did they find work with relatives? Did they sustain themselves by accepting the favors of their former fans? Did they work on low prestige jobs, such as that of bath attendant? Did the jobs they found require any training or special skills? What kind of pay did nonteachers receive? Was there competition for positions as coaches of new gladiators? Did some pursue other careers because they could not be a gladiatorial teacher?

Framing an outline and composing a first draft do not necessarily complete the research phase of a historian's work. All contingencies cannot be accounted for in advance, and few historians tie up all the loose ends of their research before they begin to write. Serendipitous finds may suggest new sources of information or require the reexamination of data already considered. And the very process of developing an outline and writing a first draft will often disclose issues needing further investigation or suggest additional evidence requiring inspection. For instance, a historian studying the enforcement of antitrust laws by the United States Department of Justice might find while writing that individual Presidents had a far more important role in antitrust policy than he had anticipated. Only by returning to collections of presidential papers, therefore, will he be able to grapple satisfactorily with his question.

Historians must take a flexible approach to the process of research. How they frame questions will guide what they look for in historical sources, but what their inspection of sources reveals may influence the questions they end up asking. At any point in an investigation, the data uncovered may impel the historian to shift the emphasis of his inquiry, to redefine his original topic, to expand or contract it, or even abandon the project in favor of a new one.

"The Informers": Bibliography

Although familiar with every nook and cranny of London and every trick of the criminal mind, Holmes does not rely solely on his own knowledge as a guide to relevant clues. Like most good detectives, he draws judiciously on a small cadre of trusted informers. There are the "Baker Street irregulars," a band of young boys who "can go everywhere, see everything, overhear everyone." There is Porlock, a distant associate of Moriarity, who offers information of "that highest value which anticipates and prevents rather than avenges crime." And there is the uncanny bloodhound Toby, whose help Holmes deemed more valuable than "that of the whole detective force of London." Similarly, the historian's own particular variety of informers—

reference librarians and bibliographic aides—point the way to relevant source material.

The process of refining a topic and formulating subsidiary questions proceeds in conjunction with the compilation of leads to sources of information. Usually historians begin at the library, making the acquaintance as soon as possible with the indispensable reference librarian. Reference librarians have been trained specially to help scholars find what they need quickly and efficiently. The researcher who goes to a reference librarian with specific inquiries will usually discover someone able and eager to direct him to relevant bibliographic aids. A researcher should acquaint himself with the nuts and bolts of major reference tools. Since no one bibliographic reference work can handle all of man's past, most tend to concentrate on specific historical periods, topics, or geographical regions. John R. M. Wilson's *Research Guide in History* offers a useful introduction to bibliographic aids for historical research.

To supplement bibliographic works, researchers should also investigate the library's main card catalogue. Most libraries maintain a subject index as well as an author–title index. The questions the historian asks should provide him with a guide through the subject headings. For example, to discover sources relevant to determining how President Harry Truman reached his decision to recognize Israel in 1948, the historian would obviously peruse such headings as "Truman," "Israel—History," "United States—Foreign Relations," or "United States—History." Librarians try to include as many books under a subject heading as possible, but subject indices in card catalogues cannot be exhaustive. Particular sources relevant to the research question may be found under only one of the several headings.

A historian's bibliographical search should encompass primary, secondary, and tertiary sources—evidence that was part of an event being investigated, firsthand accounts of the event, and historical reconstructions and interpretations of the event. Depending on the project in question, different reference works may be consulted for different categories of source material. Historians should be aware that many valuable tertiary works are unpublished, such as doctoral and masters dissertations, and papers presented at scholarly conventions. Abstracts of doctoral dissertations are published by the University of Michigan in *Dissertation Abstracts*.

Historical books, articles, and dissertations are themselves valuable bibliographical aids. Many include bibliographies of relevant sources as well as footnote citations. Given the contemporary explosion of historical publications, recent articles or dissertations may provide the historian quick access to the latest work on a particular subject. Moreover, many historical journals publish review essays or historiographic overviews of particular topics. The development of bibliography proceeds in a progressive fashion, with each consulted work suggesting yet other sources and, in turn, some of those sources providing yet other leads. As the historian adds more and more items to his bibliography, usually he will find that new items yield fewer and fewer leads.

Once the researcher begins to explore bibliographic sources, he must decide how to collect the bibliographic data in a way that will be useful and convenient for research. Historians generally employ one of two systems—the notebook or the file card. Each has its own advantages; choice of one over the other is usually a matter of personal taste. Those who use the notebook claim for it primarily the convenience of having all one's bibliographic sources in one place; unless the whole notebook is lost, one never loses track of individual entries. Those who prefer the file card system argue that a notebook is bulky whereas file cards can be carried around easily. Indeed, one can keep a few blank cards in a pocket or purse to jot down promising leads whenever or wherever one finds them. Also, a file card system allows the researcher to sort out his leads by categories; file cards can be rearranged easily—a notebook cannot.

A few simple rules apply equally well to both systems of reference. First, take down the full bibliographic citations of both the bibliographic source and of the material found in the source. A full and correct record of this material spares the historian trips back to the library when putting together the final version of a research paper. Second, do not rely on title alone to judge which books or articles include useful ideas or information. In many bibliographic aids and on most cards in a catalogue, reference to a work is accompanied by a short description of its contents. Read the descriptions before deciding to list or pass over a particular work, remembering that an incomplete survey of scholarly literature can lead to duplicating the work of others, neglecting the accomplishments of others, or failure to pursue a promising line of research. Most historians prefer to err on the side of inclusion.

However, experienced researchers know that bibliographic information alone will not tell a historian whether a proposed project can actually be accomplished. The success of a project may turn upon gaining access to a restricted collection of personal papers, to the records of a government agency or private organizations, or to one or more oral interviews. Often access cannot be determined without first contacting the custodians of sought after material or the subjects of prospective interviews. Moreover, the historian may not be able to ascertain from bibliographic citations whether sources of evidence are rich enough and comprehensive enough to sustain a research project. This determination may require actually investigating the sources or, at least, consulting with those familiar with them. Needless expenditure of time and resources can be avoided by communicating with those in charge of a historical site or a collection of records, asking for copies of detailed descriptions and finding aids, and talking to other scholars who have already explored the site or combed through the records.

"The Game": Data

The work of framing questions and compiling a bibliography leads to the heart of a research project—the systematic scrutiny of historical evidence and scholarly literature. For Holmes, "The game is now afoot." Though the historian prowls the archives rather than the streets of London, though he pursues historical truth rather than Professor Moriarity, the thrill of the hunt may be the same nonetheless. The historian must know where to track his quarry. Holmes would not have looked for evidence about an aristocratic family in the East End or Soho; nor would he have searched for a lady of the night in Buckingham Palace. The trick in finding pertinent evidence lies in knowing where to look. Like the detective, the historian must know what sources of evidence are most likely to provide the kinds of information he seeks and where to find them.

The search for historical evidence usually centers on a library or repository. Libraries contain the published secondary and tertiary sources crucial to most inquiries—books, newspapers, and scholarly and popular journals. Libraries and such repositories as national and local archives, historical societies, and museums house collections of documents and artifacts that may be unavailable anywhere else. Too often, however, historians confine their search only to libraries and similar repositories. The library with its card catalogues, bibliographic aids, shelves of books, periodicals, microfilm, and the like is an obvious starting point; but it need not, and in many cases should not, be the sole place for research. No detective works from an armchair alone—he surely investigates the scene of the crime. And as we argued in Chapter II, the historian must remember that historical evidence is anything that can be used to draw inferences relevant to his investigation. Thus, in the previous chapter on Family and Local History, we showed what can be learned from such sources as the layout of streets, the structure of buildings, the tools people worked with, and the machines they operated.

The historian investigating a topic in political history is the most likely to have a relatively full range of evidence pertaining directly to his subject. Apart from the materials in public archives (the repositories of small political units such as towns, counties, individual public agencies, as well as those of national or federal governments), the political historian can draw on memoirs, newspapers, and other contemporary accounts; and for the recent past, he has access to recordings and films of key figures and events. For example, the National Archives and Records Service of the United States contains Japanese, German, and American photographs of the Second World War. Many institutions—both private and public—will duplicate records, often at a nominal cost, or make available microfilm copies for loan or purchase. Researchers should also be aware of the growing number of personal and official papers being edited and published. Most major libraries should have such published works as *The Papers of Woodrow Wilson, The Gladstone Diaries, The Foreign Relations of the United States,* and the *Corpus Iuris Canonici.*

It might seem that political historians of the modern era would flounder in a sea of evidence. But the sheer quantity of material is not the only difficulty they face. Most government agencies classify many of their documents. All too frequently, governments classify documents as secret with no genuine national security reason for doing so. Other evidence may be available only to a few "official" or "friendly" historians. Moreover, as the last few years have made obvious, governments are not above altering documents, destroying documents, or creating documents to serve their own interests. The historian who comes along later often has virtually no way of knowing which documents represent survivals of what actually occurred, which documents have been selectively edited or even forged, and which documents have been suppressed or destroyed.

In addition, much of the communication within a government or between governmental agencies is simply not written. With the widespread use of the telephone, many crucial decisions are made orally; with a few exceptions, these conversations are lost to history. Even though political historians of the recent past can obtain far more evidence than historians of other periods, the quality and comprehensiveness of that evidence may be suspect.

The political historian also must be aware that different sources are likely to contain different kinds of information about the events to which they pertain. A historian working on British diplomatic history, for example, will find in the *British Parliamentary Papers* (also called the *Sessional Papers*) abundant data about that nation's foreign relations. Beginning in the early nineteenth century, these *Papers,* published yearly in multivolume series, contain much correspondence between the British Foreign Office and its ambassadors and other imperial and Commonwealth officials. The *Papers* are selectively edited, however, usually leaving out any material that might be detrimental to the conduct of British diplomacy. They may disclose the official rationale for policy decisions, but are likely to reveal little about the attitudes and interests that so often affect the formulation and execution of foreign policy. To gain more insight into policymaking or diplomacy, researchers must consult other diplomatic series as well as the British archives. Each year the British government issues a collection of diplomatic documents, titled *Confidential Prints,* to apprise policymaking officials of all that had transpired in the previous year. Closed to public inspection for thirty years, the *Prints* are categorized by geographical region and include all correspondence between the Foreign Secretary and the ambassadors and his correspondence with other members of the Cabinet. Compared to the *British Parliamentary Papers,* the *Prints* are likely to reveal more about the motivations of officials and the process by which decisions were made. Even though the *Prints* are extremely rich sources, containing much of what is in the archives themselves, the historian should consult the full archival record in any thorough study of British diplomacy. Finally, a historian seeking to uncover a diplomat's personal beliefs and attitudes should investigate whatever private papers are available. Only private papers are likely to include material sufficiently frank and candid to justify inferring how a diplomat's attitudes toward foreign peoples or his views on domestic politics may have influenced his policy recommendations and conduct.

Historians working in social history must generally be prepared to deal with a wide variety of sources, each one of which has a relatively low yield. A social historian might find that the evidence he seeks is scattered throughout a wide range of material—novels, magazines, artifacts in museums, paintings, photographs, newspapers, archaeological reports, surviving buildings, census lists, and government reports on taxation, sanitation, or public health. Each one of these different kinds of source material is likely to contain only snippets of information of interest to the social historian. No single source conveniently collects evidence relevant to the study of social history, as does the *Foreign Relations of the United States* series for American diplomatic history. Because his evidence usually has a relatively low yield, the social historian usually must cast his net more widely than the political, military, or diplomatic historian.

Moreover, the "silent peoples," whom the social historian often wants to study, have left virtually no written records about themselves. For many periods of western civilization, the masses were nonliterate. Peasants do not write memoirs; the personal papers of even aristocratic women have not been preserved; and from children, we have virtually nothing at all. The social historian must carefully sift written evidence to ferret out the meager number of references to nonelite groups. And he must attempt to compensate for the biases of the documents produced and preserved by the elite. Letters exchanged among plantation owners in the antebellum South, for example, might well illuminate the slave owners' attitudes about slavery, but could not be used to infer the attitudes of slaves toward their masters without first compensating for the attitudes of slaveholding whites. Moreover, the social historian must share the political historian's skepticism about official sources. Reports issued by the director of a hospital or a school will obviously be influenced by the need for public funds and popular support. If possible, the social historian should supplement these reports with the internal records of the institutions, accounts by unofficial observers, letters, diaries, and memoirs.

In part because of the "aristocratic bias" of documentary evidence, social historians often concentrate on the material remains of former societies, as well as on entries in statistical compilations. For example, a social historian of family life might explore such items as toys, child rearing equipment, clothing for men and women, the floor plans of homes, and paintings and sculptures that depict family life. Similarly, as the chapter on new history revealed, the historian may seek to construct quantitative series on groups of families from census lists; tax records; birth, death, and marriage records; wills; and deeds.

Like the social historian, the economic historian must be ready to sift through a large number of different kinds of source material to find information relevant to his inquiry. Considerable information relevant to reconstructing economic life is available, particularly for modern history. Governments often collect information about taxes, spending, land values, trade, and commerce. Moreover, such official records as wills, deeds, and marriage contracts also may yield insights into economic life. Even for so poorly documented a society as Mycenaean Greece, what written evidence we do have—the Linear B tablets—provides information about the economy. The tablets record such things as:

"The estate of the King, seed at so much: 3600 litres of wheat; so
many 'telestai' [land-holders]: 3 men."
"The deserted (?) (land) of the cult association: seed at so much:
720 litres of wheat."
and

"Kokalos repaid the following quantity of olive oil to Eumedes: 648 litres of oil."

Historians should be aware, however, that for most periods and societies, there may be vast gaps in the data collected by governments. Only since the 1930's did the government of the United States begin to collect unemployment statistics. Moreover, official data may not always be accurate. Business firms, for instance, have an incentive to underreport their margin of profit.

Economic historians also have access to another substantial body of valuable evidence—the records of private business and industry. The correspondence, inventories, orders, contracts, and memoranda of businessmen provide a huge repository of information about how and why they made the decisions they did. These same records, together with public archives, are extremely useful to historians interested primarily in the commercial and financial aspects of economic history. Business records, like government data, also may mislead the historian. Published lists of prices, for example, do not reflect necessarily the price actually charged by a company. Economic historians seeking information on prices should try to supplement such material with information in confidential company records, records of purchases, advertisements, and the personal papers of company officials. Moreover, increasing use of oral communication and telephonic decisions plagues the economic as well as the political historian. And businessmen seem no less immune to altering or suppressing the documentary record than politicians or government bureaucrats. Thus the economic historian must handle the evidence produced by the business community as carefully and skeptically as the political historian must treat official state records.

For the economic historian interested in industrial relations and labor history, the problems of obtaining and evaluating evidence are similar to those faced by the social historian. The "elitist bias" of the bulk of documentary material often obscures if not outrightly distorts the attitudes and actions of the working class. The records of organizations representing the interests of labor are of immense value; but the labor historian must remember that the leaders—the elite—of such organizations have produced and preserved the documentation. We can see today that there are often substantial differences between the leadership and rank and file of labor organizations. The historian must not assume à priori a greater identity of mind and purpose for such organizations in earlier periods.

Like the social historian the labor historian must investigate whenever possible the evidence left by the laborers he seeks to understand. Dockhands, machinists, and millworkers rarely leave personal papers. But in our modern, more literate society, workers sometimes keep diaries. More important, they have developed their own cultural vehicles and have expressed their attitudes and values in songs, manifestos, and folklore. Many newspapers and much popular literature are directed mainly to the laboring classes. The labor historian must investigate these and similar kinds of evidence to understand the mentality and social values of the workers of any society.

Historians interested in people's ideas rely primarily on the written word. The intellectual historian investigating the ideas of a single person or group of people is likely to find sources of extremely high yield. A historian investigating the political theory of Cicero could examine Cicero's philosophical treatises, speeches, and correspondence. The intellectual historian must be sensitive to several problems that complicate use of this evidence, however. First, some sources disclose what a thinker said for public consumption, whereas others better reveal that person's private opinions. Cicero's letters to his friend, Atticus, for instance, are likely to contain more candid comments on politics than are his speeches. Second, he must remember that the formal published works of any thinker usually represent the final product of his thoughts, and do not necessarily illumine the process by which these thoughts were distilled from earlier thinking and research. Again, the historian might find in Cicero's correspondence, but not in his published work, an indication of the twists and turns in Cicero's thinking as he wrote his treatises on philosophy. And third, the historian must not assume that an individual's ideas remained constant over time. People change their minds. The ideas cherished in one's youth may be entirely discarded by the time a person reaches middle age. The historian interested in Cicero's political ideas while he was still a young man should confine his investigation to those tracts, speeches, and letters written during those years of Cicero's life. Conversely, the historian seeking to survey the whole of Cicero's thought on politics should be sure to examine sources from different periods of the statesman's life. Third, not all of a subject's ideas may appear in published work. Again, by examining Cicero's private correspondence, a historian may uncover aspects of his thought totally absent from published material.

Even unpublished material must be treated critically. Prominent individuals often expect that later historians will use their private papers as source material. Indeed, Cicero's slave, Tiro, was assigned the responsibility of collecting and maintaining Cicero's correspondence so that it could be published posthumously. In contrast, the richly detailed notes and working papers of the great physicist Sir Isaac Newton seem to be just that; they do not seem to have been prepared to anticipate public scrutiny. Intellectual historians using unpublished sources must exercise the same care and dis-

crimination as political historians working with the private papers of politicians, diplomats, military officers, or administrators.

Researchers intending to use any of the New History methodologies must
be prepared to exploit their evidence in a manner appropriate to those
methodologies. As we indicated in Chapter V, psychohistorians seek information that may be used to apply one or more models of psychology. Unfortunately, much of the data needed to invoke psychoanalytic theories has
disappeared; only occasionally will the historian uncover sufficient information about an individual's early life to apply Freudian theories. Similarly,
quantitative historians may find that the available evidence is not extensive
enough to apply statistical techniques reliably; that there are gaps in the
statistical records, or that statistics are inaccurate. Moreover, he may find that
available statistics, even if reliable, do not reveal precisely what he wants to
learn. The historian may want to determine, for example, the income of
individuals but may know only the sale and rental values of the places in
which people lived.

Once the historian has identified the kinds of source material that are most
likely to provide him with the evidence he needs for his investigation, he is
ready to begin his hunt. But before setting out on the trail of his quarry, first
he must decide how to record and compile his collection of clues. He must
choose a system for taking notes that will make his information readily usable
for outlining and writing his research paper. Again, the two prevalent systems
are the notebook and the file card. For this phase of research, however, the
file card system seems inherently preferable, simply because the cards can be
arranged according to topic or subject matter, facilitating both outlining and
writing. Scholars who use the notebook find it necessary to compile an
elaborate index before beginning to write and then to flip back and forth
through the notebook while writing.

Some scholars attempt to combine the advantages of the notebook and file
card systems. Instead of including the full bibliographic citation on each file
card, they maintain a master list of references with full bibliographic citations
and assign a number to each item on each individual file card; they record
the appropriate number—often with the author's name or some other identifying word—along with the page number for that particular note. When
drafting the final version of the paper, it becomes a relatively simple matter
to work back and forth between the coded file cards and the master list of
references. Whatever system the researcher decides to use, notes should be
kept in an orderly and systematic manner. When writing a paper, nothing
is more maddening than having a vital note but no inkling of where it came
from. The researcher must either throw out the note or spend hours retracing
his steps in the library.

What does one put down in one's notes? Economy should be a guiding principle, but extreme parsimony may render notes incomprehensible later on. An especially terse or cryptic note will probably force one to reconsult the work. Avoid copying long passages. Whenever more than a few sentences verbatim are required, use a xerox or copy machine and jot down a brief description of the main points on a file card or in the notebook. Copying facilities are especially important when a researcher has only a limited amount of time to spend with a collection and cannot take detailed notes. Be sure to keep all copies in one place and indicate on each copy at least the title of the book, article, or manuscript collection from which it was taken. Whenever a verbatim quotation is taken down, make sure the note indicates just that and check the accuracy of the quotation then and there. Some researchers find it helpful to use a bright colored pen to circle direct quotations. Later, when actually writing, there can be no confusion about citing the material in the paper.

If using a notebook, leave a large margin to jot down key words to be used in indexing and commenting about the material. Some scholars find it useful to divide each page in two, one half for research notes, the other for their own commentary. In any event, make sure that personal comments are completely distinguishable from the research notes. No one wants to have to go back to the library to find out who said what.

If using file cards, the usual procedure is to take down only one note on each card. If a file card is laden with several separate notes, the value of the system will be undermined, for they cannot be sorted into subject categories later on.

The mechanics of note taking are far easier to describe than are guidelines for the appropriate contents of research notes. To record information of value and avoid transcribing useless material, research questions must be kept firmly in mind. Indeed, some people write down the research question and supplementary questions in bold letters on a piece of cardboard and keep it in view whenever doing research. This seemingly silly device can be of great help in answering the question, "Has this material anything to do with what I am looking for?" In the early stages of research, even seasoned scholars have difficulty in determining whether a piece of information or an opinion of another writer is germane to their work. When in doubt, take it down; accumulating too much material is preferable to losing valuable information.

Beyond the principles of relevance and economy, scholars subscribe to few general guidelines for recording data. Each researcher gradually gets the feel for taking notes through the experience of doing research. If an apprentice researcher senses flaws in his procedures that cannot be corrected by hewing more closely to the mechanical procedures described above, he should take his notes to an experienced researcher for criticism. Effective and efficient transcribing of information is bound intimately to the kind of research being done; thus, different projects will demand their own form of note taking.

"The Enigmas": Problems

If detective work were as elementary as Holmes so often claims, then Watson would have been able to solve most of their cases. Each case, of course, actually poses baffling enigmas that require a master detective's skill, knowledge, and experience. Possible clues may prove to be red herrings, witnesses may die or disappear, fragments of evidence may resist interpretation, promising leads may fail to materialize, the lessons of one case may be inapplicable to another, and cryptic messages may defy solution. Similar problems test the mettle of historians—forged evidence, missing evidence, fragmentary evidence, low quality evidence, noncomparable evidence, and literary and artistic evidence. Holmes resolves his cases only by confronting the enigmas of crime, and the historian reaches conclusions only by solving or circumventing the enigmas of research.

AUTHENTICATION OF EVIDENCE

On occasion, historians using heretofore unexploited documents and artifacts may have to authenticate the evidence they use. Is a piece of evidence really what it seems to be? Famous forgeries that have puzzled scholars include the Donation of Constantine, the Decretals of Pseudo-Isidore, the Protocols of the Elders of Zion, and the Viking rune stones salted in the plains of Minnesota. The Donation of Constantine, purportedly written in the fourth century A.D., was regarded as an authentic document throughout the Middle Ages. Indeed, the medieval popes had relied on the Donation of Constantine for their claim to secular authority over kings and princes, for the document allegedly records the Emperor Constantine's grant of imperial authority in the western provinces of the Roman empire to Bishop Sylvester of Rome and his successors (only in a later period was the bishop of Rome also called the Pope). In 1431, at the General Church Council of Basel, Nicholas of Cusa exposed the Donation of Constantine as a forgery by identifying a host of anachronisms within it. The document, now believed to have been fabricated in the eighth century A.D., reflects the language, style, and legal and political terminology of that later period, not of the era some four centuries earlier. The authentication of evidence usually requires technical skill and highly specialized knowledge. In Chapter II we briefly discussed some of the issues considered by experts in authentication—the provenance of the evidence, traces of fabrication, and consistency between an artifact or document and similar pieces from the period it purportedly comes from.

AVAILABILITY OF EVIDENCE

The historical record is not intact. Not all the documents, artifacts, and memories that once existed still exist. Not all of those that still exist are within the reach of every historian. Records of local governments, for example, are often incomplete; officials discard quantities of documents; and fire, flood, or even insects destroy others. Records of national governments pertaining to foreign policy are often classified as confidential. Houses, public buildings, and fortifications can succumb to wind, sand, or demolition.

If a historian fails to obtain particular items of evidence, he may not be able to infer reliably historical reports relevant to his work. Without that evidence, several contradictory reports may seem equally likely to be true. Sometimes historians can circumvent problems of missing evidence by redirecting their thinking or constructing chains of argument that rest on other, accessible evidence.

When apparently crucial evidence appears to be unavailable, the historian need not abandon his search immediately. If a family historian finds that the vital records of a local government have been destroyed, he still may be able to infer with assurance the same historical reports from the records of local churches. A document missing from a local archive may be available in microfilm at a state or provincial archive. Copies of letters and diplomatic despatches may be kept by both senders and recipients. Papal Bulls of the Middle Ages may be preserved by several monasteries, as well as in the Vatican archives.

In some cases, problems of obtaining evidence may apply even to sources actually cited in scholarly literature. A researcher working on the history of pediatrics may encounter several references to a work of Hippocrates. If unfamiliar with classical texts, the researcher may not know that the particular work cited has been published only in a nineteenth–century, French edition of the complete works of Hippocrates, is not translated into any modern language, and is available only in a handful of libraries. What to do? The researcher has two choices. He can either request his library to borrow the work through its interlibrary loan system and hope to find someone who can translate the relevant passages, or he can rely on descriptions of these passages offered by other scholars. The former choice is potentially time-consuming and expensive but preferable, if the work of Hippocrates seems to be important for the project. The latter course of action is permissible only if the passages seem tangential to the topic under investigation.

When crucial evidence is indeed unavailable, the historian must be prepared to recast the inquiry itself. This would be advisable if his work depends on confidently selecting one of several conflicting reports, yet neither a diligent search for alternative evidence nor the most ingenious arguments justify any particular selection. Since the historian cannot magically summon unavailable evidence and should not disregard the canons of reliable inference, he must redirect his inquiry instead.

SAMPLES OF DATA

In the chapters on new history and family and local history, we discussed problems of inferring historical reports from samples of information. Yet sampling problems similar to those of statistical inference confront virtually every researcher, not merely those using quantitative methods or doing case studies. Frequently historians are able to examine only fragments of a potentially complete corpus of evidence—samples of despatches from the full correspondence between two Foreign Ministeries, a few remaining sculptures from a once extensive collection held by a monastery, or a few gravestones still legible in a seventeenth–century cemetery. Before inferring historical reports from such samples of evidence, the historian must first try to determine the features of the entire corpus from those items still extant or accessible.

To illustrate the conundrums of sampling that might beset historians, consider the plight of this biographer. His subject had an illicit love affair during his adult life, and the biographer obviously would try to learn about the affair from letters exchanged by the lovers. But surviving letters might represent only a portion of the correspondence that they actually exchanged. Not only may letters have been discarded mistakenly or lost during changes of residence, but either of the lovers may have destroyed letters in fits of anger or jealousy. And members of either family may have disposed of those missives that seemed especially embarrassing. Thus before the biographer begins to infer reports about the affair itself, he must determine if letters are likely to be missing and, if so, infer features of the full collection of correspondence. How many letters are missing? Are missing letters concentrated in particular periods of time? Are missing letters likely to stress particular subjects? Are missing letters likely to express bitter or bruised feelings? The biographer might seriously go astray without first pondering the problems involved in trying to infer what the full collection might be like from the sample of letters that are within his reach. He might, for instance, infer false harmony between the lovers or understate the depth of their passion.

No easy answers await historians who have to rely on fragmentary evidence. They must try to ascertain what proportion of the full corpus of evidence is available to them and how the attrition of time may have distorted the sample still remaining. The reliability of efforts to reconstruct a corpus of evidence from a sample depends both on the size and characteristics of the sample. The historian examining a collection of love letters should be alert for references to letters that seem to be missing, for unexplained gaps in the sequence of correspondence, and for the failure of the letters to mention issues that almost certainly had been broached. He should carefully trace the provenance of the letters, and consider the personalities and circumstances of the lovers as well as anyone else in a position to destroy or withhold some of the correspondence. If possible, he should question those who might have some knowledge of the letters. At best he might be able to uncover some of the missing letters. Otherwise he must rely on inferences derived from his knowledge of the existing letters, the individuals involved, and the history of their affair. He will have to construct arguments to infer the nature of the omissions before he develops arguments to infer the nature of the affair. In some cases, samples might accurately reflect the full corpus of evidence, but in other instances they may not. Historians should not misrepresent a sample as the entire body of evidence. Nor should they fail to discuss problems raised by having to rely on a sample.

Even when a full corpus of evidence is potentially available to the historian, he might find it too time-consuming or expensive to examine every item. In this case, he must devise his own scheme for sampling the information. Assume that a historian sought to study German newspaper reaction to the Treaty of Versailles during the early 1920's. Obviously he would not try to examine every newspaper published during the period. But given the nature of German newspapers, he would also want to avoid simply selecting a random sample from among all available papers. German newspapers of this period were closely affiliated with the nation's political parties. A random sample might yield several restatements of the position taken by one party and entirely omit the position of another. A more sensible scheme of sampling would be to select at random at least one paper affiliated with each of the important political parties—Communist Party, Social Democratic Party,

German People's Party, German National People's Party, and Nazi Party—
and at least one of the large independent papers of Berlin and Frankfurt.
Following this plan, the historian will be sure to survey a wide range of
political opinion from which he can draw further inferences.

QUALITY OF EVIDENCE

Evidence is not inherently of low or high quality. Rather, the quality of
evidence depends upon how and why it is used. A historian considers evidence to be of low quality when he cannot link it realiably with generalizations to infer reports relevant to his work. Just like missing evidence, poor
quality evidence may make it impossible for the historian to decide confidently which of several contradictory reports is likely to be true. As we indicated
in the preceding discussion of sources, researchers often must wrestle with
the problems posed by low quality or low yield sources. When confronted
with these problems, the historian can do one of two things. He can either
cast his net more widely, accumulating, if possible, a sufficient range of
sources to allow him to infer reliable reports, or he can recast his initial
questions.

Consider the case of a diplomatic historian interested in how policy recommendations were formulated in the field. He might decide to investigate the
post records of several United States embassies in Latin America. To his
chagrin, he might find a wealth of detail in these documents about entertaining in foreign lands and how American diplomats handled requests made by
their traveling countrymen, but precious little about how they arrived at
recommendations for the State Department. Confronted with such a disap-
pointing yield, the historian would not be able to infer reliably either the kind
of recommendations sent to Washington or the procedures officials used to
keep abreast of developments in their capitals. If still committed to his
original enterprise, the historian could search for other kinds of evidence,
such as the personal memoirs or letters of foreign service officers, that might
enhance the reliability of his inferences. Or, recognizing that low quality
evidence for one inquiry may be high quality evidence for another, the
diplomatic historian could pose questions that the post records could answer.
He could investigate the people entertained by United States ambassadors,
the social ambiance of the foreign posts, or what embassy personnel were
willing and able to do for American nationals abroad. Historians must be
prepared for dry wells, especially when working on poorly documented societies or exploring sensitive matters. High quality, useful evidence may simply
not be available.

COMPARABILITY OF DATA

Historians often use evidence for purposes of comparison. But the questions of what to compare with what and how to make comparisons at all introduce complex problems of inference. As we indicated in the chapter on new history, in order to compare and contrast ideas, individuals, groups, institutions, trends, or processes, historians place these items into classes or categories based on either qualitative or quantitative distinctions. Such categorization is necessary whenever research calls for comparison, irrespective of the methods employed. Thus historians might compare crime in the city and the countryside, public opinion among different religious groups, occupation of family members from different generations, or attitudes toward old age in different eras.

To make sure that their comparisons are valid, researchers should be certain that their classification schemes fulfill the following four criteria. First, the standards for placing items into categories should be clear and precise. Serious errors will result if historians place into the same category items that differ with respect to characteristics that would properly place them in different categories. A historian of crime, for example, using urban and rural crime statistics, should determine whether the police in the city and the police in the country have used the same criteria for classifying an activity as criminal. If urban and rural criteria are not identical, the historian probably should not place urban and rural crime statistics in the same category for purposes of comparing criminality in the city and country. Second, categories should be homogeneous for whatever factor or variable is being analyzed. For example, a historian studying temporal changes in the incidence of death at different ages would be ill–advised to categorize as infant mortality all deaths occurring between birth and age five. This scheme obscures the sharp break in death rates that occurs after the first year of life and might suggest misleadingly stable rates of infant mortality. Third, categories should be mutually exclusive so that items properly fit into one and only one category. For example, a scheme dividing political opinion as radical, moderate, liberal, conservative, capitalist, and socialist would present perplexing classification problems since many individuals or groups could obviously be placed into several of these categories. Finally, categories should be inclusive of all items of interest to the researcher. Obviously a historian studying social mobility would be served poorly by a scheme for classifying occupations that excluded domestic service or migrant labor.

After developing a sound scheme of classification, the historian must be careful to place each item that he considers into the correct category. An improper or misleading categorization might occur, for instance, if he fails to adjust for the changing meanings of certain words. A historian comparing how prominent American educators in the seventeenth and twentieth centuries looked on the aged might classify as hostile to older people those individuals who frequently used such terms as "hag" and "fogey" to describe them. But the recent work of David Hackett Fischer on attitudes toward old age clearly indicates that in the seventeenth century these words did not carry the same pejorative connotation they have today. The meaning of many terms that refer to old age, Fischer suggests, changed in the late eighteenth century from merely designating a person as aged to implying that old age was bad.

Historians also should be wary of comparisons based on questionable inferences from available evidence. Making comparisons compounds the problem of reliable inference since errors can arise if either or both of the items being compared are classified improperly. Ancient historians should be cautious about making comparisons between the Athenian and Megarian economies. While we know little enough about the economy of Athens—at least relative to what we know about modern economies—we know far less about Megara, except that she was a trading city and exported cheap clothes, vegetables, and fruits.

ART AS EVIDENCE

History and art long have shared an uneasy coexistence. Competitors for similar audiences, interpreters of the same experience, art and history are also sources of inspiration for one another. As historical evidence, art offers the researcher matchless insight, creating effects, as Oscar Wilde observed, "incomparable and unique." But if interpreted too literally, art can deceive the most dedicated scholar.

Literature and the fine arts offer the historian vivid and immediate impressions of life in other eras. To read a novel, recite a poem, or contemplate a painting is to see life through the creative vision of another. Absorption in literature and art is useful especially during the exploratory stage of a research project when the historian seeks an intuitive grasp of his problem, sifts through ideas, and speculates about hypotheses to be tested. The historian's imagination expands as he sees medieval England with Chaucer, Napoleonic France with David, Czarist Russia with Dostoevsky, Victorian England with Virginia Wolfe, turn of the century Dublin with Joyce, the Weimar Republic with Hesse, the Spanish Civil War with Picasso, and contemporary America with Mailer.

But generalizations about the creative process offer little guidance for reliably inferring historical reports from literature or art. We still know little about creativity and the connections between art, the artist, and society. Art proceeds according to a logic of its own and may be a dark and distorted mirror of the artist and his world. Oscar Wilde expressed this notion well.

> Art takes life as part of her rough material, recreates it and refashions it in fresh forms, is absolutely indifferent to fact, invents, imagines, dreams, and keeps between herself and reality the impenetrable barrier of beautiful style, or decorative or ideal treatment. . . . Art never expresses anything but itself. It has an independent life, just as Thought has, and develops purely on its own lines. It is not necessarily realistic in an age of realism, nor spiritual in an age of faith. So far from being the creation of its time, it is usually in direct opposition to it, and the only true history that it preserves is the history of its own progress.

Historians, of course, still draw upon art as evidence for historical reports, especially when arguments cannot be fashioned from other information. Used selectively and not pressed too far, evidence from fiction, painting, and sculpture can be valuable to historians. For thinly documented periods, art can reveal what people at least imagined, if not necessarily what they actually did. Changes in the predominant form and content of art can suggest trends in popular opinion and cultural values, as can audience reaction to particular works of art. But historians will be led astray if they assume too literal a connection between art and the artist's milieu, or if they fail to divine that artistic works have an internal logic of their own. Philippe Ariès, we noted in the previous chapter, inferred medieval views of children from how artists depicted little boys and girls. He maintains that the failure of medieval painters and sculptors to portray children realistically as distinct from adults indicates that people then probably did not differentiate between childhood and adulthood. Yet the work of these artists actually may have reflected artistic style and convention (the internal logic of art) rather than ideas about real children. The generalizations that sustain Ariès' argument would also imply that ancient Egyptians, who almost invariably drew faces in profile with a single eye showing, were unaware of what a face actually looked like; or that those who drew without perspective had no realistic concept of space or distance. Again Mr. Wilde offers pertinent commentary. "What the imitative arts really give us are merely the various styles of particular artists, or of certain schools of artists. Surely you don't imagine that the people of the Middle Ages bore any resemblance at all to the figures on mediaeval stained glass, or in mediaeval stone and wood carving, or on mediaeval metal-work, or tapestries, or illuminated MSS. . . . The Middle Ages as we know them in art, are simply a definite form of style . . . No great artist ever sees things as they really are."

"The Wrap Up": Conclusion

Even Holmes does not solve all of his cases to his own satisfaction. After a successful bout with Moriarity, he realizes that the professor will likely return again to prey on the innocent people of London. But he can still sit back with Watson and review what he has already accomplished. Similarly, the historian must sit down and write up the results of his research, knowing full well that his inquiry may not be conclusive. Indeed the historian's research is never complete. Evidence he has uncovered almost invariably will suggest new problems to examine; an account of a single incident may suggest the asking of larger historical questions; and general discussions will suggest particular events that need more scrutiny. In fact, one of the major practical problems facing the historical researcher is knowing when to stop. Even the most diligent detective cannot accept every case, or chase down every single lead.

Once the historian has examined the source material suggested by his original plan of study, he should assess whether his findings will allow him to answer adequately and reliably both the major question and supplementary questions that guided his research in the first place. During this assessment, he may find, as Holmes occasionally does, that he must search for still more clues to sustain his reconstruction of the past and his interpretative arguments. This additional research usually involves only minor details. If he finds that his data are sufficient for the task, the historian can turn to the job of writing up the results of his research, mindful that while outlining or writing, he may have to return again to research to tie up loose ends or to fill in any gaps in his evidence or argument.

VIII

Historical Writing

Historians usually communicate their findings through a written manuscript. In planning and executing a research project, no historian can afford to ignore the craft of historical composition. The content and form of historical work cannot be separated neatly. Historical writing does not simply present information and arguments. Unlike purely scientific writing, it offers more than equations for building bridges or formulas for concocting new pesticides. History, although bound by rules of logic and the demand for empirical evidence, is also a form of literature; historians write to affect people, to influence their thinking, and to kindle their emotions. What a work of history conveys to a reader will depend, in part, on its structural design, its pace and emphasis, the clarity and grace of its prose, and the tone of its rhetoric. Contorted structure, turgid prose, and sloppy diction may influence the impact of a work as much as skimpy research and shallow thinking.

Written work in history may take the form of a paper or article, a book-length study, or even a multivolume opus. Since different principles of composition and style may apply to different types of work, we focus here on the writing of papers or articles. The principles of article writing we discuss are applicable to the writing of student papers as well as to work destined for scholarly journals. In this chapter we consider the formulation of a strategy for presenting the results of research and the tactics best suited for organizing and writing a paper. We emphasize the production of papers that require research in primary sources, but also discuss papers that require critical analysis of the work accomplished by other historians. We assume no specialized knowledge or familiarity with the writing of articles.

After substantially completing the research phase of a project, the historian must devise a strategy of persuasion for presenting his results. Like the general who fails to develop battle plans before deploying troops, the historian who fails to plan his writing risks squandering his resources, in this case the evidence he has gathered and the ideas he has hit upon. To convey most effectively what he has learned about the past, the writer does not necessarily recapitulate for the reader the sequence of steps followed in his research. Neither does he write up his conclusions without attention to the style, tone, organization, and emphasis of his work. The historian must plan carefully the composition of a paper, presenting his findings according to whatever strategic design makes them seem most convincing. The historian marshals his evidence and deploys his literary skills to persuade readers to accept his own understanding of a period, an event, an individual, or a process.

Developing a strategy of persuasion entails consideration of six issues. First, the writer must decide how to deal with at least three audiences— himself, his immediate readers, and a universal audience. Second, bearing in mind all three audiences, the historian must decide what is important about his work and then choose those points that best convey to the readers the significance of his research. Next, the historian must decide whether to use a format that is primarily narrative or analytic, whether to tell a story or to develop the analysis and solution of a problem. Fourth, the historian must create a structure for his article that highlights the points he considers important and accommodates either the narrative or the analytic form of presentation. Fifth, the historian must decide upon the most appropriate language and style for his audiences. And finally, the historian must also choose how to present the scholarly apparatus of his paper, what to relegate to footnotes or appendices, or how much bibliographic detail to include in citations. Only if the historian keeps these six issues in mind and recognizes that how he resolves any one of them will affect the resolution of all the others, can he hope to create a convincing article that does justice to his work.

The Audiences

As the philosophers of rhetoric Chaim Perelman and L. Obrecht-Tyteca have pointed out, a speaker or writer must recognize that, in formulating a strategy of persuasion, he is simultaneously addressing three distinct audiences. The first audience is the author himself. A historian who does not write for himself is likely to get little satisfaction from his work. One of the greatest joys of writing history is the elation that comes from having crafted a work that faithfully and forcefully represents your own ideas and reflects the hard work devoted to research and analysis. Moreover, through self–deliberation, the author decides how to address the other two audiences. The philosopher Pascal has insisted that an essential guide to the truth is "your own assent to yourself, and the constant voice of your own reason."

The second audience consists of those individuals most likely to read and ponder the work (in the case of the student, this audience includes the instructor). If the author expects his work to be read only by authorities in the field, he would adopt a strategy different from that for a popular audience. Aiming at both specialists and nonspecialists, the author might devise a composite strategy designed for both groups, relegating technical or specialized material to footnotes or an appendix.

The third audience is the "universal audience" of all men, or perhaps all "reasonable" men, both now and in the future. The historian must address the universal audience if he wants his work to stand the test of time and be respected by whoever might read and understand it. The best historians respond to the diverse requirements of all three audiences.

Students often complain that in order to write a successful history paper, they feel that they must "write for the professor." However, two distinct issues are usually conflated in the phrase, "writing for the professor"—(1) saying what the student thinks the professor wants to hear, and (2) expressing the student's own views and interpretations in a manner calculated to persuade the professor to take seriously his arguments. An understanding of the concept of the second audience can enable the student to reconcile his desire to express his own views and to please his instructor. A student need not parrot an instructor's interpretations in order to "write for the professor." If a student realizes that, like the playwright, he must craft the presentation of his thought so as to convey that thought in the most persuasive and convincing manner possible, the student will be able to remain faithful to his own interpretations and may expect usually a favorable review of his work from the second audience.

Historians may have to wrestle with conflicting demands of the three audiences. For example, conflicts may arise between the second audience (assume in this case, a professor) and the third or universal audience. A student working in quantitative history, for instance, might know that he can slip questionable assumptions past a professor who is uncomfortable with math beyond multiplication. Indeed, the student might know that if he tried forthrightly to discuss these assumptions, he would only confuse the professor and make him less receptive to the study's historical conclusions. Yet, he may realize that to satisfy the universal audience, he must either explain why these assumptions are viable or modify his work accordingly. To resolve such conflicts, the historian must think carefully about why he is writing the paper and the compromises he can and cannot tolerate. He might direct his strategy to one of the audiences only or adopt a composite strategy that tries to mediate between the demands of each audience.

What Is Important?

An effective strategy of persuasion identifies the main points that the writer wishes to communicate and indicates what must be emphasized in order to make these points as clear and convincing as possible. The historian must decide why his work is worth relating and guide his writing accordingly. Perhaps he is trying to explain why one event rather than a contrasting event occurred, or to explain a pattern of change over time. Perhaps he is trying to convey the emotional texture of past experience, to tell us what life was like for people living in circumstances different from our own. He might be trying to describe precisely how a historical event came about; he might be exploring the ethical implications of decisions made by men and women. Or he may be trying to synthesize several of these varied objectives of historical study.

A historian's work may be directed also toward revising or expanding what we think we already know about the past, offering new responses to old questions, redefining the questions, or opening up new areas of inquiry. The historian may apply new methods of research and analysis, use new generalizations or covering laws, or exploit a body of evidence that other scholars had ignored. What he is attempting to do should determine how he defines his questions and places his work in the context of scholarship accomplished by others. This clear-cut definition of purpose will also help him to decide how much time he should spend describing and explaining his methodology and presenting the evidence upon which his work relies and will help him to determine what to emphasize in his summary and conclusion. To understand the point of a study is to know what to include and what to omit, what to emphasize, and what to skim over.

Narrative and Analytic Modes

Having decided what points are important, the historian can decide whether a narrative or analytic form will best put them across. The distinction between these forms of presentation is not hard and fast, but is useful for illustrative purposes. The narrative paper is devoted to telling a story—to recounting the flow of events over time. The analytic paper, which is becoming increasingly popular among professional historians, is devoted to the analysis and solution of a problem or puzzle. The body of an analytic paper sets forth the problem and its component parts, presents evidence gathered by the historian, and shows, through reasoned argument, how an examination of this evidence helps solve the problem being considered. Almost all articles classified as "new history" are written in the analytic form.

A historian of the family may want to know if the peasants of a medieval province tended to form nuclear families of parents and children or extended families, including grandparents, uncles, aunts, and other relatives. In presenting the findings of his research, he may, after appropriate introductory remarks, explain the methods used to reconstruct the composition of medieval families. Then he may present his data in a series of tables and, using arguments founded on principles of statistical inference, test various hypotheses about the nuclear versus the extended family. Using yet other generalizations and historical reports, then he may discuss the historical significance of his quantitative results.

The historian using the narrative mode can apply the same principles that guide dramatists or short story writers. He can expand or contract the actual flow of time to create a tempo best suited to his narrative; like the dramatist, he has the signal advantage of knowing how everything turns out in the end. The historian may decide to follow events over an extended period of time, or focus on what happened during a brief span, perhaps only a few days or even a few hours. He might decide to tell the story from the point of view of the omniscient author, of an individual participant, or abandon a point of view altogether. He might follow the story in chronological order or develop a nonlinear design that uses such devices as flashbacks and cutaways. The historian might choose to emphasize the convergence of several themes that he has been tracing through the narrative, perhaps culminating the account with a single, graphic episode. Or he might plan his narrative to highlight a dramatic turning point in the events being followed.

Unlike the dramatist, however, the narrative historian is bound to his evidence. Narrative history is an art produced within a strict set of constraints. Just as the author of a sonnet is constrained by requirements of length, meter, and rhyme, the narrative historian is constrained by the logical and empirical requirements of historical inquiry. If the poet abandons the requirements of the sonnet, he still may write great poetry, but he will not have written a sonnet. If the historian abandons the constraints of his discipline, he still may write great literature, but he will not write history.

The best narrative history is written by scholars who can achieve literary excellence while convincing their audiences that their stories faithfully recount events as they actually occurred. The literary and scholarly goals of history sometimes coincide. Aside from arguments used to sustain the reports of a narrative, the quality of its rhetoric will influence its credibility. The coherence and flow of a narrative, the polish and sophistication of its prose, and the images summoned by its use of words and phrases, all affect the audiences' willingness to accept its veracity. Unfortunately, the artistic and scholarly goals of narrative history sometimes also contradict one another. Methodically explaining how one has reached his conclusions may burden the narrative with tedious and difficult material. All historians must struggle with the problem of how to balance the literary and scholarly demands of their work.

The historian working in the analytic form also must attend to questions of composition and style. The structural integrity of an analytic article, the logical progression of its arguments, the grace and elegance of its prose, will influence the impression it makes on its second and third audiences. Moreover, the historian using the analytic form too may hope to touch the emotions and human sympathies of his audiences and create in their minds a greater appreciation of unfamiliar experiences. He also may feel the need to shape his rhetoric for the precise purpose of overcoming resistance to his methodology or interpretative conclusions. Even the historian who takes science for his ideal model can never achieve the alleged emotional neutrality of technical writing, for it is impossible not to elicit an emotional response when dealing with thought, feelings, and behavior of our fellow men. Just because a historian intends to use statistical methods to portray the composition of families does not mean that he can avoid using language that invites his readers to think about what it might have been like to grow up in one kind of family or another. No literary device can overcome fully our proclivity to identify with people, to imagine what their lives were like, to empathize with them, or to be repulsed by them. The historian who tries to be scientific by anesthetizing his prose may alter, but not quench, the emotional reactions to his work.

Structure

Whether the historian intends to tell a story or analyze a problem, he must organize his work in a way that enhances its credibility and significance. The paper as a whole must form a coherent structure and supply the information necessary to understand and appreciate the historian's accomplishments. The following model, though it does not represent the only format appropriate for a historical paper, demonstrates a form of organization that is adaptable to most types of work and is easy to analyze and explain. This model is deliberately designed to encompass nearly every conceivable component of a historical article; obviously, many works could be designed more simply.

    I. Introduction.
        A. "The Hook."
        B. Statement of the Problem and Significance of the Work.
        C. Historiographic Context.
        D. Foreshadowing of Findings.
        E. Methodological Discussion.
    II. The Body: Evidence and Arguments.
    III. Conclusion.
        A. Synthetic Conclusions.
        B. Broader Implications and Further Research.
    IV. The Scholarly Apparatus.
        A. Footnotes.
        B. Bibliography.
        C. Appendices.

THE INTRODUCTION

The Hook. We call the initial paragraph of a paper "the hook," because its purpose is to captivate the reader, to pique his interest, and to motivate him to read the rest of the paper. "The hook" generally should be limited to a single paragraph and focus on whatever material the author believes would be most appealing to his second audience. Written solely for the second audience, "the hook" can ignore the interests of the author or first audience and the third or universal audience. The author can try to catch the reader's attention by referring to the subject matter of his work, its methodology, its scope, its historical significance, its relationship to other work, or its problem area. The choice makes no difference as long as "the hook" does the job. Historians dealing with naturally appealing topics such as freedom of speech or American slave insurrections may "hook" the reader merely by stating their topics and indicating that important details are still unknown. Historians offering more obscure or prosaic themes may have to entice their audiences with references to the big questions their work helps resolve, or how their work illustrates the application of new historical concepts and methods.

Statement of the Problem and Its Significance. After his effort to "hook" the reader securely, a writer may devote one or more paragraphs to describing the problem he is addressing and to explaining why this problem is significant. Although this section should be as appealing as possible to the second audience, its primary objective is to inform rather than to allure the reader. By reading these paragraphs, the reader should be able to ascertain what he might expect to learn from the whole paper.

Historiographic Context. Historiography refers to the production of written history. No historian works in a vacuum. Invariably, others have written on the same or closely related subject matter. The historian can set forth what other writers have said about the subject and specify where his own work is located in this ongoing historical tradition. He might be filling a gap in the historiography of a given problem, extending the work of other scholars, contributing another case study to a corpus of completed work, challenging conventional wisdom, or resolving a standing interpretative dispute. How much space to devote to historiography depends both on the nature of the work and the prior knowledge the author can assume from the second audience. Historians confronting a rich historiographic tradition and introducing new interpretations may find that previous work must be described and evaluated, in detail, especially when addressing a second audience unfamiliar with the literature. However, the historian moving into relatively unplowed territory reasonably might decide that historiography merits only a few succinct remarks.

Foreshadowing of Findings. Before the main dish, historians sometimes offer readers a taste of what is to come in the body of the paper. This gives the reader a better chance to decide whether it is worthwhile to digest the rest of the paper. Foreshadowing is especially useful when the historian has reached conclusions that contradict prevailing beliefs or are otherwise striking or novel. The historian also might choose to foreshadow his findings when readers are asked to plow through material they might find difficult or tedious. Generally, a separate section foreshadowing findings is appropriate for analytic papers. Historians working in the narrative mode can borrow techniques from the novelist, integrating foreshadowing into the telling of their story.

Methodological Discussion. The results of historical research can be only as good as the methods used by the historian. Thus there is good reason for any historical article to include a discussion of methodology. This discussion can be handled in two ways. The writer can either devote a section of the article to an explicit description of the methodology employed or he can describe the methodology as he goes along. If he is using a nontraditional methodology such as quantification or psychohistory, we think it is preferable to discuss that methodology in a separate section. Such a separate discussion prepares the reader for the procedures that will be used to evaluate evidence and reach conclusions. If, on the other hand, the writer will be employing traditional historical analysis, he can discuss his methodology within the main body of the essay. Even those historians who use the most time-honored methods should explicitly state how they have linked historical reports to causal arguments and, when necessary, what generalizations they have used to infer historical reports from available evidence. Suppressing such generalizations can be justified only when they are both obvious and noncontroversial.

THE BODY: EVIDENCE AND ARGUMENT

This section of an article will usually be the longest, the fullest in presentation of evidence and elaboration of argument. Because the body of the paper is rich with material, historians sometimes find it difficult to keep the main points of their thinking prominent, high-lighted against the background of supporting and sometimes subsidiary material. But a historian sensitive to persuading his audiences will keep his spotlight trained on those points he has already determined are important. Organization of this section of the article is far from mechanical; it requires close attention to both forest and trees. If the organization loses sight of the forest—the main points—the impact of the article is diminished. But if the organization does not arrange the trees—evidence and argument—into the configuration of the forest, the article will simply be unpersuasive.

CONCLUSION

Synthetic Conclusion. This section of the article is akin to the dramatic climax of many a well-wrought play. All the themes and tensions are somehow knit together so the audience understands what the drama is all about. In the synthetic conclusion, the historian draws together the threads of arguments into a coherent whole, and states clearly and forcefully the conclusion he has reached after studying the evidence, establishing historical reports, linking those reports together into causal arguments, and evaluating historical scholarship. The synthetic conclusion may have been foreshadowed in an earlier part of the paper, but its most powerful exposition usually should be reserved for the end. The statement of the synthetic conclusion need not be too lengthy; the tactic here is enough exposition for full understanding but sufficient compression for power and punch. A mere summary usually lacks the persuasive power of a true synthetic conclusion, and a simple listing or précis of the findings is often flat; the readers have been primed for a climax and they will not be satisfied with mere recapitulation of the plot.

Broader Implications and Further Research. A synthetic conclusion often does not exhaust the results of energetic research. The historical enterprise not only produces "conclusions"—ends to discussion—but also suggests promising new ideas. A study of the patterns formed by presidential elections in twentieth–century America, for example, may suggest a new scheme for periodizing all of American political history. Obviously, in the context of an article on twentieth–century elections, the historian could not develop fully this scheme or offer much supporting evidence. But he could sketch in its general contours and indicate how further research could test its validity.

However, we should note here that not all historians approve of concluding sections that suggest broader implications. Some label these conclusions "mere speculation"; others object to them as "surprises," unwarranted by preceding evidence and discussion. The wise writer, if he can, ascertains his second audience's views on such discussion in advance.

SCHOLARLY APPARATUS

Footnotes. No two historians are likely to apply the same criteria for what should go into footnotes. Some historians write with an abundance of footnotes; others use them sparingly. While we cannot, therefore, provide a set of rules for what material should be included in footnotes, we can describe the ways in which historians use them. Footnotes may be either referential or substantive. Referential footnotes guide the reader to sources of the citations, quotations, and ideas included in the text. Authors use substantive footnotes to provide the readers with additional content and commentary.

Referential footnotes can include the following kinds of information:

(1) Identification of quotations. Any quotation must have a footnote. This is an unbreakable rule for research papers.

(2) Identification of ideas and information. Too often students are unaware that they must acknowledge their debt to other historians. If a historian includes in his discussion a report or explanation found in another scholar's

work, he must acknowledge his debt in a footnote, another unbreakable rule. We will probe this issue more fully in a later section of this chapter, "Intellectual Honesty and Plagiarism."

(3) Identification of other scholarly works. For example, a historian writing about the assassination of Julius Caesar and confining his discussion to three other historians' views, can nonetheless use a footnote to mention other scholarly works on the subject. This is often done through the device of saying, "See also . . ." or "Cf." (an abbreviation meaning "compare," from the Latin, *confer*). Frankly such a listing of other scholarly works sometimes is used to convince the reader that the author has done his homework and to anticipate the question, "I wonder if the writer has considered the work of X?"

An author also can refer readers to works relevant to further exploration of issues broached in the text. A historian describing the use of a particular psychological model, for example, can refer readers to other studies that further elaborate or evaluate the model.

Substantive footnotes may be used for the following material:

1. Occasional presentation of evidence. The strategy of persuasion an author devises may call for presenting a chart, a table, or a document's full text in a footnote rather than the main text. In general, however, evidence should be displayed in the body of the paper.

2. Brief discussion of methodological issues. If the historican has not included a section on methodology in the first part of his paper, he may decide to take up such questions in the body of his paper. However, the introduction of a methodological discussion may disrupt the flow of an article or clash with the pace and tone of its prose. In such circumstances, writers frequently relegate brief discussions of methodological questions to footnotes.

3. Further explanation of ideas or arguments. Footnotes can be used to elaborate on ideas or arguments when further discussion would detract from the flow or focus of the text. The historian might want to use a footnote to develop a point only peripherally relevant to his main theme, lest further discussion of it in the text distract the reader's attention from more central issues. Some writers deplore the use of footnotes for this purpose, arguing that any point worth discussing is important enough to be set on center stage. Whether to use footnotes for further explanation or development of material is a matter of personal preference. However, if a writer finds himself resorting to this kind of footnote frequently, we advise a reconsideration of strategy. In many cases, material that a writer relegates to a footnote might better be used to vary the pace or to add a touch of humor to the text itself.

4. Historical controversies. Historians may use footnotes to discuss controversies arising in the work of other scholars. Such controversies are appropriately relegated to footnotes if their discussion is not central to the author's argument or detracts substantially from the flow of the text.

5. Technical matter. Some of the material essential for an understanding of the argument or evidence might be too cumbersome or arcane to be included in the text itself. For example, a definition of technical terms such as standard error, an explanation of the value of a statistical coefficient, a discussion of differing definitions of an oedipal complex, or a description of the reading of a papyrus fragment all might be considered technical material and as such handled through footnotes.

6. Identifying remarks. Occasionally historians may resort to the footnote as a means of identifying an individual or event mentioned in the text. This technique is particularly appropriate for people and events not likely to be familiar to the second audience, but not meriting full elaboration in the text itself.

7. Digressions. Sometimes a historian's evidence will suggest insights and information unrelated to arguments developed in the text. On rare occasions, historians may consider such material sufficiently interesting to warrant discussing it in a footnote. For example, a historian using a hitherto unexploited survey of American political leaders to determine what issues they considered most important in a presidential election might note in a footnote evidence from the survey relevant to judging how accurately these leaders were able to predict the outcome of that election. However interesting a historian may find his superfluous material to be, he should remember that a footnote is not a dumping ground for fascinating but irrelevant trivia or a place to prove how hard he has worked.

Just as no two scholars are likely to agree on what material should or should not be relegated to footnotes, so also do authorities differ about the form in which footnotes are written. The sensible historian ascertains from his second audience (whether professor, scholarly journal, or popular magazine) the preferred format. Regardless of format, the overriding criterion for referential footnotes is that the information provided enable the reader to find the item cited easily and accurately. Few things provoke greater frustration in a reader than being unable to locate the material cited in a footnote because the information is inaccurate, incomplete, or ambiguous.

Many colleges and universities have adopted a standard form for footnotes. Two of the most commonly used formats are those propounded by Kate L. Turabian's *A Manual for Writers of Term Papers, Theses, and Dissertations,* 4th edition (Chicago: University of Chicago Press, 1975), and the *MLA Style*

Sheet, 2nd edition (New York: The Modern Language Association, 1970).

Bibliography. The bibliography is a special part of the scholarly apparatus. Its primary function is to inform the reader quickly and conveniently of the sources—primary, secondary, and tertiary—that the researcher used in the preparation of the article or paper. Few articles published in scholarly journals include a bibliography; the information about sources is contained in the footnotes. However, since research papers often must include a bibliography, we offer a brief discussion of it here.

Some historians follow the rule that no item may appear in the bibliography that has not appeared in a footnote. Unfortunately, this rule may serve to diminish rather than to enhance the value of a bibliography, especially for a research paper. A diligent researcher usually consults many more sources than he eventually cites in the paper. Other historians interested in the same subject may find the additional references valuable for their own work. And by knowing the range of material that an author has gone through, readers can evaluate better his use of evidence and perhaps gain a clearer understanding of what he is arguing. At the very least, a complete bibliography will tell a reader whether or not the author consulted certain sources not cited in footnotes.

Bibliographies are most useful to the reader when they are divided into categories. The categories may be as simple as divisions among primary, secondary, and tertiary sources; or as detailed as divisions among such sources as letters, public documents, photographs, oral interviews, books, and articles. The key to creating categories is to make the bibliography convenient and useful to the reader; the author already knows what he has consulted.

Bibliographies also may be annotated. Authors may evaluate general categories of sources or individually consider each entry in the bibliography. In the latter case, entries may be accompanied by a brief commentary on the source's particular worth, contents, or relevance. An author also might note those potentially relevant sources unavailable to him, or discuss the strengths and weaknesses of the full corpus of research material.

For the proper form for bibliographies, consult either of the two handbooks mentioned above.

Appendices. Appendices serve the same purposes as substantive footnotes. They can be used to present evidence or commentary that is unusually technical or tangential to the paper's main arguments. But an appendix also can serve as a place to record far more lengthy material than would normally be put in a footnote. For example, an author writing about lawmaking in fifth–century Athens might confront ancillary problems not strictly germane to the main topic but requiring some kind of attention. One such issue might be how the allotment machines worked that were used to choose members of the Athenian Boule, or council. The working of allotment machines is important because lawmaking well could be affected by the composition of the council. Yet if the paper's main theme was how debate within the council influenced decision making on laws, the whole allotment machine issue, if manageable in a brief discussion, might well be treated as an ancillary issue and be dealt with in an explanatory footnote. A more detailed description suitably would be consigned to an appendix.

Some writers rely heavily on appendices, preferring not to clutter their texts with a host of subsidiary issues. Others, however, think that appendices are necessarily too disconnected from the text of an article to include at all. Whether or not to use appendices should be part of a historian's overall strategy of persuasion, not a matter of whim.

Style and Language

Having taken into account the demands and expectations of his audiences, the writer is finally ready to decide upon appropriate style and language. Most research papers should be cast in a formal style. The second audience usually is accustomed to papers that use formal prose and will be upset, if not outraged, to find slang, colloquial expressions, or a "chatty" tone. A research paper is not a letter to a friend, a short story, or an entry in a diary or journal. A paper written in a casual style is likely to offend and distract the second audience, diminishing the impact of the work.

However, "formal" does not mean stilted or stylized. Everyone should strive to develop his own personal and distinctive formal style, infusing his own personality into his prose. In a formal paper, however, the writer's personality always must take second place to the argument.

Several good handbooks for English composition are currently available; we need not recapitulate their contents here. Instead we will consider briefly several simple "Do's" and "Don'ts" of sound writing. The art of writing, of course, cannot be reduced to any set of rules and guidelines. Such superbly gifted authors as James Joyce and Gertrude Stein have produced masterpieces in creative defiance of the advice usually offered in textbooks on writing. But to violate such guidelines requires either extraordinary creativity or long experience with the written word. Our brief list of "Do's" and "Don'ts" are intended as suggestions to be pondered by prospective authors; they are not meant to deter innovation or to stifle imagination.

DO'S

Be Consistent. More than a century ago, Emerson warned that "a foolish consistency is the hobgoblin of little minds." For those who write the formal prose of history, however, the struggle for consistency usually is wise rather than foolish. Inconsistency in style and word usage is likely to confuse and annoy the second audience, impeding understanding and appreciation of the historian's work.

The good writer tries to present a consistent self or persona throughout the article; to be consistent about such details as spelling and capitalization; to be consistent about the use of tenses; and, above all, to maintain a consistent style and tone. The writer must decide whether to present himself to readers in the first person singular; the third person singular, "the writer" or "the author"; or in the even more impersonal, "this study" or "this paper." Some argue that "I" is an inappropriate voice for scholarly work; but others contend that "the author" or "the paper" sounds too stilted and formal. Whatever the individual historian's decision, once he chooses a voice, he should speak only in that voice throughout the paper. Moreover, once the historian decides how to spell or capitalize a word and how to use technical terminology he should maintain consistency. Variation in this realm creates confusion rather than pleasing variety. In addition, he should not arbitrarily shift the tense used to present an idea or describe an event. If, for example, in a historiography section, he summarizes the work of one author in the present tense, he should not switch to the past tense for the next author. Finally, he should not abruptly change the style or the tone midway in the paper. He should avoid sudden switches from simple, concise, and direct prose to long, complex, and elliptical sentences. He should not barrage the reader suddenly with technical language in an article using ordinary prose. He should not suddenly switch from a matter-of-fact style to one laden with metaphors, images, and allusions.

Aim at Simplicity. In *The Elements of Style,* a classic guide to good writing, E. B. White recalls how his teacher, Professor William Strunk, Jr., had "leaned forward over his desk, grasped his coat lapels in his hands, and, in a husky conspiratorial voice said 'Rule Thirteen. Omit needless words! Omit needless words! Omit needless words!'" Knowing that his second audience has a limited amount of time and energy to spend on a paper, the historian sensitive to persuasion will heed this advice, striving for economy of expression. As Strunk reminds us, the omission of needless words "requires not that the writer make all his sentences short, or that he avoid all detail and treat his subjects only in outline, but that every word tell."

Moreover, the quest for economy of expression does not mean that historians must necessarily forgo the multiplication of detail, repetition, or accentuation designed to impress a point on the reader's mind. But words unrequired by a strategy of persuasion have no place in a well-wrought article. The historian must study his work sentence by sentence, paring away needless words, and recasting sentences to make them more concise and forceful. Consider, for instance, the following two sentences:

> It was Gobineau's theory of race that mixtures of blood of the different races was something unfortunate because it would contaminate the Aryan race, which was the superior race. (29 words)

> According to Gobineau's theory of race, mingling the blood of different races unfortunately contaminates the superior Aryan race. (18 words)

The second sentence is shorter by eleven words, is cleaner, and has more punch. The historian should be aware of indirect phrases (e.g., "was something unfortunate," "because it would contaminate") that add needless words and grate upon the reader's ear. He should be sensitive also to such weak and needless expressions as "there are," "it is," "which was," "the fact that," "in terms of."

Economy can be achieved also by combining a series of short sentences into a single sentence. Consider again an actual example:

> Franklin D. Roosevelt ran for a third presidential term in 1940. He was a member of the Democratic Party. Roosevelt was also a shrewd campaigner. During the campaign of 1940 he promised that American boys would not fight in the European war. Wendell Willkie was his Republican opponent in this election. Willkie had emerged as a dark-horse nominee at the Republican Convention of that year. (66 words)

> In 1940, contending for a third presidential term against Wendell Willkie, the dark-horse Republican nominee, Franklin D. Roosevelt shrewdly promised that American boys would not fight in the European war. (31 words)

Of course, the historian must be careful not to create monster sentences that twist and coil into grotesque shapes.

If sentences should contain no extra words, paragraphs should include no extra sentences. A paragraph that grows to the length of a page has probably gotten out of hand. Paragraphs often balloon beyond control when authors fail to frame workable topic sentences. The careful writer begins each paragraph with a sentence that simultaneously tells the reader what the paragraph will discuss and restricts the scope of the paragraph. Consider, for example, a topic sentence such as, "As everyone in the community knew, John Smith played an important role in all aspects of the small town's life." If the writer intends to present a lengthy discussion of John Smith's influence, this topic sentence should be followed by another qualifying sentence that indicates to the reader how the discussion of Smith will proceed. He could handle Smith's role in local education in this paragraph and then, in separate paragraphs, treat Smith's role in politics, economics, and society. An extended discussion of Smith's influence cannot be contained in one paragraph. By breaking up a long discussion into shorter paragraphs, the persuasive writer lightens the reader's burden, letting the topic sentences lead him step by step through the argument.

Be specific, concrete, and precise. Readers understandably become frustrated and cross when they must struggle to grasp what a writer is talking about. Readers are not miracle workers; they cannot divine what might be in the mind of an author. They only know what actually appears on the written page. "But I really meant to say . . ." is a sad lament often expressed by beginning writers. Only the writer knows what he meant to say; his second and third audiences know only what he actually did say. Write as though you have no opportunity to explain later what you truly were trying to say. The reader should be able to comprehend your message the first time around.

You should not try to appear learned and erudite by using fancy words or contrived phrases in place of simple, descriptive words and expressions. Try to use concrete language that conveys your thoughts to the reader as precisely as possible. Consider, for instance, the following two sentences:

Cowering behind barricades erected for defense, the protomorphic practitioners of warfare were too disaffected to unleash their weapons.

Cowering behind sandbags, the inexperienced soldiers were too frightened to fire their rifles.

The revised sentence is not only less wordy, pedantic, and labored than the first, but it relates more information and summons a sharper image to the reader's imagination. If you really mean "sandbags," why say "structures for defense," which could range from fortresses to foxholes? If you really mean "fire their rifles," why say "unleash their weapons," which could range from letting loose their guard dogs to launching a nuclear rocket? Why disguise "soldiers" as "practitioners of warfare"? Why strain to use "protomorphic" instead of "inexperienced," "disaffected" instead of "frightened"? Historians should not automatically avoid big words and elaborate phrases or emulate the style of a grade school reader. But they should have good reason for using unusual language, not merely to flex their intellectual biceps.

Once resolved to use concrete language that most closely reflects your ideas, you must pay close attention to the meaning of words. Careless choice of words creates confusion and misunderstanding. Words in our language usually have a definite set of meanings; despite similarities, few words are truly synonymous. If you mean that Theodore Roosevelt had a "stocky" build, do not say that he was "fat." If you mean that Franklin Roosevelt was "crippled," do not say that he was "immobile." If you mean that Achilles was "brave," do not say that he was "noble." Many words also sound alike, but have different meanings. Do not confuse imminent and immanent, farther and further, constant and continual, ingenious and ingenuous. Few good writers work without a dictionary at hand. Their problem is not spelling. Rather, they recognize the need for precision in the use of vocabulary. If experienced writers need to consult a dictionary to verify definitions, certainly the novice should follow the dictum, "When in doubt, look it up."

Understanding is further sacrificed when a work includes such undefined phrases as "Many leading scholars believe," or "Proponents of the Marxist interpretation argue." Unless your footnotes name the scholars or proponents you have in mind, your reader will not know to whom you are referring. The innocent may be indicted along with the guilty. Do not be afraid to use names, writing for example, "Such leading scholars as Macaulay, Trevelyan, and Namier contend. . . ."

Errors in grammar can also mar the precision of a work. A common error that can lead to comic results is the failure to link pronouns with their proper antecedents. One prominent Greek historian, for instance, wrote of Philip of Macedon that, at the seige of Methone, "He lost the sight of his right eye during the seige, but he captured it by assault before an Athenian fleet arrived." Few of us, if any, know of anyone who restored his own sight by assaulting it. However, too often, such errors provoke simple confusion rather than mirth. What information can one glean from these sentences? "The king decided to declare war against France and to cut off the head of his wife. This gave him a headache and an upset stomach." What does "this" stand for? The king's decision? The results of the decision? And which decision? In the second sentence, "this" must be replaced by a specific description of what caused the king's headache and upset stomach. Consider another example. "The Senator was rebuked by the President, berated by his wife, and expelled from the Senate. It was the most humiliating experience of his life." What does "it" refer to? The most dedicated reader could not determine what the writer actually meant; even worse, the reader might suspect that the writer did not know what he meant either. Once that suspicion lodges in a reader's mind, he becomes very hard to persuade. Historians should cast a hard eye at every pronoun in their work, insuring that a reader could easily determine to whom or to what it refers.

Other forms of grammatical errors also leave readers wondering what an author is trying to say. These include, for instance, the dangling or misplaced modifier (e.g., "Sitting on his haunches and howling at the moon, the prospector finally spotted the coyote."); the omission or improper use of punctuation (e.g., "At dusk crouching to avoid detection the Kings troops slowly approached the fortress."); and careless arrangement of words ("In the forest the conspirators met at night, concealed by dense growth."). In each case, a few revisions yield perfectly respectable sentences:

> "The prospector finally spotted the coyote, sitting on his haunches and howling at the moon."

> "At dusk, crouching to avoid detection, the King's troops slowly approached the fortress."

> "At night, the conspirators met, concealed by the forest's dense growth."

Those who disdain attention to grammar might consider an observation of James Russell Lowell: "Precision of thought is expressed by precision of language and is largely dependent on the habit of it."

Finally, the writer should explain all abbreviations, numbers, equations, symbols, charts, and graphs in words. These explanations can be handled in footnotes, appendices, a list of symbols and abbreviations, or in the text itself. But they must be there lest the writer risk losing the reader's good will. Symbols without identification both annoy readers and impede their ability to follow the argument. Arguments that cannot be followed will rarely seem convincing.

Strive for Balanced Structure. Sentences might be considered as being balanced on a scale—the subject and its modifiers on one side, the predicate and its modifiers on the other. If too much material or too many words are packed into either the subject or the predicate, the sentence is out of balance. The phrases, "out of balance," "out of kilter," "askew" all suggest that something is amiss. Thus the careful writer will see to it that he has not overloaded either his subjects or predicates. The principle of balance applies to both short and long sentences.

A properly balanced sentence also maintains parallel structure; it does not mix incompatible elements. Sentences that break the rule of parallel structure mix apples and oranges. The effect is usually as hideous as oranglesauce. Nouns, for example, should be balanced with other nouns, adjectives with other adjectives, adverbs with other adverbs. Failure to maintain such balance results in limping, awkward prose.

"That politician is arrogant, deceitful, and a bigot."

"That politician likes to play rough and winning every battle."

"That politician not only is greedy, but also takes bribes."

While the meaning of the author may be clear, the language is jarring. In each case, these ungainly sentences can be restored to a state of balance.

"That politician is arrogant, deceitful, and bigoted."

"That politician likes to play rough and to win every battle."

"That politician is not only greedy, but also bribable."

Moreover, in a balanced sentence, the predicate is appropriate for the subject. Beginning writers frequently commit the error of predicating the impossible.

"Huey Long was able to arouse charisma in his audiences."

"The organization of this paper will state stages in the history of Tammany Hall."

"A race riot in Colfax, Louisiana, murdered fifty-nine people."

Unfortunately for the authors of these three sentences, charisma cannot be aroused, organization does not state anything, and riots do not commit murder.

Balance in the structure of prose also means varying the pace of the writing. The simplest way to achieve variety in pace is to balance long and short sentences within a paragraph. Prose is not poetry. Good prose has rhythm, but its rhythm is not constant. A string of long sentences has a sonorous cadence and can put a reader to sleep, whereas a string of short sentences produces a staccato effect. Occasionally a rapid–fire barrage of short sentences can be very effective. But a steady stream of short sentences soon grates on the reader's ears. The great rhythmic power of prose lies in its ability to change its beat, to move smoothly from one tempo to another. Changing the tempo is not a mere mechanical process of alternating long and short sentences. It is not easy to develop a distinctive and attractive prose rhythm or pace, but the good writer works hard on this aspect of his composition. Many find it helpful to read their writing aloud, to listen to the sound and rhythm of their words and sentences. At the minimum, the apprentice writer must be aware of pace and edit his work accordingly.

Work for Smooth, Natural Transitions. As in a fine garment sewn together from separate pieces, the seams of a well-made article should not mar its smooth and elegant lines. Segments of a paper should flow together without awkward interruption, and gracefully written transitions should guide the progress of a reader. Sentences that knit together the paragraphs and sections of a paper are among the most difficult to write. The vexation of composing transition sentences, however, does not excuse resorting to such "clanking machinery" as "In terms of," "We shall now turn to," "We shall now demonstrate." If you find yourself losing the struggle with transitions, you might ask how well you really understand the connection you are trying to forge. Reconsidering the link itself may lead you to the language you need. Another technique is to form a transition by repeating words or phrases that have just been used in a previous paragraph or section. Another transitional device is the insertion of sub-headings into the text. If, regardless of such techniques, you can discern no clear connection between segments of your paper, you ought to reconsider its structural design. No technique can compensate for chaotic organization.

DON'TS

Avoid the Hallmarks of Casual Prose. Slang, colloquial expressions, dialect, idioms, clichés, trite phrases, jargon, neologisms, and foreign words or phrases are all avoidable. Good writers use a lively style and shun the hackneyed. Phrases like "the panorama of the past," "a crushing defeat," "wheel of fortune," and "play it by ear" have become so worn that they no longer carry the punch they had when first written. The clichés that seem to dominate casual prose by no means exhaust the possible combination of words. A good writer creates new phrases, phrases born from precision of thought, from familiarity with a subject, and from sensitivity to artistic expression.

Jargon and what some call "bureaucratese" are becoming increasingly difficult to avoid. Government reports are full of bastard words—"saleswise," "air-minded," and "finalize." These ungainly creations often lend themselves to double meanings. For example, does "sales-wise" mean "possessing good sense in the market place" or "concerned with commercial exchange"? Does "air-minded" mean "concerned about the atmosphere" or "a person whose ideas are light and thin"? Good writers avoid these words and phrases not only because they are ugly, insipid, and tired, but also because they lack precision.

Avoid Both Too Many and Too Lengthy Quotations. Quotations should be used to fulfill three major functions: (1) to corroborate a claim, (2) to illustrate its meaning, and (3) to enhance its impact. Quotations thrown into the text to add length merely detract from substance. If, for instance, one wanted to argue that John Adams believed that Plato's *Republic* was a satire, he might want to quote a part of one of Adams' letters to Thomas Jefferson that makes that argument. If one wanted to argue that John Adams often saw American political problems in light of his knowledge of Greek and Roman history, he might want to include a few quotations from Adams' writings, speeches, or letters, illustrating this theme. If one wanted to argue that Adams did not understand ancient political theory, he might want to select a quotation with an egregious misinterpretation of an ancient text. The point is to know why you are quoting.

Used judiciously and in accordance with strategic calculations, quotations can both add to the historian's persuasiveness and vary the pace of his writing. But a paper that is simply a string of quotations, however artfully linked together, is not an argument at all and will not persuade the reader to accept either the interpretations or findings. The historian would do well to heed the advice of the debate coach. "Argue. Don't just be a human transition between quotation cards." The novice writer should try to compose his first draft without using quotations at all. He can insert them later if they will truly add force to his argument.

Historians must also be wary of letting quotations speak for them. The writer should try to state in his own words his understanding of the message or meaning of a quotation and not rely on the reader to extract this information on his own. Readers may draw their own conclusions from quotations, but the historian should make sure that the reader can easily comprehend how he interprets and uses any material quoted in the paper. Moreover, the historian should use language that leads naturally into a quotation, rather than relying on such clumsy constructions as, "he said, . . ." or "Let me quote from . . . ."

Long quotations may also disrupt the text of a paper. Unlike a short quotation that can vary the tempo of writing, a long quotation usually brings a paper to a dead stop. The reader is interested primarily in what the writer is saying, not in what someone else has already said. If the historian has a piece of primary evidence that must be quoted in full, he should try to put it into a footnote or an appendix. Other material, such as the views of other scholars, ought to be paraphrased, with the historian taking care to cite those scholars properly in a footnote. On those rare occasions when it seems imperative to include a long quotation in the text, it should be set off as a block quotation, that is, single-spaced and properly indented.

Avoid the Passive Voice. Sentences written in the passive voice usually fall flat; even more important, they fail to identify the agent or agents responsible for the action specified in the sentences. Instead of telling the reader "who did something," the passive voice says only that "something was done." Sentences constructed in this fashion not only lack vitality, but also rob us of important information. Consider the following simple sentence. "In this fight, the President was defeated." Although the sentence informs the reader that the President lost a battle, it does not disclose who or what defeated the President. If the historian knew that a coalition of senators from the South thwarted him, he ought to say so in the active voice. After all, a political battle is full of action and the prose should reflect it.

The passive voice can be used effectively only when the agent of the action is unknown. The historian knows that the action took place, but not who or what did it. The effective writer confines his use of the passive voice to this situation.

Avoid Abuse of Rhetorical Figures. Overuse of rhetorical figures such as metaphors, similes, irony, puns, hyperbole, rhetorical questions, alliteration, or repetition, may induce the reader to scream out, "Enough is enough!" Rhetorical figures are a bit like rich desserts. A little is satisfying; too much is cloying. The apprentice writer, having discovered the power of hyperbole or the impact of irony, is often tempted to abuse these devices. Indeed, it is fun to see how long one can sustain a metaphor, how many times one can pun, and how much can be packed into a single simile. But after tasting the delight of such an exercise, the sensitive writer recognizes that his reader is not likely to find the result appetizing and edits accordingly. This very paragraph itself comes close to commiting the sin it warns against. The experienced writer learns to stop before he has pushed a good thing too far. The apprentice writer, with perhaps less sensitivity to how much the reader can comfortably endure, is advised to err on the side of caution. Because abuse of rhetorical figures irritates the reader and overshadows the argument being made, the persuasive writer takes care to use these devices sparingly, so that their effect is to enhance rather than detract from the meaning of his work.

Politicians, striving for public attention, often resort to jarring hyperbole. Thus, for Richard Nixon, a reshuffling of federal agencies and departments was the "second American Revolution;" and for Jimmy Carter, the current American tax system was a "disgrace to the human race." Verbal overkill makes an argument seem ridiculous rather than persuasive. Thus the careful writer generally avoids such hyperbolic words and "greatest," "enormous," "exceedingly," or "stupendous."

Similarly, inexperienced writers frequently reach for inappropriate metaphors. A metaphor describes one kind of object or idea by using words or phrases that literally denote another. For example, when we speak of a ship plowing the sea, we are describing the ship's movement in water by analogy to a plow's movement on land. Used properly, metaphors have great power. But metaphors also may be trite, strained, or illogical. Eager to show how large corporations flourished in the absence of government regulation, a student once wrote that "the trusts were wallowing in the filth of *laissez-faire.*" Although the student laudably did not turn to a commonplace, worn-out analogy, the image of trusts wallowing in filth, like pigs, clashes with the tone of a scholarly work. Moreover, the term "filth" is an inappropriate physical analogy for a policy or process like *laissez-faire.* The careful writer also avoids mixing incompatible figures. The mixed metaphor is sometimes unintentionally comic, but usually just absurd. Consider the following passages that were actually printed in the *New York Times:*

> "The Assemblymen also were miffed at their Senate counterparts because they have refused to bite the bullet that now seems to have grown to the size of a millstone to the Assemblymen whose necks are on the line."

and

> "Breaking of the urban renewal logjam in Englewood came upon the heels of long-smoldering and occasionally explosive unrest in the public school."

In the first passage, the inattentive writer made a bullet expand into a millstone (clearly impossible), and then conflated two different sayings ("having a millstone around one's neck" and "putting one's neck on the line"). In the second passage, the writer had a logjam following the footsteps of turmoil. The copy editor of the *New York Times* calls these gaffs "mixaphors," a neologism almost as ungainly as the error itself.

Tactics of Argumentation

Tactics borrowed from the domain of argumentation or debate can be used profitably to reinforce the historian's strategy of persuasion. But the historian does not assume a posture identical to that of the debater or the attorney. Advocates in debate or in law assume positions in advance of inquiry which they must defend against the onslaughts of adversaries assuming contrary positions. This form of advocacy reflects the conviction that truth emerges from competition between advocates defending alternative theses as ably as possible. The historian, however, is not expected to take positions before completing research or to anticipate immediate refutation and response to his work by those equally concerned with advancing other points of view. Yet the historian inevitably becomes an advocate for what he has learned about the past. If necessary, he is willing to engender controversy, to challenge the conclusions of other historians, and to assail their methods of inquiry. He may even turn the tables on a scholarly adversary, using the other's own material to advance a contrary thesis of his own.

For most audiences, historical work loses credibility if the historian assumes the posture of the debater or lawyer responsible for defending a preset position against an immediate adversary. A more persuasive posture is that of the judicious inquirer—serious, open-minded, committed to seeking truth, and receptive to new evidence and fresh perspective. The historian should not appear bound dogmatically to his conclusions. He should accord due credit to intellectual adversaries and not try to belittle or browbeat them, to drown them in rhetoric, or to defeat them on technicalities. Moreover, to establish his competence and credibility, the historian must demonstrate that he has considered all relevant evidence reasonably within his purview, and alternative hypotheses reasonably within his range of knowledge and expertise. Unlike the debater, the historian will not be excused by the second audience for suppressing evidence contrary to his positions. We might laugh at Soviet history that recreates the Russian Revolution without Leon Trotsky. But the historian who more subtly shades the presentation of conflicting evidence commits the same error and leaves himself open to ridicule, disparagement, and telling refutation of his work.

We recommend honest persuasion. Even as a judicious inquirer, the historian can employ tactics of the debater in his strategic calculations. But the historian should not deliberately mislead the second audience or use arguments that he believes could not withstand scrutiny by the universal audience.

PREEMPTION

No matter how carefully planned and executed, an historical work may still possess weaknesses likely to be perceived by the second audience. As a means of preempting potential criticism, authors sometime mention and refute expected objections in the text or footnotes of the paper itself. By anticipating his critics, the author can express potential objections to his work in a form amenable to convincing retort. Moreover, faced with a preemptive strike, a critic can no longer address his objections directly to the author's work. Instead he must now consider the work, the objections, and the author's response to the objection before delivering his own rejoinder. Charles B. Dew, for instance, in his article "Disciplining Slave Ironworkers in the Antebellum South: Coercion, Conciliation, and Accommodation," attempts to preempt objections to his reliance on the operations of ironmasters "whose furnaces and forges lay in the Valley of Virginia."

> More detailed evidence is available on the antebellum Virginia iron industry than for any other Southern state, but research in the surviving records of iron establishments that were located in other areas of the South indicates that Virginia's labor practices were characteristic of the industry throughout the slave states. The emphasis on a specific group of men in a specific area also reflects a conviction that only through close and detailed case studies of the ways in which slavery functioned on day to day basis can we begin to understand what it meant to be a slave in any phase of the American slave system, industrial or agricultural, urban or rural.*

Although effective response to Dew's preemptive argument still might be possible, his case is likely to be far more convincing than if he had simply ignored the issue.

Preemption is a perfectly legitimate tactic; the historian should not fear to employ it so long as he does not misstate an objection or consciously devise a fallacious response. Preemptive arguments must be used sparingly, however, lest a work appear excessively defensive or lest the author raise objections that may never have ben considered or given much credence by the second audience. Preemptive arguments often are better presented in sub-

---

*Excerpt from Charles B. Dew, "Disciplining Slave Ironworkers in the Antebellum South: Coercion, Conciliation and Accommodation," *American Historical Review* 79 (1974), copyright © 1974 by American Historical Association. Reprinted by permission.

stantive footnotes than in the main text of an article. Tucked away in the footnotes, they protect the author without calling undue attention to possible shortcomings of his study or forcing him to adopt a defensive tone.

SPREADING

In the parlance of debaters, "the spread" is an effort to overwhelm opponents with more arguments than they can effectively answer in the alloted time. The victims of this technique face the unhappy dilemma of either passing over some opposition arguments or weakening their own responses by abbreviation. Moreover, by using the spread, advocates protect their own position from an unexpected but convincing refutation by an opponent. The spread is an especially powerful tactic for a historian advancing a thesis that is controversial or that runs against the inclinations of the second audience. One of the authors, for instance, has used this tactic as part of his effort to refute the widely held conviction that the presidential election of 1928 in the United States was a "critical" or "turning point" election that ushered in the New Deal era of political competition. Instead of relying on a single procedure for identifying a "critical" or "turning point" election, he used several. Instead of confining his analysis and argument to general elections, he investigated primary elections and changes in the party registrations of voters. All the separate lines of argument led to the single conclusion that the election of 1928 did not significantly change patterns of American electoral politics. Thus, even though a critic might effectively refute one of his arguments, there are still three or four more arguments that support the interpretation offered.

Good historians, like good debaters, shun the mindless spread, carefully avoiding arguments devoid of merit. The accumulation of specious or irrelevant arguments will serve only to destroy the credibility of a scholar, thus defeating his efforts at persuasion. The historian considering the persuasive effectiveness of the spread would do well to remember a sage trial lawyer's advice to a novice attorney, "If you think you've won your case, stop talking."

THE EITHER-OR

Logicians recognize that arguments with contradictory premises still can yield the same conclusions. This insight is of use to historians who must rely frequently on controversial reports for the derivation of other historical reports or the formulation of historical explanations. Historians can advance persuasively a thesis in the face of conflicting opinion on the credibility of relevant reports by contending that the outcome is the same regardless of which of several possible reports the audience accepts. The historian exploiting this technique maintains that a particular conclusion is likely to be true if either one or another report is correct. For example, Edward J. Epstein uses this technique to challenge the finding of the Warren Report that a single bullet fired by Lee Harvey Oswald struck both President Kennedy and Governor John Connally. Epstein insists that, on the contrary, separate bullets fired by two different assassins wounded each man. He argues that either the conclusion of the FBI report that no exit wound was present on the President's body or the conclusion pieced together from several reports that the alleged exit wound in the President's throat was below the wound in his back imply that a bullet could not have entered Kennedy's back, traveled through his body, and struck Governor Connally. Those using the either-or technique, however, should be aware that an adversary could respond by pointing to yet another possibility not considered in the initial argument. Thus defenders of the Warren Report have disdained to entertain either of Epstein's alternative reports, arguing instead that available evidence shows the entrance wound in Kennedy's back to be higher than the exit wound in his throat. The either-or tactic should be employed only when the historian is fairly sure that the possibilities he proposes are the only likely inferences from available evidence.

REFERENCE TO AUTHORITY

Since the Middle Ages, arguments based on appeal to authority have fallen into disrepute. No longer can an advocate credibly sustain a conclusion merely by citing the pronouncements of a recognized sage. Yet by referring to the work of prominent scholars who have dealt with the subject matter of the paper, the historian can suggest to the second audience that he is part of the "big picture," that he keeps company with the luminaries of his field. Appropriate references to authority suggest that an author is engaging in discussion with high-powered intellects and is grappling with questions that have concerned the most notable of scholars. Andrew A. Appleby, for example, in the second sentence of his article, "Agrarian Capitalism or Seigneurial Reaction? The Northwest of England 1500–1700," sets his study in the context of work accomplished by two of England's most prominent historians —Eric Kerridge and the late R. H. Tawney.

Moreover, historians sometimes become giant killers, deliberately challenging the Goliaths of a field in order to establish the significance of their own contributions. Kathleen Conzen, in the conclusion of her article on residential patterns in Milwaukee, takes on Frederick Jackson Turner and his seminal work on the American frontier. In history, as well as in biblical epics and fairy tales, giant killing is dangerous but rewarding, if successful. Historians should beware, however, that gratuitous attacks on respected scholars will probably offend rather than impress the second audience. Golden eggs do not await all who try to scale the beanstalk.

Historians also may cite authorities as models for particular approaches to an historical issue. Although the second audience's acceptance of an approach will not be determined solely by reference to authority, historians can strengthen the credibility of their position by drawing upon the prestige earned by other scholars. For instance, French scholars of family history often invoke the name of Louis Henry, distinguished pioneer in the application of demographic techniques to studying historical families.

BALANCING EVIDENCE AND DISCUSSION

Reports and explanations advanced by either a debater or a historian are founded ultimately on the application of generalizations to empirical evidence. Yet not every report and explanation merits the same emphasis on evidence and inference. A historical report may be so well accepted by scholars that no evidence need be presented to establish its credibility. Even the most timorous student would not feel compelled to cite documents proving that George Washington was the first President of the United States or that John F. Kennedy was assassinated on November 22, 1963, in Dallas, Texas. In contrast, the historian inferring reports from new evidence, challenging entrenched positions, or entering a standing controversy will describe thoroughly his evidence and reasoning process. A historian may enter the controversy over the paternity of Brutus, exploring the thesis that Brutus was, in fact, the son of Julius Caesar, and was conceived during a long lasting affair between Caesar and Brutus' mother, Servilia. Obviously, without detailed analysis of the available evidence, an historian could not hope to persuade the second or third audience that Brutus was Caesar's son, that Brutus was not Caesar's son, or even that either report is equally likely to be true.

Yet another category of reports and explanations may require some elaboration of evidence and argument. A historical conclusion, although solidly supported by available evidence, may simply be unfamiliar to the second audience. For instance, archeological findings indicate that little girls of ancient Greece probably played with dolls that had articulated limbs. Yet even those who specialize in ancient history are unlikely to be aware of these findings. If they considered the matter, historians would agree surely that Greek girls probably had such dolls. To compensate for the unfamiliarity of the report, however, an author should cite evidence for it in his article. The citation need not be exhaustive, embracing every archeological report that mentions a doll with articulated limbs. A few examples will suffice because the credibility of the report is not likely to meet serious challenge.

A historical work not only should contain enough evidence and argument to sustain its findings, but also should include sufficient information for a reader to follow its internal logic. Writers should not encumber their work with clanking machinery or dwell upon minutia, but must be careful not to leap from point to point without a clear indication of the route being followed. A historian may be familiar with all the steps of his reasoning, but the reader may not be. A reader who loses the thread of the logic will not be very receptive to the conclusions. Internal summaries may help lead a reader through the pathways traced by historical argument. Summaries also create variation, perhaps slowing the hectic pace of an article or offering respite from the absorption of difficult material. The more complex the work, the more apposite the classic dictum: "Tell them what you're going to tell them; tell them; tell them what you've told them."

When exploring a topic little known to the second audience, a historian may supply the audience with background information. Although sometimes necessary for comprehension, background data may also bog down a work and detract from its central motif. Background discussion should be kept to a minimum and integrated into the structure of a paper. If necessary, refer the reader to other books and articles. Too often, beginning historians lose their audience before their paper really begins by including a lengthy, tedious, and disconnected section of background information. These sections usually attempt to encompass far more material than can be treated compactly. Without new evidence or illuminating insights, they both bore the reader and risk affronting him with distortions produced by unsubstantiated generalizations or excessive compression. Moreover, these sections rarely include information that could not be obtained elsewhere. For example, if a historian were writing about a riot in France in the early 1790's, he should not begin with a background section on the French Revolution; if he were writing about the funding of the Apollo Project, he should not begin with a background section on the history of the American space program.

CREATING PRESENCE

Following a strategic blueprint, authors often seek to create "presence" for aspects of their work. They strive to impress a message or feeling on the consciousness of a reader, to awaken his interest, and to advance conclusions to the forefront of his attention. While a writer creates presence through command of a subject, logical argument and mastery of formal prose, he can also draw judiciously on rhetorical techniques. The following list describes some of the more useful techniques.

Rhetorical Figures. Although we earlier warned against abuse of rhetorical figures, they can, when skillfully used, enhance the presence of a work. In his masterful description of Hamilton Fish's sense of integrity, for instance, Allan Nevins creatively revives an otherwise lifeless metaphor. "He [Fish] sometimes chipped the cube of truth to make it roll." And Samuel Flagg Bemis cleverly uses assonance to introduce his discussion of a diplomatic controversy over the hunting of seals. "Amphibious is the fur seal, ubiquitous and carnivorous, uniparous, gregarious and withal polygamous."

Anecdotes and Illustrations. Brief accounts of interesting events and concrete illustrations can bring a work down to earth, offering easy points of contact for a reader. Anecdotes and illustrations also help convey the atmosphere of place or period and reveal the rough edges of experience that abstraction and generalization necessarily smooth over.

Flagging. To supplement strategic decisions on what to emphasize in a paper, writers occasionally flag or signal especially significant ideas or information. In verbal discourse we often flag items by pausing, changing the tone and volume of our voice, and varying the speed of our delivery. In written discourse, we rely on the words themselves, perhaps using such familiar flag terms as "key," "central," "crucial," "essential." To avoid overselling ideas or striking a tone that seems labored or patronizing, however, flag terms should be used sparingly and selectively.

If pressed too far or used ineptly, the tactics of argumentation can subvert the goal of persuading the second audience. An author must be alert to writing that seems labored or contrived and to signs that the bare bones of his tactics protrude through the flesh of his paper. Moreover, he should not allow tactics to become red flags, calling attention to potential flaws in his work. Thus an author may shun the explicit use of an either-or argument, unless fairly certain that he has considered all likely possibilities. He may try to avoid spreading techniques or rhetorical devices that spotlight weak links in a chain of argument. And he may decide to forgo preemption of an objection not likely to be raised by the second audience.

The Process of Writing: Outlines and First Drafts

The production of a finished paper is a process. That is, it proceeds in stages, usually beginning with an outline, then a first draft, and concluding with a succession of revisions.

An apprentice writer using the model we have just described would be well-advised to compose a detailed outline before beginning the first draft of his paper. The very process of drawing up a detailed outline of the body of a paper virtually compels the historian to plan his presentation carefully and keep it from swirling aimlessly from point to point. Since an outline is also likely to take care of organizational problems, it leaves the writer free to concentrate on his prose. Though some writers manage to organize effectively as they write, and regard the outline as a nuisance or hindrance, even those who disdain a preliminary outline would do well to outline their work once a first draft has been written. The process is invaluable for discovering structural flaws in a paper and in forcing a precise definition of the subtopics, their relations to one another, and to the general topic.

Once you have established a detailed outline, you will be in a position to fine tune decisions about emphasis. Which subtopics need fullest development? Which ones can be handled by reference to existing scholarship? Which ones are most important to the main topic? When such questions still seem unanswerable, the need probably still exists to think about the whole project or to read more in the scholarly literature, or both. It will probably save countless hours of wasted effort to resolve these questions as soon as you identify them.

Finally, the historian should compare his detailed outline to the material he has gathered. Does the outline raise questions for which he has insufficient evidence to answer? If so, he has at least pinpointed the specific areas needing further research. At this point, the historian should also make a thorough assessment of the "fit" between his own tentative conclusions and other scholarly interpretations. Sharp divergence between his views and those of other historians also will indicate areas for further, intensive investigation.

Historians generally begin the task of formal composition by producing a preliminary or first draft of their paper. Some historians follow their rough outline, writing down everything that comes to mind, without worrying much about structure or style. They try to express and develop all of their ideas, returning later to reexamine the paper's argument, hone its prose, and tighten its organization. Their first drafts may be twice as long as the paper they ultimately produce. Other historians follow a different procedure, composing lean and spare skeletons to be fleshed out in later efforts. They focus on the sequence of arguments, the layout of evidence, and the internal structure of their paper. Since they do not expect to say everything they know or fully develop their insights at this stage, they are likely to write drafts substantially shorter than the final paper. Still other historians try to approximate the length of the final paper in the first draft, writing with the intention of making only minor adjustments during revision. Historians also may write their first draft in separate segments, later fusing them into a coherent work. An especially common procedure is to compose the main body of the paper first, and then to add the introductory and concluding sections.

Although historians approach a first draft in a way that best suits their personal style and temperament, most follow a few basic procedures. First, historians spend time—as much as it takes—reviewing the material they have collected. They may reorganize subject categories if it seems advantageous and make lists of supporting evidence and illustrations in the approximate order suggested by their outline. Then they carefully review this augmented outline, paying attention to how the narrative flows or argument progresses. If a tentative organization seems disjointed or confused, this is the time for revision. It is far easier to restructure an outline than reorganize an already written paper.

When you are finally ready to write the first draft, make sure to work where you can concentrate. Constant interruptions and noise are enemies of effective writing. A historian working alone, in a quiet room, will be best able to channel his energy and intelligence to the immediate task of composition. Another elementary thing to remember at the drafting stage, which will later need revising, is to leave plenty of space between lines and at the top, bottom, and side margins of each page. Whether you type or write your first draft in longhand, having this space available will make it far easier to make additions and editorial corrections on the first draft itself, thus dispensing with an intermediate copy. In addition, by writing on only one side of the page, a historian can place drastic revisions on the reverse side as well as rearrange, cut up, and scotch tape back together sections of the draft.

There are several ways to handle footnotes while drafting. One method is to include the full citation within the text itself, setting it off in square brackets, or writing it in a differently colored ink. Another is to number footnotes consecutively while keeping a separate and corresponding list with full bibliographic citations. This latter method, however, is inadvisable, because if you have to reorganize the first draft even slightly, the sequence of numbers will be disrupted and a citation might end up tied to the wrong sentence. A few writers manage to write first drafts without paying any attention to footnotes, a proceduure that invites disaster and should generally be avoided. However you decide to cope with footnotes in your draft, be consistent. A misstep here may cause you to waste hours later, frantically shuffling through notes, looking for the card or page that corresponds to the quotation or idea needed for a footnote. If you pay attention to these details while working on your first draft, it will save you much time and anxiety later on.

Finally, a word about time and effort. Writing is hard work. Only when we are forced to commit thoughts to paper do we face having to think hard. We may feel that we understand something, but the real test is to express formally what we think we know. Historians need ample time to write; few professional scholars expect to turn out more than five to ten good pages a day. Do not deceive yourself into thinking that you can write a research paper in a couple of evenings. The effort devoted to choosing a topic, framing questions, gathering material, devising arguments, and making an outline will be wasted unless you devote comparable effort to writing.

Intellectual Honesty and Plagiarism

Some teachers tell their classes a story to illustrate the problem of plagiarism. An unmarried, intelligent, and educated woman lived in a society in which job opportunities for women were extremely limited. She wrote a fine book about an important historical question. But, because she was a woman and because she was relatively unknown, only a few copies of her work were sold. Much to her dismay two years later, she read a book by another prominent and male historian dealing with the same question she had treated in her book. She was not upset at finding another book on the topic, for she relished scholarly discussion and debate. What did cause her grief was finding in the other writer's book the same argument she had presented in her study without a single reference to her book. She felt robbed and could not endure to let the intellectual thievery go by unnoticed. She sent the offending author a terse and tart letter. "Dear Sir," she wrote, "If you will prevent me from making my living with my ideas, I fear I shall be forced to earn it with my body."

Intellectual theft does not always produce such dire consequences, at least for the person who is robbed. But theft is theft and the offender, if caught, is likely to suffer severe penalties. In one way, theft of an idea is even worse than theft of money or goods. Money or merchandise can be restored. But an idea is irreplaceable. You cannot give back to a person another idea for the one you stole.

Plagiarism, the theft of another's research and thinking, has reached the level of a plague. Its most heinous manifestation is the purchased research paper, passed off to the professor as the student's own work. Another common manifestation is the paper that contains significant amounts of material, sometimes lifted verbatim, from books and articles without any footnote or indication in the text that the material was produced by someone other than the student. We cannot ignore this form of theft any more than we can ignore having our own pockets picked. Students who engage in intellectual thievery should not be surprised to find themselves punished if caught.

Moreover, writers commit more subtle forms of plagiarism, thefts that occur without the writer being fully conscious of what he is doing. This lack of awareness causes many acts of plagiarism. The honest author can guard against accidental theft by making himself scrupulous about the way he takes his notes and writes his article. In the chapter on research, we suggested several ways the writer can make sure that his research notes indicate clearly which words and ideas belong to the author he is reading and which are his own comments on that author's work. By following those procedures, the conscientious writer can guard against unintended plagiarism.

A few rules of thumb can be followed to help resolve the often difficult problem of knowing when to acknowledge an idea found in another writer's work. First, if the idea has been expounded by only one historian, by all means, confess your indebtedness. This acknowledgment can come in the text itself (this is the more gracious manner) or in a footnote. If the idea is part of the general scholarly opinion, you need not fear plagiarizing. Judgments like "George Washington was one of America's finest Presidents" need not be accompanied by citations of the opinions of other scholars.

Most ideas, however, fall into that vast middle ground between the unique and generally accepted. The safest policy is to acknowledge secondary sources, lest your second audience feel that you are trying to pass off the idea as your own original creation. Most working historians cherish honesty in scholarship. Any other course risks affronting your audience or perhaps even suffering sanctions ranging from demands for revision to outright rejection, or even to lawsuits for plagiarizing published scholarship.

Language as well as ideas can be stolen from an author. During our research, we often come across beautifully written sentences or phrases; we exclaim to ourselves, "I wish I had said that." Despite our wish, the reality is that someone else said it first. An inviolate rule among scholars is that language written by another must appear in quotation marks when reproduced in a paper. The quotation of especially elegant language can cast reflected glory on your own work, showing the reader that you too appreciate a finely wrought sentence or phrase. But if you fail to acknowledge your debt to another writer, and if the second audience recognizes the theft, he will be sufficiently outraged to discount any other strengths of your work. You need not run such risks, especially since proper acknowledgment can work to your benefit. Like any other tactic quotation of another's words simply because those words are so elegantly arranged must not be overdone. In a relatively short research paper of 15 to 20 pages, the tactic is effective only once or twice. Used more often, it becomes tedious.

Contrary to supposition, paraphrasing is not a foolproof way of avoiding plagiarism. Indeed, the act of paraphrasing often encourages plagiarism. Historians paraphrasing someone else's work should reveal what has been done in the text or in a footnote. Second, minor alteration in the text of another's work is not a true paraphrase. Those marginal changes are but a thin disguise for theft of language. To paraphrase means to restate another person's ideas *in your own language.* Changing a verb or two, reordering clauses within sentences, is not paraphrasing. It is still theft, even though you have tinkered with the words you stole.

Any honest and conscientious writer will try to avoid any hint of plagiarism. This form of theft discredits both the credibility of the paper and the reputation of the author.

Critical Book Reviews

Like the research paper, the critical review is a mainstay of historical scholarship and a frequent assignment in history classes. By describing and evaluating the labors of others, as well as by performing original research, historians advance our understanding of past events. Criticism places scholarship in appropriate context, reveals its major contributions, exposes inadequate evidence and flawed reasoning, and may point to the synthesis of disparate work or suggest new questions and programs of research.

Skill in description and criticism also extends beyond historical study. From television ads to newspaper editorials to government reports, we confront communication urging us to purchase a product, accept an idea, or follow a course of action. The same knowledge and skills required for criticizing the work of historians can be applied to evaluating the messages of daily life and communicating our judgments to others.

Those seeking guidance on how to organize a critical review can follow the model outlined below. Although not the only appropriate format, the model is straightforward and easy to follow.

I. Introduction.
II. Brief summary of contents, including major arguments and descriptive material.
III. Place of work in current historiography.
IV. Internal analysis of the work.
V. Aesthetic analysis of the work.
VI. Summation.

INTRODUCTION

A good critical review usually opens with a crisp introductory paragraph. This paragraph should "hook" the reader just as in a research paper. The introduction can focus on the book's thesis, the reviewer's assessment, or the historical problem being addressed; it must have impact and lead the reader directly into the brief summary of the contents of the book. Ronald L. Hayes, for example, introduces a review of Julian Jaynes' *The Origin of Consciousness in the Breakdown of the Bicameral Mind* with the following provocative yet informative lines: "Moses was a schizophrenic. The Code of Hammurabi and large portions of the Old Testament are the products of people who today would be shuffling through the back wards of mental institutions. Indeed, the entire history of human activity until about 3500 years ago—the development of language, writing, law, geometry, cities, calendars, art and architecture—all can be attributed to people whose thought processes would be labeled psychotic by contemporary standards."

SUMMARY OF CONTENTS

A critical book review, although not a book report, incorporates a book report into its text. Too often beginners simply summarize a book and claim to have produced a review. A critical review goes beyond recapitulation of a book's contents to evaluate the work and show how it relates to other scholarship. But reviewers often ground their analysis on a brief description of a work.

A reviewer's description should disclose a book's outline and reveal the issues addressed by the author. But the reviewer should concentrate his attention on the book's most important conclusions and their supporting arguments. Thus evaluation cannot be separated from description; a reviewer cannot decide what to emphasize in his summary without first determining the major contribution of a book. Side issues only need to be mentioned in passing or omitted entirely if space is constrained. A reviewer may choose to abstract and synthesize the contents of a book, supplemented perhaps by a brief summary, chapter by chapter. Or he may isolate one or more chapters for detailed discussion.

Because a work's significance can be determined only in relation to the scholarship of others, reviewers must indicate how a book relates to work already accomplished in the field. Readers will surely want to know what is original about an author's approach, methods, evidence, reasoning, and conclusions. Books that fail to break new ground generally are dismissed summarily by reviewers. Moreover, readers may want to know how a work can be synthesized with other contributions to broaden understanding of historical questions. Those unfamiliar with relevant work can turn to other book reviews and to historiographic essays. For reviews, one can draw upon newspapers (e.g., *New York Times Review of Books, London Times Literary Supplement*); review periodicals (e.g., *New York Review of Books*); magazines (*New Republic, Harpers, Saturday Review*); scholarly journals (e.g., *History, American Historical Review, Journal of American History*); and two new publications, *Reviews in American History* and *Reviews in European History*. The *Book Review Digest* can also guide one to journals reviewing a particular book.

Historians may also consider in this section how the climate of opinion at the time the book was written may have affected the work under review. Scholarship is not an isolated enterprise; historians are influenced by the times in which they write and by the work of others. Contemporary affairs may have influenced the questions asked and the conclusion reached. For example, historians' views of Woodrow Wilson and the aborted League of Nations have changed dramatically over time. The 1920's, a period of profound disillusion in Europe, saw many historians arguing that Wilson's ideas were hopelessly utopian and absolutely unworkable. Later in the mid 1940's, when there arose a strong sentiment in favor of forming a new world organization—the United Nations—a revision of previous historical opinion took place. While scholars debated Wilson's role in the failure of the League, most believed that the ideals represented by the League were sound. In more recent years, with the availability of far more abundant documentation about the Peace Conference at Versailles, historians have revised their earlier view that Wilson was an uninformed and unrealistic diplomat. The now declassified records have shown Wilson to have been remarkably well-informed on many details and a vigorous negotiator.

INTERNAL ANALYSIS

This section of a review usually is the most lengthy and demanding. Evaluation of a book requires more than a statement of whether you liked the book. While strategic plans may call for an expression of your feelings about the book, these impressions cannot substitute for critical appraisal. Reviewers must clearly indicate the criteria against which they choose to measure an author's work. And reviewers should signify the importance of their criticisms.

Assessment of a book turns on a variety of issues. Reviewers may dissect the questions framed by an historian, probe the sufficiency of his evidence, assess the inner logic of his arguments, and examine the theories he uses to explain and judge historical events. Reviewers may also evaluate the structural design of a book, attending to such matters as the sequence of arguments, the development of sub–themes, and the clarity and ease of transitions. To guide your analysis, you can consider the models of inference and explanation sketched in Chapters II and III, the discussion of question framing in Chapter VII, and of organization in this chapter. For work using psychological theory or quantitative inference, you may also consider the delineation of psychohistory and quantitative history in Chapter V.

The following checklist of questions, although not exhaustive, illustrates how a reviewer begins to penetrate beneath the surface of a historical work.

1. What questions guide the author's research and thinking?
   a. Does the author exclude relevant and significant questions?
   b. Do his questions fulfill the logical requirements of question framing?
   c. How do his questions shape the course of inquiry?
2. Does the author examine all relevant and available evidence?
3. Does the author systematically consider alternative hypotheses?
4. What explanatory models does the author employ, e.g., Marxist economics or Freudian psychology; and how do these models influence his conclusions?
5. Does the author have any specific biases or interests that affect his work?

6. Does the author attempt moral judgments?
    a. What standards does he use?
    b. Are his standards set forth explicitly?
    c. Does he separate moral and empirical analysis?

7. How does the author organize his work?

AESTHETICS

Reviewers frequently comment on the aesthetic qualities of a book. As we noted earlier, form and content are inseparable. Clarity and elegance of prose, consistency of style, adherence to proper scholarly form, and other aesthetic issues all affect the contribution of a book. Robert L. Beisner, for instance, justly chides a scholar for flaws in his writing style.

> In addition, the book suffers from poor writing, especially in the first three-and-a-half chapters. One quotation will illustrate [the author's] penchant for obscure verbiage: "That the President in the all-out pursuit of a national policy objective did not take time out to deliberate studiously on the grounds for his action in order to determine some priority of motivation does not prove that there was no such priority, however unconscious, plus a blending of various motivational factors into what can be termed instinct." (!) If [the] publisher had played the role of rigorous editor, everyone would have been better off.

SUMMATION

Because a critical book review usually has a rather stringent limitation on its length, the summation is often very short, a paragraph or two at the most. In the summation, the reviewer synthesizes the points he has made in his evaluation and presents his estimation of the book's worth and importance. The following passage exemplifies a terse and informative summary of a critical review:

> The author appears to have scaled the historical mountain of post-World War I America simply because it had not been done before. The climb, however, has provided neither a coherent perspective on the period nor any new eye-catching insights or information. But he does present material that is not readily available elsewhere about a generally neglected period. I hope that his work will stimulate more systematic research.

APPENDIX:

EXPLANATORY MODELS

In Chapter III, "Historical Explanation," we briefly described the structure of an explanation positing that Marcus Brutus murdered Julius Caesar because Brutus believed that Caesar would make it impossible to preserve the Roman Republic. The diagram below further elaborates that explanation, filling in details that for the sake of simplicity we omitted from our earlier discussion.

The diagram shows how the historian uses covering laws and statements of conditions to justify his explanation. It includes both a factual and a theoretical component. The factual component consists of the historical reports inferred from empirical evidence; the theoretical component consists of the covering law, the statement of conditions under which the law applies, and the transformation rules (definitions that show what real–world observations correspond to the terms of the theory). The single direction arrows indicate the flow of causality in the model: from the causal event to the effect or event to be explained, and from the alternative event to the contrasting event.

Although formidable in appearance, the model actually has a fairly simple structure that includes all aspects of a causal explanation, and brings together the notions developed in Chapter III. The model shows how causal explanation depends upon inferring historical reports from evidence and applying causal theory to these reports. It discloses the importance of specifying alternative events as well as causal events and

FIGURE VIII

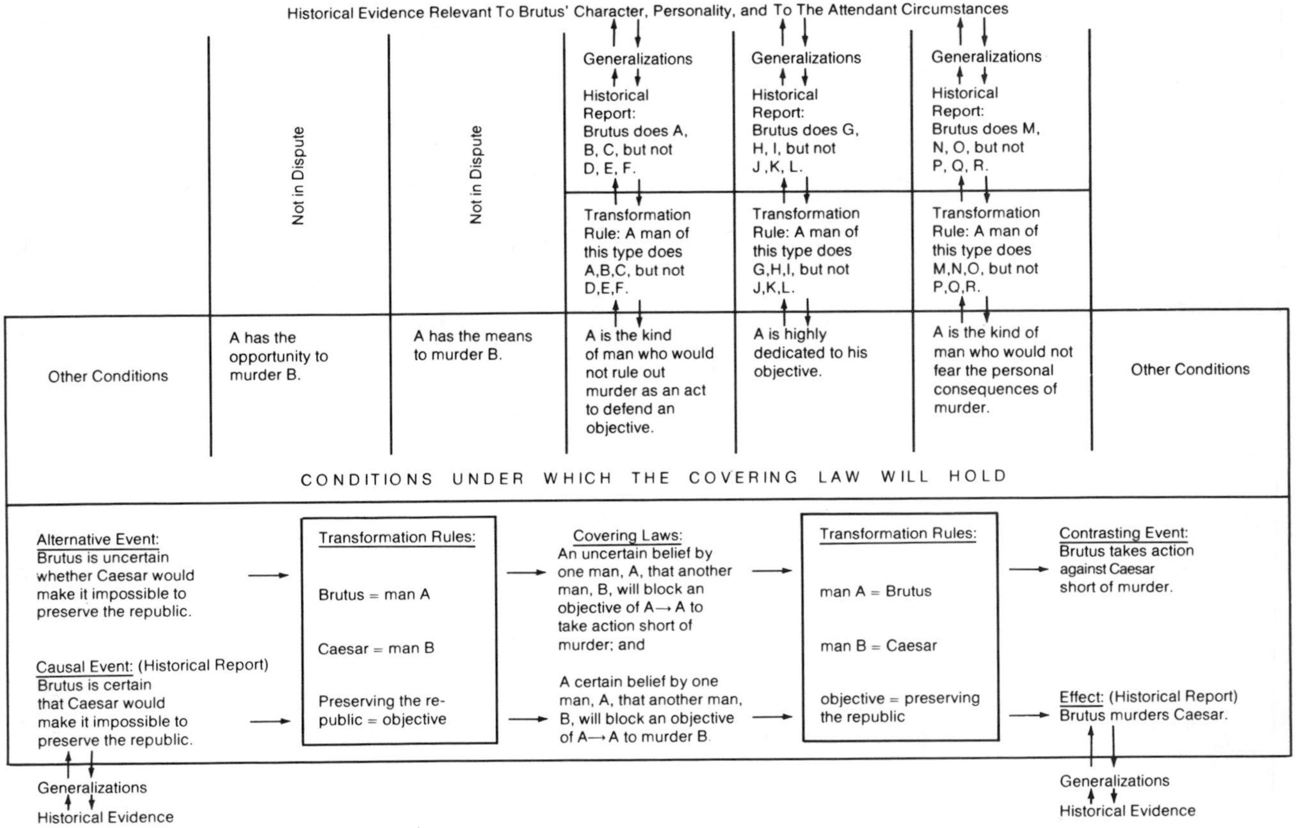

Historical Evidence Relevant To Brutus' Character, Personality, and To The Attendant Circumstances

Other Conditions	Not in Dispute	Not in Dispute				Other Conditions

Column entries:

A has the opportunity to murder B.

A has the means to murder B.

Generalizations → Historical Report: Brutus does A, B, C, but not D, E, F.
Transformation Rule: A man of this type does A,B,C, but not D,E,F.
A is the kind of man who would not rule out murder as an act to defend an objective.

Generalizations → Historical Report: Brutus does G, H, I, but not J, K, L.
Transformation Rule: A man of this type does G,H,I, but not J,K,L.
A is highly dedicated to his objective.

Generalizations → Historical Report: Brutus does M, N, O, but not P, Q, R.
Transformation Rule: A man of this type does M,N,O, but not P,Q,R.
A is the kind of man who would not fear the personal consequences of murder.

CONDITIONS UNDER WHICH THE COVERING LAW WILL HOLD

Transformation Rules:
Brutus = man A
Caesar = man B
Preserving the republic = objective

Covering Laws:
An uncertain belief by one man, A, that another man, B, will block an objective of A → A to take action short of murder; and

A certain belief by one man, A, that another man, B, will block an objective of A → A to murder B

Transformation Rules:
man A = Brutus
man B = Caesar
objective = preserving the republic

Contrasting Event: Brutus takes action against Caesar short of murder.

Effect: (Historical Report) Brutus murders Caesar.
← Generalizations
← Historical Evidence

Alternative Event: Brutus is uncertain whether Caesar would make it impossible to preserve the republic.

Causal Event: (Historical Report) Brutus is certain that Caesar would make it impossible to preserve the republic.
← Generalizations
← Historical Evidence

contrasting events as well as events to be explained. It demonstrates how transformation rules take reports about particular historical events and translate them into the general terms included in covering laws and statements of conditions. It reveals how a statement of conditions is applied to a covering law, producing a model that can be tested by reference to the real world. Moreover, the diagram indicates the key points at which a critic may attack an explanation of an event and how the historian can marshal his defense.

The historian would use this model to justify an explanation asserting that Brutus murdered Caesar, because he believed that Caesar would make it impossible to preserve the Roman Republic. The model includes the covering law that establishes a causal connection between the murder and Brutus' belief, the conditions that warrant applying the law to this particular case, and the transformation rules that translate the historian's knowledge of Brutus and his situation to the general terms of the law and the conditions. Both Brutus' belief that Caesar would make it impossible to preserve the republic (the causal event) and his murder of Caesar (the event to be explained) are historical reports that must be inferred from historical evidence. As we indicated earlier, unless these reports of cause and effect are reliable, the explanation as a whole will not be credible. In this case, the contrasting event to the effect is that Brutus took action against Caesar less drastic than murder. This hypothetical event clarifies the puzzle that the explanation is designed to solve: Why did Brutus murder Caesar as opposed to adopting another form of opposition short of murder? By stating as an alternative to the causal event the hypothetical report that Brutus was uncertain whether Caesar would destroy the Republic, the historian sets forth his answer to the puzzle: Brutus killed Caesar rather than taking some action short of murder because he was certain rather than uncertain that Caesar would make it impossible to preserve the Republic.

The model also includes the covering laws that justify connecting the causal event with the effect and the alternative to the cause with the contrasting event. Specifically, the historian proposes that a certain belief by one man, A, that another man, B, blocks an objective of A will lead to A's murder of B. He further proposes that an uncertain belief by A that B blocks an objective of A will lead A to take action short of murder against B. The covering law is a statement connecting completely general terms; it makes no reference to time, place, or specific people. A few simple transformation rules are therefore needed to show how the historical reports of the cause, alternative event, effect, and contrasting event correspond to the terms of the theory. Without such transformation rules, we would not know whether the general law proposed actually covers the particular events in question. In this case, the transformation rules simply define Brutus and Caesar as men and "preserving the republic" as an objective. Once transformed, the causal event becomes A believes for certain that B will block an objective of A. The effect becomes A murders B. The contrasting event becomes

A takes action short of murder. The covering law states that given the conditions, the effect always will follow the cause and the contrasting event always will follow the alternative event.

As we indicated in Chapter III, the covering law is supposed to hold only under a specified set of conditions. For the murder in question, the diagram reveals that these conditions include general statements about the means at hand, the opportunity to commit murder, the willingness not to rule murder out, the degree of dedication to the objective, and the willingness to disregard the personal consequences of murder. Of course, the historian must show that these conditions actually are fulfilled in the case being considered. Thus the diagram indicates that the historian must infer from evidence reports about Brutus' character and personality as well as the circumstances he faced. He must then apply another set of transformation rules that relate these particular reports to the general statements included in the conditions. These rules enable us to translate what we know about Brutus and his circumstances to the general conditions set forth in the model. The two–headed arrows connecting historical reports to the statement of conditions indicate that the historian could begin with a general statement of conditions and use transformation rules to see how well Brutus fits those conditions. Or he could begin with reports about Brutus and use transformation rules to turn those reports into a general statement of conditions. The transformation rules connecting reports and conditions in this model are far more complex than those used to connect the cause and effect with the terms of the covering law. They must express our notions about the kind of person who would not rule out murder, who was highly dedicated to a cause, and who would disregard the personal consequences of a murder committed for the cause. We would not expect such a person to disparage the objective in private correspondence, or personal conversation; to offer secretly advice or comfort to those opposing the objective; or to previously have shown great inconsistency in the objectives that he pursued.

The transformation rules listed in the model indicate that the type of man described in statements of each condition would be expected to perform certain types of acts and not to perform others. For purposes of illustration we have represented these acts with letters: A,B,C,D,E,F, etc. To give some content to these representations we might expect a man highly dedicated to an objective to spend a great deal of his time and energy advancing the objective, to sacrifice his other interests in pursuit of the objective, and to support the objective with generous contributions of personal funds. For purposes of illustration we also assumed that reports about what Brutus does and does not do precisely correspond to acts mentioned in the transformation rules. Actually, a historian could never expect so neat a fit.

We indicated also in the model that the conditions pertaining to the murderer's means and opportunity are not in dispute. The model does not indicate that the historian sought to determine the applicability of these conditions through historical inference and transformation rules. Rather, for purposes of the explanation, he simply assumes that Brutus had the means and the opportunity to murder Caesar and does not actually try to demonstrate that this was the case. Such assumptions simplify historical explanation, in this case focusing attention on Brutus' motives. Only when challenged does the historian need to justify assumptions by reference to historical evidence.

The full development of a model like the one sketched here would require a scholarly article or perhaps even a book length monograph. Most of the historian's work would probably come in the effort to demonstrate that the stated conditions actually hold for Brutus' murder of Caesar. This demonstration would require virtually all our knowledge about Brutus, detailed theoretical knowledge about the conditions under which the covering law holds, and an elaborate argument relating our empirical knowledge to these conditions. Was Brutus really *that* dedicated to the Republic? Did he *really* disdain the personal consequences of murder? The historian would have to justify each of his historical reports, each of his transformations from report to the terms of the conditions of the covering law. Moreover, the historian would also have to justify the reports of cause and effect as well as the application of the covering law itself under the stated conditions. The following checklist indicates the issues that might be raised by a critic of the explanation proposed by the historian.

1. The reports of the causal event and event to be explained are likely to be false.
2. The reports about Brutus' character, personality, and circumstances are likely to be false.
3. The reports about the cause and effect cannot be connected logically to the terms of the covering law.
4. The reports about Brutus' character, personality, and circumstances cannot be connected logically to the statement of conditions.
5. The historian has omitted conditions relevant to the application of the law.
6. The covering law is not likely to hold even under the stated conditions.

The model sketched here reveals how explanations are revised and new explanations developed. Historians may infer new historical reports or discredit earlier reports relevant to a causal explanation. They may also use new theory to undermine one model and increase the credibility of an alternative model. A scholar of the ancient world, for instance, might discover new information that questions Brutus' dedication to the Republic, indicating that one of the crucial conditions for the model set forth above may not actually hold. Or he might find evidence that enables him to infer that Brutus suspected that Caesar actually was his father. (Most ancient historians believe that Caesar had a long-standing affair with Brutus' mother, Servilia.) This historical report then could become part of the causal event for an alternative explanation of the murder. Similarly, the historian might use the principles of Freudian psychology to challenge the connection between murder and dedication to an objective proposed in the model above. He might argue that an understanding of motivation must be sought in the unconscious rather than in the conscious mind. Moreover, the historian then could use covering laws derived from Freudian psychology to build a model that asserts that Brutus killed Caesar because of an unconscious hostility toward the father that had spurned him.

Disputes over aspects of causal explanation provide much of history's vitality. We learn a great deal from challenging and defending the explanations put forward by one another. This process improves our understanding of what happened and expands our vision of the ways in which events can be explained. Yet without a clear understanding of explanatory models, debate becomes muddled and confused. Historians begin talking at cross-purposes, uncertain of precisely what issues are at stake. Those who study the past need to pay greater attention to the structure of the explanations they propose.

SUGGESTIONS
FOR FURTHER READING

American Genealogical Research Institute Staff. *How to Trace Your Family Tree.* Garden City, New York: Doubleday, 1975. A competent and readable introduction to genealogical research.

Aydelotte, William O., Allan G. Bogue, and Robert William Fogel, eds. *The Dimensions of Quantitative Research in History.* Princeton: Princeton University Press, 1972. Essays on quantitative history, covering both Europe and America.

Baker, Sheridan. *The Practical Stylist,* 3rd ed. New York: Crowell, 1973. A straightforward primer on writing a solid, clean, convincing essay.

Barraclough, Geoffrey. *An Introduction to Contemporary History.* Baltimore: Penguin, 1967. A prominent medieval German historian's attempt to formulate a structure or framework for historical discussion of the world since 1900.

Barzun, Jacques. *Simple and Direct: A Rhetoric for Writers.* New York: Harper & Row, 1975. A powerful and eloquent argument for clear, crisp prose.

Barzun, Jacques, and Henry F. Graff. *The Modern Researcher,* rev. ed. New York:

Harcourt Brace Jovanovich, 1970. The best traditional guide to researching and writing history.

Berkhofer, Robert F. *A Behavioral Approach to Historical Analysis.* New York: Macmillan, 1969. An argument in favor of looking to the behavioral sciences for ways of explaining human action in the past.

Blalock, Hubert M., Jr. *Social Statistics,* 2d ed. New York: McGraw-Hill, 1972. For the ambitious reader; the best introduction to statistical methods for those engaged in social science research.

Bloch, Marc. *The Historian's Craft.* New York: Vintage, 1964. A sensitive and trenchant discussion, setting forth this remarkable French historian's thoughts on "how and why a historian practices his trade."

Brown, Robert. *Explanation in Social Science.* Chicago: Aldine, 1963. A sophisticated introduction to how social scientists explain the phenomena they study.

Carr, Edward H. *What Is History?* New York: Knopf, 1961. A provocative book that ranges over most of the problems facing practicing historians.

Collingwood, R. G. *The Idea of History.* New York: Oxford University Press, 1946. An excellent description and penetrating analysis of the development of the concept of history from the classical era to the present; suffused throughout with Collingwood's own idea of what history should be.

Doane, Gilbert H. *Searching for Your Ancestors: The How and Why of Genealogy,* 4th ed. Minneapolis: University of Minnesota Press, 1973. First published in 1937, a classic introduction to genealogy.

Dray, William H., ed. *Philosophical Analysis and History.* New York: Harper & Row, 1966. The best introduction for the beginning student; includes lucid statements on the controversy over historical explanation.

Felt, Thomas E. *Researching, Writing, and Publishing Local History.* Nashville: American Association for State and Local History, 1976. Advice for the novice in local history.

Finberg, H. P. R., ed. *Approaches to History.* Toronto: University of Toronto Press, 1962. An anthology of essays on the values of different fields of historical specialization.

Fischer, David Hackett. *Historians' Fallacies: Toward a Logic of Historical Thought.* New York: Harper & Row, 1970. One historian's view of how his colleagues have gone wrong.

Follett, Wilson. *Modern American Usage.* New York: Hill and Wang, 1966. A safe refuge when in search of the "standard" usage amidst the chaos of bureaucratese and slang; written by a firm traditionalist.

Frankfort, Henri and H. A. Frankfort, et al. *Before Philosophy.* Baltimore: Penguin, 1949. A seminal and powerful exposition of how mythopoeic explanation differs from rational, empirical thought.

Gilbert, Arthur N., ed. *In Search of a Meaningful Past.* Boston: Houghton Mifflin, 1972. An anthology of sixteen selections by eminent historians on the importance of historical study in the contemporary world.

Gilbert, Felix, and Stephen R. Graubard, eds. *Historical Studies Today.* New York: Norton, 1972. A useful collection of essays setting "new" history into the context of the traditional approaches taken by historians.

Gordon, Michael, ed. *The American Family in Social-Historical Perspective.* New York: St. Martin's, 1973. An excellent collection of essays; the best introduction to American family history.

Gottschalk, Louis R. *Understanding History: A Primer of Historical Method.* New York: Knopf, 1950. Especially useful for its discussion of historical sources.

Greenwood, Val D. *The Researcher's Guide to American Genealogy.* Baltimore: Genealogical Publishing Co., 1973. A detailed guide to genealogical techniques and resources; excellent as a reference work.

Hoogenboom, Ari, and Olive Hoogenboom, eds. *An Interdisciplinary Approach to American History,* 2 vols. Englewood Cliffs, New Jersey: Prentice-Hall, 1973. Essays selected for their reliance on insights, methods, and models borrowed from other disciplines.

Kaplan, Abraham. *The Conduct of Inquiry: Methodology for Behavioral Science.* Scranton: Chandler Publishing Co., 1964. A detailed and systematic exposition of methods that can be used to understand human behavior.

Kirk, G. S. *Myth: Its Meaning and Function in Ancient and Other Societies.* Berkeley and Los Angeles: University of California Press, 1970. A lucid and comprehensive treatment of modern scholarly discussions of mythic thought.

Kren, George M., and Leon H. Rappoport, eds. *Varieties of Psychohistory.* New York: Springer, 1976. An anthology of seventeen articles pertaining to four topics: "The Nature of Psychohistory," "Psychobiography," "The History of Childhood," and "Group Processes and Historical Trends."

Lichtman, Allan J. *Your Family History: How to Use Oral History, Family Archives, and Public Documents to Discover Your Roots.* New York: Vintage, 1978. A comprehensive guide to the study of personal family history that goes beyond both genealogical questions and sources.

Lifton, Robert J., ed. *Explorations in Psychohistory: The Wellfleet Papers.* New York: Simon and Schuster, 1974. An anthology of thirteen essays by prominent practitioners of psychohistory.

Marwick, Arthur. *The Nature of History.* London: Macmillan, 1970. An urbane, readable guide to interpretations of the past, emphasizing the work done in this century.

May, Ernest R. *"Lessons" of The Past: The Use and Misuse of History in American Foreign Policy.* New York: Oxford University Press, 1973. May warns against the dire effects that a superficial understanding of the past can have on the formulation of American foreign policy.

Muller, Herbert J. *The Uses of the Past: Profiles of Former Societies.* New York: Oxford University Press, 1952. A sociologist's study of former societies that stresses the ambiguities, complexities, and paradoxes of the past in order to emphasize these same features in the present.

Nevins, Allan. *The Gateway to History.* Garden City, New York: Doubleday, 1962. A literate, perceptive, extraordinarily humanistic, and thoroughly traditional collection of essays on the theory and practice of historical study.

Rabb, Theodore K., and Robert I. Rotberg, eds. *The Family in History: Interdisciplinary Essays.* New York: Harper & Row, 1971. A wide ranging collection of essays taken primarily from a special issue of the *Journal of Interdisciplinary History.*

Shafer, R. J. *A Guide to Historical Method,* rev. ed. Homewood, Illinois: Dorsey, 1974. A straightforward, practical approach to the use of historical evidence.

Skotheim, Robert Allen, ed. *The Historian and the Climate of Opinion.* Reading, Massachusetts: Addison-Wesley, 1969. An anthology of selections from major twentieth-century American historians, illustrating how the ideas of an age may shape historical inquiry and interpretation.

Thompson, James W., and Bernard J. Holm. *A History of Historical Writing,* 2 vols. New York: Macmillan, 1942. These volumes contain a sound but often cursory description of the western historical tradition; valuable as a reference tool.

Weitzman, David. *Underfoot: An Everyday Guide to Exploring the American Past.* New York: Scribner's, 1976. A breezily written beginners' guide that touches upon photographs, objects, cemetaries, and buildings.

Winks, Robin W., ed. *The Historian as Detective: Essays on Evidence.* New York: Harper & Row, 1968. Entertaining and informative essays about how historians infer reports from their evidence.

INDEX

accidents (historical), 102
allegorical interpretation of myth, 82
American foreign policy
  economic interests approach to, 11–12
  ethnocentrism in, 7–8
  military strength as a determinant of, 9
  "moralistic-legalistic" approach to, 6–11
  public opinion vs. professional
    determination of, 9, 11–12
  revisionist approach to, 11–12
analytic form of historical writing, 214
anecdotes in historical writing, 239
Annales school of historians, 112
anti-American sentiment and Open–Door
  policy in China, 7
appendices in historical writing, 221–222
argumentation tactics used in historical
  writing, 233–39
  balancing evidence and discussion,
    237–38
  creating presence, 238–39
  either-or, 235–36
  preemption, 234
  reference to authority, 236–37
  spreading, 235
Ariès, Philippe, 155–156, 207
art as historical evidence, 17, 206–8
audiences for historical writing, 210–12,
  215, 216, 218, 220, 222, 233, 234,
  239

Augustine, St., 89–90
authenticity of historical evidence, 27,
  34–35, 200–201
  use of additional evidence to verify,
    36–37
  and the Zapruder film of the Kennedy
    assassination, 34–36.
autobiographical interviews, 164
axioms, defined, 50

balance of power
  defined by Kennan, 8
  effect of World War II on, 8–9
  effectiveness of maintaining, 12
  importance of maintaining, 8–9
balanced structure in historical writing,
  227–29
Bandura, Albert, 133
begging the question
  in historical research, 186–87
  in interviews, 166
behaviorist school of psychology
  use in historical explanation, 132–33
Berkhofer, Robert F., 103
bias
  in interview questions, 166
  and use of moral judgment, 74